PROGRESS OF THE WORLD'S WOMEN 2005

WOMEN | WORK | & | POVERTY

Martha Chen • Joann Vanek • Francie Lund • James Heintz
with Renana Jhabvala • Christine Bonner

Advisory Team

Debbie Budlender
Community Agency for Social Enquiry
Cape Town, South Africa

Diane Elson
University of Essex
Colchester, Essex
United Kingdom

Guadalupe Espinosa
Institute of Social Development
Mexico City, Mexico

Noeleen Heyzer
Executive Director
UNIFEM
New York, NY, USA

Selim Jahan
Bureau of Development Policy - UNDP
New York, NY, USA

Francesca Perucci
UN Statistics Division
New York, NY, USA

Anne Trebilcock
ILO
Geneva, Switzerland

Data Analysis Teams

Canada:
Leah Vosko and Sylvia Fuller
York University
Toronto

Costa Rica:
Jesper Venema
ILO Regional Office
Panama City

Egypt:
Mona Amer and Alia El Mahdi
University of Cairo
Cairo

El Salvador:
Edgar Lara López, Reinaldo Chanchán,
Sara Gammage
Fundación Nacional para el Desarrollo
San Salvador

Ghana:
James Heintz
Political Economy Research Institute
University of Massachusetts
Amherst, Mass.

India:
Jeemol Unni
National Commission for Enterprises in the
Unorganized Sector
New Delhi

South Africa:
Daniela Casale, Colette Muller, Dorrit Posel
University of KwaZulu Natal
Durban

Editor: Karen Judd, UNIFEM
Consulting Editor: Gloria Jacobs
Copyeditors: Tina Johnson, Anna Grossman
Production: Barbara Adams, Nanette Braun, Jennifer Cooper, Heather Tilbury, UNIFEM
Design: VanGennep Design
Cover design: Cynthia Rhett
Printing: ProGraphics

Contents

5	**Acknowledgements**
6	**Preface**
8	**Overview: Women, Work and Poverty**
14	**Chapter 1: Employment and Poverty Reduction**
	Poverty and Gender Inequality in the 21st Century
	Employment in the 21st Century
	Employment in the MDGs and PRSPs
	Organization of this Report
22	**Chapter 2: The Totality of Women's Work**
	Understanding and Measuring Women's Work
	Mapping Women's Paid and Unpaid Work
	The Dynamics of Women's Paid and Unpaid Work
	Gender and Other Sources of Disadvantage: Implications for Poverty Reduction
36	**Chapter 3: Employment, Gender and Poverty**
	Informal Employment: Definition and Recent Data
	Millennium Development Goal 3: Recommended Employment Indicators
	Labour Force Segmentation, Earnings and Poverty: Developed Country Data
	Labour Force Segmentation, Earnings and Poverty: New Data from Developing Countries
	Labour Markets and Labour Force Statistics
	Table Notes
58	**Chapter 4: The Reality of Women's Informal Work**
	Nature of Informal Work
	Benefits of Informal Work
	Costs of Informal Work
	Close-up: Occupational Groups
	A Causal Model of the Informal Economy
	Poverty, Gender and Informal Employment
74	**Chapter 5: Women's Organizing in the Informal Economy**
	Benefits of Organizing
	Identifying as Workers
	Strategies and Forms of Organizing
	Influencing Policy Decisions: National, Regional and International Networks and Alliances
	The Next Stage
86	**Chapter 6: A Framework for Policy and Action**
	Policy Debates on the Informal Economy
	Framework for Policy and Action
	Close-up: Good Practice Cases
	The Way Forward
105	**References Cited**
111	**About the Authors**
112	**Index**

Tables and Figures

Page	
28	**Table 2.1:** Risks and vulnerabilities associated with employment at different stages of the life cycle
40	**Table 3.1:** Wage and self-employment in non-agricultural informal employment by sex, 1994/2000
45	**Table 3.2:** Percentage distribution of women's and men's informal employment by employment status
46	**Table 3.3:** Percentage distribution of women's and men's formal employment by type
47	**Table 3.4:** Hourly earnings as a percentage of the hourly earnings of formal, private, non-agricultural wage workers by employment status category
48	**Table 3.5:** Average wages per worker and women's share of employment for small and microenterprises by size, Egypt, 2003 (expressed in 2002 Egyptian pounds)
48	**Table 3.6:** Women's hourly earnings as a percentage of men's hourly earnings
49	**Table 3.7:** Hourly earnings in selected employment status categories, Ghana (in cedis and purchasing power parity adjusted U.S. dollars)
50	**Table 3.8:** Average weekly hours of work by sex and employment status
50	**Table 3.9:** Total hours worked per week in employment and unpaid care work, employed population (15+), Ghana, 1998/1999
51	**Table 3.10:** Working poor as a percentage of employment (15+) in selected employment statuses by sex, 2003, El Salvador
52	**Table 3.11:** Relative poverty rates: working poor poverty rates by sex and employment status category and formal and informal employment, as a percentage of the poverty rate for formal, private non-agricultural wage workers
53	**Table 3.12:** Poverty rates by household type, South Africa, 2003
53	**Table 3.13:** Poverty rates among persons in households sustaining themselves on informal income, urban India, 1999/2000
54	**Figure 3.1:** Segmentation of Informal Employment by Average Earnings and Sex
54	**Figure 3.2:** Poverty Risk of Households by Sources of Income
54	**Figure 3.3:** Poverty Risk of Households by Primary Source of Income

Acknowledgements

The authors are deeply grateful to UNIFEM for commissioning this report on informal employment and the working poor, especially women, and their importance in efforts to eliminate poverty. In particular, we want to express our gratitude to Noeleen Heyzer, Executive Director, for her leadership, her interest and expertise on issues of women, work and poverty, and for her substantive and financial support, without which the report would not have been possible.

We would also like to acknowledge Joanne Sandler, UNIFEM Deputy Director for Programme for her inputs and support and Meagan Bovell, Nisreen Alami, Leyla Sharafe and Ellen Houston in UNIFEM's Economic Security and Rights section for research support. Special thanks are due to Karen Judd, UNIFEM editor, and Gloria Jacobs, consulting editor, who provided valuable inputs and shepherded the report to completion.

Other UNIFEM staff with whom we consulted include Meenakshi Ahluwalia, Aileen Allen, Letty Chiwara, Nazneen Damji, Sandra Edwards, Eva Fodor, Chandi Joshi, Yelena Kudryavtseva, Osnat Lubrani, Lucita Lazo, Firoza Mehrotra, Zina Mounla, Natasha Morales, Sunita Narain, Grace Okonji, Teresa Rodriguez, Amelia Kinahoi Siamoumua, Damira Sartbaeva, Alice Shackelford, Stephanie Urdang, Marijke Velzeboer-Salcedo. Thanks also to UNIFEM interns Michael Montiel and Inés Tófalo for translation of material in Spanish and to Marie-Michele Arthur and Tracy Carvalho for their management of contracts and payments.

We would also like to express our thanks to the UNDP and the ILO for both substantive advice and additional financial support. In addition, Selim Jahan of UNDP and Anne Trebilcock of the ILO served on the Advisory Team and provided valuable comments. Debbie Budlender, of CASE in South Africa; Diane Elson, coordinator of UNIFEM's first *Progress of the World's Women* in 2000; and Guadalupe Espinoza, former UNIFEM Regional Programme Director in Mexico provided many helpful comments. Ralf Hussmanns of the ILO provided statistical guidance and Francesca Perucci of the UN Statistics Division provided additional statistical inputs. Other ILO staff with whom we consulted include Amy King-DeJardin, Marie-Thérèse DuPré, Rakawin Lee, Katarina Tsotroudi, María Elena Valenzuela, Linda Wirth and Sylvester Young.

Very special thanks are due to the members of the Data Analysis Teams who carried out the data analysis in seven countries for Chapter 3. Special thanks also to WIEGO team members Marais Canali, who compiled references, wrote some of the good practice cases and assisted the authors throughout; Shalini Sinha, who worked closely with the authors on Chapter 5; Anna Marriott, Cally Ardington and Kudzai Makomva, who assisted with research for different chapters; and Suzanne Van Hook, who managed the contracts for the data analysis team. Others in the WIEGO network who were consulted on the cases studies featured in Chapters 5 and 6 include Kofi Asamoah, Stephanie Barrientos, Ela Bhatt, Mirai Chatterjee, Nicole Constable, Dan Gallin, Pat Horn, Elaine Jones, Paula Kantor, Martin Medina, Winnie Mitullah, Pun Ngai, Fred Pieterson, Jennefer Sebstad, and Lynda Yanz.

Finally, we would like to thank the working poor women and men around the world who inspire our work.

Martha Chen, Joann Vanek, Francie Lund,
James Heintz, Renana Jhabvala,
and Christine Bonner

Preface

The modern global economy is now a reality. Yet everywhere in the world, there are people working in conditions that should no longer exist in this 21st century, for income that is barely enough for survival. Home-based workers put in long hours each day, yet are paid for only a fraction of their time. Rural women spend backbreaking hours on family plots, often for no payment at all. Those in urban areas work in unregulated factories, earning pennies for products that are shipped via sub-contractors to markets far away, or they find jobs as waste-pickers, scavenging garbage heaps for items to sell. The working poor are both men and women. However, the further down the chain of quality and security, the more women you find. Yet it is their work — including their unpaid work in the household as well as their poorly paid work in insecure jobs or small enterprises — that holds families and communities together.

Informal workers are everywhere, in every country and region. Globalization has brought new opportunities for many workers, especially those who are well educated, with the skills demanded in the high-tech global economy. But it has deepened insecurity and poverty for many others, including women, who have neither the skills needed to compete nor the means to acquire them. The lives of these working poor people are the message of this report: too many of them, both women and men, are in unregulated and insecure jobs, in conditions that are frequently unhealthy and often unsafe.

Increasingly, rather than informal work becoming formalized as economies grow, work is moving from formal to informal, from regulated to unregulated, and workers lose job security as well as medical and other benefits. What we are seeing is that growth does not automatically 'trickle down' to the poor. It can in fact widen the gap between rich and poor. As globalization intensifies, the likelihood of obtaining formal employment is decreasing in many places, with "footloose" companies shifting production from one unregulated zone to an even less regulated one elsewhere, employing workers in informal contract or casual work with low earnings and little or no benefits.

In many developing countries, with the collapse of commodity prices and the persistence of agricultural subsidies in rich countries, many rural communities are disintegrating, forcing both women and men into the informal economy. That is partly the reason why, in developing countries, informal employment comprises from 50 to 80 per cent of total non-agricultural employment. When agricultural workers such as coffee harvesters or cocoa growers who are unable to compete in the world market are included, the percentage of informal workers is dramatically higher. In nearly all developing countries (except for North Africa) the proportion of working women in informal employment is greater than the proportion of working men: over 60 per cent of working women are in informal employment outside of agriculture.

Women workers are not only concentrated in the informal economy, they are in the more precarious forms of informal employment, where earnings are the most unreliable and the most meagre. While in some instances, their income can be important in helping families move out of poverty, this is only true if there is more than one earner. This is a sobering fact to consider as we redouble our efforts to implement the Millennium Development Goals, including the elimination of poverty and the achievement of gender equality. Not achieving these goals is unthinkable. Widening gaps between rich and poor, and women and men can only contribute to greater instability and insecurity in the world.

And this is the other message of this report: decent work is a basic human right, one that governments, corporations and international policymakers can make a reality for all working people. Change is possible, and innovative solutions are already being acted upon. This report shows how and where change has happened, and describes how governments, UN and NGO partners and socially responsible corporations can work together to ensure that informal workers, especially women, receive an equitable return for their labour.

To make this happen, four things need to be made a priority:

First, organizing women informal workers to obtain legal and social protection. Unless women are empowered to demand services, protection and their rights, the basic structures that govern their lives will not change. Women acting alone can only bring about limited change. This therefore means supporting women's organizing, along with unions and member-based workers' organizations, to ensure that more workers receive the labour rights to which they are entitled.

Second, for the self-employed, greater effort must be made to deliver services to these workers, to improve access to credit and financial markets and to mobilize demands for their products and services. Women's skills and assets must be upgraded so they can compete more effectively in these markets. In Burkina Faso, we saw firsthand the difference that skills can make. UNIFEM helped women who produced shea butter learn how to improve the quality of their product. This in turn helped them move up the value chain, establishing a specialized, niche market for their product that is now bought by corporations at better prices than the women were receiving previously.

Third, there must be appropriate policies in support of informal workers. This requires that informal workers are visible and that the totality of their work — especially in the case of women — is valued. The starting point for meaningful policy decisions is to make women's informal work visible through gender-sensitive, disaggregated statistics on national labour forces. This data must be developed, analysed and used in creating policy that focuses on economic security and rights.

Finally, there is a need to strengthen strategies that can transform basic structures that perpetuate gender inequality. What kind of global rules are required to regulate markets, and guide the priorities of international economic institutions towards globalization that improves lives and working conditions? Closing the gender income gaps, ensuring safe and healthy working conditions for all, must be central to policy and rule-setting. Socially responsible corporations can lead the way in this. At the same time, all corporations can be held accountable through standard-setting and the independent monitoring and verification that are a necessary part of implementation.

This report is a call to action to achieve the goals outlined here. Advocates and the working poor themselves have done much to improve conditions already and to ensure that the working poor in the informal economy remain on the international agenda. Socially responsible campaigns and ethical marketing initiatives have helped to raise awareness around the importance of better working conditions for informal workers. The Clean Clothes Campaign and the Women's Principles, a set of goals for corporations that use sub-contractors or run factories in developing countries, created by the Calvert Investment Group, working with UNIFEM, are part of an effort by consumers in developed countries to insist that the goods they buy be created under humane conditions. Governments are also recognizing the importance of protecting the lives and well-being of their citizens — their human capital — and have insisted that certain standards be maintained and minimum wages paid.

These efforts should not be the work only of socially responsible companies, or concerned consumers, or of organizations of informal workers. Corporations and entities active in the global marketplace must alter their policies to "make poverty history." Advocates can use the tools provided in this report to reach beyond their core constituencies. They can assess the impact of economic policies on women and men and insist on those that offer concrete solutions to the deplorable conditions prevalent in the informal economy.

Noeleen Heyzer
Executive Director, UNIFEM

Overview: Women, Work and Poverty

2005 marks the fifth anniversary of the UN Millennium Declaration, adopted in 2000 and the tenth anniversary of the Beijing Platform for Action in 1995. In the decade since Beijing, the number of people living on less than $1 a day has fallen; the gender gap in primary and (to a lesser extent) secondary education has been reduced; and women enjoy greater participation in elected assemblies and state institutions. In addition, women are a growing presence in the labour market– the global indicator used to approximate women's economic status (UN 2005).

However, the decline in overall poverty masks significant differences not only between but also within regions. Asia experienced the greatest decline in extreme poverty, followed by Latin America, but sub-Saharan Africa experienced an increase. Even where the numbers of extremely poor people have declined, notably China and India, poverty persists in different areas and social groups, reflected in rising inequalities (UN 2005).

For women, progress, while steady, has been painfully slow. Despite increased parity in primary education, disparities are still wide in secondary and tertiary education—both increasingly key to new employment opportunities. And while women's share of seats in parliament have inched up in all regions, women still hold only 16 per cent of parliamentary seats worldwide. Finally, although women have entered the paid labour force in great numbers, the result in terms of economic security is not clear. According to the United Nations' *Millennium Development Goals Report 2005*: "Women's access to paid employment is lower than men's in most of the developing world…. Women are less likely than men to hold paid and regular jobs and more often work in the informal economy, which provides little financial security" (UN 2005).

Today's global world is one of widening income inequality and for many, increasing economic insecurity. Informal employment, far from disappearing, is persistent and widespread. In many places, economic growth has depended on capital-intensive production in a few sectors rather than on increasing employment opportunities, pushing more and more people into the informal economy. In others, many of the jobs generated by economic growth are not covered by legal or social protection, as labour markets are de-regulated, labour standards are relaxed and employers cut costs (see Chapter 4). As a result, a growing share of the workforce in both developed and developing countries is not covered by employment-based social and legal protection.

Moreover, in the process of economic growth and trade liberalization, some informal workers get left behind altogether. This includes wage workers who lose their jobs when companies mechanize, retrench or shift locations. It also includes the smallest-scale producers and traders who have little if any access to government subsidies, tax rebates or promotional measures to help them compete in export markets or against imported goods. These 'losers' in the global economy have to find ways to survive in the local economy, many resorting to such occupations as waste picking or low-end street trading.

Progress of the World's Women 2005 makes the case that strengthening women's economic security is critical to efforts to reduce poverty and promote gender equality, and that decent work is basic to economic security. It provides data to show that:

- the proportion of women workers engaged in informal employment is generally greater than the proportion of men workers;
- women are concentrated in the more precarious types of informal employment; and
- the average earnings from these types of informal employment are too low, in the absence of other sources of income, to raise households out of poverty.

The report concludes that unless efforts are made to create decent work for the global informal workforce, the world will not be able to eliminate poverty or achieve gender equality.

Statistical Findings

Statistics from a variety of developing countries show that, despite differences in size, geographic location and income level, fully 50 to 80 per cent of non-agricultural employment is informal. Between 60 and 70 per cent of informal workers in developing countries are self-employed, including employers, own-account workers and unpaid contributing family workers in family enterprises (ILO 2002b). The remaining 30 to 40 per cent are informal wage workers, including the employees of informal enterprises, casual day labourers, domestic workers and industrial outworkers.

In terms of earnings, average earnings are higher in formal employment than in informal employment and in non-agriculture than in agriculture activities. Average earnings also vary across segments of the informal labour force. Informal wage employment is generally superior to informal self-employment. However, a hierarchy exists: informal employers have the highest average earnings followed by their employees, then own-account workers, and then casual wage workers and domestic workers. Related statistical analyses have found that industrial outworkers have the lowest average earnings of all (Charmes and Lekehal n.d.; Chen and Snodgrass 2001).

The risk of poverty is lower in formal employment relative to informal employment and in non-agricultural employment relative to agricultural employment. The risk of poverty also varies across segments of the informal labour force. Generally, informal wage workers – with the exception of domestic workers, casual wage workers, and industrial outworkers – have lower poverty risk than own account workers.

Gender inequality in employment has multiple dimensions. First, women are concentrated in more precarious forms of employment in which earnings are low. In developed countries, women comprise the majority of part-time and temporary workers.

In developing countries, except in those with large low-wage export sectors, women typically account for a relatively small share of informal wage employment. However, informal employment generally represents a larger source of employment for women than formal employment and a greater share of women's employment than men's employment. In developing countries over 60 per cent of women workers are in informal employment outside of agriculture—far more if agriculture is included. The exception is North Africa, where 43 per cent of women workers, and a slightly higher per cent of men workers, are informally employed.

Within the informal economy, women are concentrated in work associated with low and unstable earnings and with high risks of poverty. Outside of agriculture, women are more likely than men to be own account workers, domestic workers, unpaid contributing workers in family enterprises and industrial outworkers. A significant proportion of women working in agriculture are also unpaid contributing workers on the family farm.

Second, within employment categories, women's hourly and monthly earnings are generally lower than men's. A gender gap in earnings exists across almost all employment categories – including informal wage employment and self-employment. A few exceptions exist among public sector employees in certain countries, such as El Salvador, and in cases like Egypt where most of women's employment involves unpaid work on family enterprises and the few women who do participate in paid employment tend to be highly educated. In these exceptional cases, women's average hourly earnings can be higher than men's.

Third, in the countries for which data are available, women work fewer hours on average in paid work than do men. In part, this is due to women's long hours in unpaid household labour. Responsibilities for unpaid household work also reinforce labour force segmentation – women can be restricted to own-account or home-based employment, even if they have to work longer hours and earn less than they would in other types of employment.

Finally, despite the low earnings and precarious nature of much of women's paid work, in both developed and developing countries, women's labour force participation can help keep a family out of poverty – provided there are additional sources of family income.

Research Findings

The links between work and poverty reflect not only how much women and men earn but how they earn it and for how long. Each *place of work* is associated with specific costs, risks and benefits, depending variously on security of site tenure, costs of securing it, access to needed infrastructure, such as light, water, toilets, storage, garbage removal, etc.; access to customers and suppliers; ability of informal workers to organize; and the different risks and hazards associated with the site.

Several broad categories of informal workers can be distinguished according to their *employment relations*: employers, their employees, own account workers who do not hire others, unpaid contributing family workers, casual wage workers and industrial outworkers. Industrial outworkers, the vast majority of whom are women, lack firm contracts, have the lowest average earnings and often are not paid for months on end. The small amount and insecurity of their income is exacerbated by the fact that they have to pay for non-wage costs of production, such as workplace, equipment and utilities (ILO 2002b; Carr et al. 2000).

The modern industrial system has not expanded as fully in developing countries as it once did in developed countries. In many developing countries industrial production takes place in micro and small units, in family businesses or in single person units, while traditional personalized *systems of production and exchange* still obtain in agricultural and artisan production. But in today's globalizing economy, both traditional and semi-industrial relations of production and exchange are being inserted into or displaced by the global system of production. Authority and power tend to get concentrated in the top links of value chains or diffused across firms in complex networks, making it difficult for micro-entrepreneurs to gain access, compete and bargain and for wage workers to bargain for fair wages and working conditions. Highly competitive conditions among small-scale suppliers and the significant market power of transnational corporations mean that the lion's share of the value produced across these value chains is captured by the most powerful players.

For the rest—those who can't compete—some may become suppliers in these chains or networks, others struggle as subcontractors while still others are forced to hire out their labour to subcontractors. In today's global economy, it is hard to imagine a greater physical and psychological distance, or a greater imbalance – in terms of power, profit and life-style – than that between the woman who stitches garments or soccer balls from her home in Pakistan for a brand-name retailer in Europe or North America and the chief executive officer (CEO) of that brand-name corporation.

The consequences of working informally go far beyond the income dimensions of poverty to include lack of human rights and social inclusion. Compared to those who work in the formal economy, those who work in the informal economy are likely:

- to have less access to basic infrastructure and social services;
- to face greater exposure to common contingencies (e.g., illness, property loss, disability and death);
- to have less access to the means to address these contingencies (e.g., health, property, disability or life insurance);
- to have, as a result, lower levels of health, education and longevity;
- to have less access to financial, physical and other productive assets;
- to have fewer rights and benefits of employment;
- to have less secure property rights over land, housing or other productive assets; and
- to face greater exclusion from state, market and political institutions that determine the 'rules of the game' in these various spheres.

Together these costs take an enormous toll on the financial, physical and psychological well-being of many informal workers and their families.

New Analytical Tools and Promising Examples

This report offers several new conceptual and methodological frameworks that provide fresh insights into the links among informal employment, poverty and gender inequality and serve as a basis for future research. These include:

- an analysis of the linkages between the gender division of labour, women's unpaid work and informal paid work along different dimensions (Chapter 2);
- a framework based on the proposed new employment indicators for Millennium Development Goal 3; analysing differences by sex in types of employment and earnings (Chapter 3);
- a statistical method for assessing the 'poverty risk' of different employment statuses by sex, linking national labour force and household income data to show the links between gender, employment and poverty risk (Chapter 3);
- an expanded definition and a multi-segmented model of labour markets that takes into account labour market structures in developing countries and changing employment relations in developed countries (Chapter 3);
- a typology of the costs – both direct and indirect – of informal employment that can be used to carry out a full accounting of the social and distributional outcomes of different types of informal work (Chapter 4);
- a causal model of the informal economy, which posits that some people operate informally by *choice*, others do so out of *necessity*, and still others do so because of *tradition* (e.g., hereditary occupations) (Chapter 4);
- a new policy analysis tool, modelled on gender budget analysis, called *informal economy budget analysis* (Chapter 6).

To ensure that appropriate policies, institutions and services are put in place, the informal workforce needs to be visible to policy makers and government planners. To date, relatively few countries have comprehensive statistical data on the informal economy, and the collection of such data needs to be given greater priority. More countries need to collect statistics on informal employment in their labour force surveys, and countries that already do this need to improve the quality of statistics they collect. Moreover, data that is collected needs to be analysed to bring out the linkages between informal employment, poverty and gender equality, as done for the first time for seven countries in this report.

There are many promising examples of what can and should be done to help the working poor, especially women, minimize the costs and maximize the benefits of their work. This report features a selection of these. They come from all regions and are initiated by governments as well as civil society and the private sector, women's organizations as well as labour organizations, and demonstrate the power of working in partnership.

Future Directions

The overarching future policy goal is to stop the ongoing generation of informal, insecure and badly paid employment alongside the constriction of formal employment opportunities. This requires expanding formal employment opportunities, formalizing informal enterprises and jobs, and increasing the returns to their labour of those who work in the informal economy. For labour and women's rights advocates it means demanding a favourable policy environment and specific interventions in order to increase economic opportunities, social protection, and representative voice for the working poor, especially women, in the informal economy.

A favourable policy environment

Both poverty reduction and gender equality require an economic policy environment that supports, rather than ignores, the working poor. Most (if not all) economic and social policies – both macro and micro – affect the lives and work of the working poor in various direct ways:

- as workers
- as consumers
- as users of infrastructure, finance and property, including urban space and natural resources
- as potential recipients of tax-funded services or transfers (World Bank 2005a).

Economic policies that discount the real-life structure and behaviour of labour markets cannot be assumed to be neutral towards labour. Similarly, economic policies that ignore the fact that most unpaid care work is done by women cannot be assumed to be neutral towards women's labour in particular. Economic planners must take into account the size, composition and contribution of both the formal and informal labour forces in different countries and recognize that policies have differential impacts on formal and informal enterprises and workers, and on women and men within these categories. To assess how economic policies affect the working poor, it is important to analyse how class, gender and other biases intersect in labour markets. More specifically, it is important to identify inherent biases in favour of capital (over labour), formal enterprises (over informal enterprises), formal labour (over informal labour) and men (over women) within each of these categories.

A new tool, *informal economy budget analysis*, modelled on gender-responsive budget analysis, is designed to assess whether and how the allocation of resources by government at different levels (local, provincial/ state and national/ federal) and across different ministries or departments (trade, labour, housing, health) serves to (a) lower or raise the costs of those working informally, and (b) provide or deny access to benefits that could help them grow their enterprises and otherwise take steps along the path to steady and secure incomes. Used in conjunction with gender-responsive budget analysis, informal economy budget analysis can also shed light on the intersection of gender and other sources of disadvantage (by class, ethnicity or geography) in the realm of work.

Targeted interventions

In addition to a favourable policy environment, targeted interventions are required to address the costs of working informally. These should aim:

- To increase the assets, access and competitiveness of the working poor, both self-employed and wage employed, in the informal economy

For the working poor to be able to take advantage of the opportunities offered by a more favourable policy environment, they need greater market access as well as the relevant resources and skills with which to better compete in markets. Over the past three decades, there has been a proliferation of projects designed to provide microfinance and/or business development services to microenterprises. While the vast majority of the clients of microfinance are working poor women, business development services are not typically targeted at the smallest enterprises, particularly those run by women. Future microfinance and business development services need to target working poor women more explicitly, and with context-specific and user-friendly services.

- To improve the terms of trade for the working poor, especially women, in the informal economy

To compete effectively in the markets, in addition to having the requisite resources and skills, the working poor need to be able to negotiate favourable terms of trade. This involves changing government policies, government-set prices or institutional arrangements as well as the balance of power within markets or value chains. This requires that the working poor, especially women, have bargaining power and are able to participate in the negotiations that determine the terms of trade in the sectors within which they work. Often what is effective in this regard is joint action by organizations of the working poor and like-minded allies who can leverage access to government policy makers and to rule-setting institutions.

- To secure appropriate legal frameworks for the working poor, both self-employed and wage employed, in the informal economy

Workers in the informal economy, especially the poor, need legal recognition as workers and the legal entitlements that come with that recognition, including the right to work (e.g., to vend in public spaces), rights at work and rights to property. Strategies to secure the rights of women informal wage workers include international labour standards and conventions; national labour legislation; corporate codes of conduct; and collective bargaining agreements and grievance mechanisms.

- To address risk and uncertainty faced by poor workers, especially women, in informal employment

All workers, and informal workers in particular, need protection against the risks and uncertainties associated with their work as well as the common contingencies of illness, property loss, maternity and child care, disability and death. Providing needed protections requires a variety of interventions, including different safety nets (relief payments, cash transfers, public works); insurance coverage of various kinds (health, property, disability, life); and pensions or long-term savings schemes. Governments, the private sector, trade unions, non-governmental organizations and other membership-based organizations can all play active roles in providing social protection to informal workers.

Support for organizing by women informal workers

To hold other players accountable to these strategic priorities, the working poor need to be able to organize and have representative voice in policy-making processes and institutions. Informal workers, especially women, cannot count on other actors to represent their interests in policy-making or programme planning processes, including national Millennium Development Goals reports and the Poverty Reduction Strategy Papers (PRSPs). Securing this seat at the decision-making table requires supporting and strengthening organizations of informal workers, with a special focus on women's organizations and women's leadership. These organizations also require creative linkages with and on-going support from women's organizations and other social justice organizations, including trade unions; governments; and UN partners, such as UNIFEM, UNDP and the ILO.

While most of these priorities have been on the international development agenda for some time, this report highlights two strategic concerns that do not get sufficient attention.

First, poverty and inequality cannot be reduced by expecting economic policies to generate employment and social policies to compensate those for whom there are no jobs, or only bad jobs. Economic growth often fails to generate sufficient employment or employment that pays enough to live free of poverty, while compensation through social policies is typically inadequate or neglected altogether.

Second, poverty reduction requires a major reorientation in economic priorities to focus on employment, not just growth and inflation. To be effective, strategies to reduce poverty and promote equality should be *employment-oriented and worker-centred*.

In recent years, many observers have called for people-centred or gender-responsive approaches to poverty reduction. What is called for here is an approach that focuses on the needs and constraints of the working poor, especially women, *as workers*, not only as citizens, as members of a vulnerable group or as members of poor households. A worker focus will provide coherence and relevance to poverty reduction strategies because most poor people work, because earnings represent the main source of income in poor households, and because working conditions affect all dimensions of poverty (i.e., income, human development, human rights and social inclusion).

The Way Forward

Combating poverty and achieving gender equality require a major reorientation of economic and development planning. Governments and their international development partners need to recognize that that there are no short-cuts in this effort: economic growth, even if supplemented by social policies, too often fails to stimulate the kind of secure, protected employment needed to enable the working poor to earn an income sufficient to pull themselves out of poverty. Women's entry into the paid labour force on the terms and under the conditions identified in this report has not resulted in the economic security needed to improve gender equality

The creation of new and better employment opportunities – especially for the working poor – must be an urgent priority for all economic policies. The experience of the last two decades, especially in developing countries, has shown that policies targeted narrowly towards containing inflation and ensuring price stability, such as those frequently promoted by the IMF and the World Bank, often create an economic environment that is hostile to an expansion of more and better employment opportunities. Successful efforts to combat poverty require a radical change in the economic policies promoted by these institutions and adopted by many governments.

In the short term, however, there are things that can be done short of the complete overhaul of development thinking and planning called for. What is needed is a critical mass of institutions and individuals at all levels to work together on a set of core priorities. These include:

Core Priority # 1 - To promote decent employment for both women and men as a key pathway to reducing poverty and gender inequality. A concerted effort is needed to ensure that decent employment opportunities are viewed as a target rather than an outcome of economic policies, including national MDG strategies and Poverty Reduction Strategies.

Core Priority # 2 - To increase visibility of informal women workers in national labour force statistics and in national gender and poverty assessments, using the employment by type and earnings indicators recommended for Millennium Development Goal 3.

Core Priority # 3 - To promote a more favourable policy environment for the working poor, especially women, in the informal economy through improved analysis, broad awareness building and participatory policy dialogues.

Core Priority # 4 - To support and strengthen organizations representing women informal workers and help them gain effective voice in relevant policy-making processes and institutions.

This report shows that workers in the informal economy, especially women, have lower average earnings and a higher poverty risk than workers in the formal economy. The meagre benefits and high costs of informal employment mean that most informal workers are not able to work their way out of poverty. In the short term, they are often forced to 'over-work' to cover these costs and still somehow make ends meet. In the long term, the cumulative toll of being over-worked, under-compensated and under-protected on informal workers, their families, and their societies undermines human capital and depletes physical capital.

In conclusion, the working poor in the informal economy are relegated to low paid, insecure forms of employment that make it impossible to earn sufficient income to move out of poverty. So long as the majority of women workers are informally employed, gender equality will also remain an elusive goal. Progress on both of these goals therefore demands that all those committed to achieving the MDGs, including the UN system, governments and the international trade and finance institutions, make decent employment a priority – and that corporations be made more socially responsible. Informal workers, both women and men, organized in unions, cooperatives or grassroots organizations, are ready to partner with them in this vital endeavour.

CHAPTER 1
Employment and Poverty Reduction

Woman selling ackee in a street market, Kingston, Jamaica. Photo: Christopher P. Baker/Lonely Planet

"Poverty means working for more than 18 hours a day, but still not earning enough to feed myself, my husband, and my two children."

Working poor woman, Cambodia (cited in Narayan 2000)

At the Millennium Summit in September 2000, the largest-ever assembly of national leaders reaffirmed that poverty and gender inequality are among the most persistent and pervasive global problems. After a decade or more of relative neglect, poverty had pushed its way back to the top of the global agenda. After three decades of women's advocacy, gender equality had moved from the margins to the centre of that agenda (UNIFEM 2002b). Moreover, the Millennium Declaration, adopted by the world's leaders, recognized that the two are linked, noting the centrality of gender equality to efforts to combat poverty and hunger and to stimulate truly sustainable development (UN 2000). In so doing, the Declaration honoured the vision of the Platform for Action adopted at the 1995 Fourth World Conference on Women in Beijing.

Progress of the World's Women 2005 marks the fifth anniversary of the UN Millennium Declaration and the tenth anniversary of the Beijing Platform for Action. It focuses on a key pillar of both the Millennium Declaration and the Beijing Platform: strengthening women's economic security and rights. Within that framework, it looks particularly at employment, especially informal employment, and the potential it has to either perpetuate or reduce both poverty and gender inequality. It provides the latest data on the size and composition of the informal economy in different regions and compares official national data on average earnings and poverty risk across different segments of both the informal and formal workforces in several countries. It looks at the costs and benefits of informal work and provides a strategic framework for promoting decent work for women informal workers.

Poverty and Gender Inequality in the 21st Century

The persistence of poverty worldwide is a major challenge of the 21st century. Five years after the Millennium Summit, more than 1 billion people struggle to survive on less than $1 a day (UN 2005). Of these, roughly half – 550 million – are working (ILO 2003a). By definition, 550 million people cannot work their way out of extreme poverty. They simply do not earn enough to feed themselves and their families, much less to deal with the economic risks and uncertainty they face.

The 2005 Millennium Development Goals Report shows that progress is possible. The number of people living on less than $1 a day fell by nearly 250 million from 1990 to 2001. But the decline in overall poverty masks significant differences between regions: Asia showed the greatest decline in extreme poverty, followed by a much slower decline in Latin America; while Sub-Saharan Africa experienced an increase in extreme poverty. China and India account for much of the poverty decline in Asia (UN 2005). But in India, deep pockets of poverty persist and regional disparities have increased (Deaton and Dreze 2002). And in China, income disparities between rural and urban areas and between different regions remain large, as reflected in the large numbers of rural to urban migrants from the late 1980s to the end of the 1990s.[1]

For poor people who are working, how they make a living – their sources of income or livelihood – is a major preoccupation. Poverty, however, is multidimensional. Today, there are several broad approaches to understanding and measuring poverty and well-being, including:

- **income and basic needs**: focusing on the income, expenditures, and basic needs of poor households;
- **human development**: focusing on health, education, longevity and other human capabilities and on the choices or freedom of poor people;
- **human rights**: focusing on the civic, political, economic and social rights of the poor; and
- **social inclusion**: focusing on the access of poor people to what they are entitled to as citizens and on giving them representative 'voice' in the institutions and processes that affect their lives and work.

The lives of the working poor in the informal economy come up short along each of these dimensions of poverty and well-being.

What about gender equality? While the understanding of this concept may vary, depending on

---

1 The numbers of rural to urban migrants are estimated to have peaked at around 75 million in the period from the late 1980s to the mid-1990s and to have tapered to around 70 million by the end of 2000 (Chen and Ravallion 2004, Weiping 2001). The decline in the poverty rate in China appears to have flattened after 1996 despite per capita GDP growth rates around 7% through 2001 (Chen and Ravallion 2004).

Vendors in a street market, Hanoi, Viet Nam. Photo: Martha Chen

the lived experiences of different groups in different countries, the Millennium Declaration provides a consensus understanding according to which gender equality means "equality at all levels of education and in all areas of work, equal control over resources and equal representation in public and political life" (UN 2005).[2] By 2005, in most regions, the gender gap in primary and (to a lesser extent) secondary education had narrowed; women's representation in national parliaments had increased; and women had become a growing presence in the labour market. But higher education remains an elusive goal for girls in many countries; women still occupy only 16 per cent of parliamentary seats worldwide; and they remain a small minority in salaried jobs in many regions, while they are overrepresented in the informal economy (ibid.).

In addition, some of the measures of progress may have contradictory outcomes for women. For example, women's share of non-agricultural wage employment, one of the four indicators under Millennium Development Goal 3, simply shows whether the share of women in such employment has increased or decreased; it does not show the conditions under which women work or the returns to their labour. If women are concentrated in low-paid and unprotected forms of non-agricultural wage employment, then an increase in their share of such employment does not represent an increase in gender equality (see Chapter 3).

Employment in the 21st Century

For much of the 20th century, economic development – at least in Europe and North America – was predicated on the model of state-based social and economic security as embodied in the welfare state, the goal of full employment and related protective regulations and institutions (ILO 2004a). However, by the 1980s, a new economic model began to take shape: one that is centred on fiscal austerity, free markets and the 'rollback' of the state. Under this model, there are three main policy prescriptions for economic development and growth: market liberalization, deregulation and privatization. While inflation has been brought under control in many countries, financial crises and economic volatility have become more frequent and income inequalities have widened (UNRISD 2005; ILO 2004a). More critically, the central goal of this new model – long-run, sustainable growth as the solution to uneven development – has not been achieved in many of the countries that have embraced it.

The consequences of these policies in terms of poverty or gender inequality are rarely discussed in mainstream economic debates, nor are the cuts in domestic social spending and legal protection that are often part of the orthodox policy mix. At best, there is a call for these policies to be complemented by investments in public goods such as education, health, infrastructure and by social policies to compensate the 'losers' in the processes of liberaliza-

---

2 As UNIFEM and others have pointed out, gender equality also entails the transformation of gender hierarchies and social and economic structures that perpetuate inequality; and ensuring women's personal security and right to live free of poverty and violence (see Heyzer 2001a,b; UNDP 2005).

tion, deregulation and privatization. But the fundamentals of free-market reforms, including the expectation that employment and standards of living will increase along with economic growth and that market interventions create distortions that may upset this relationship, remain largely unchallenged.

In fact, these economic reforms, unless properly managed, can have contradictory outcomes in terms of poverty and gender inequality. They can offer many opportunities for poverty reduction provided that steps are taken to enable people who are poor to gain rather than lose from the changes involved. On the other hand, they can leave poorer countries of the world – and the poorer section of the population within them – worse off than before. The consequences for those who are poor, especially women, depend on who they are, where they live, whether they are allowed to earn a livelihood and what they do to earn it.

Without an explicit focus on increasing the demand for labour, economic growth will not generate as many jobs as needed, resulting in jobless growth. Moreover, without an explicit focus on the quality of employment, the jobs that are created may not be regulated or protected. Recent economic growth has been associated with flexible labour markets, outsourcing of production and the growth of temporary and part-time jobs.

Countries around the world have adopted labour laws that tolerate and even promote labour market flexibility without much concern for the social outcomes of such policies in terms of poverty and gender inequality, and therefore without putting in place safety nets or unemployment compensation schemes (Benería and Floro 2004). During the 1990s in Ecuador, for example, as part of the reforms initiated by the International Monetary Fund (IMF) and the World Bank, measures to increase labour flexibility were incorporated in the labour code, including: (a) the replacement of indefinite labour contracts with fixed-term contracts and the use of temporary, part-time, seasonal and hourly contracts in hiring; and (b) restrictions on the right to strike, collective bargaining, and the organization of workers (CELA-PUCE 2002, cited in Floro and Hoppe 2005). As another case in point, the Government of Honduras is currently considering a new 'temporary work law' that would permit garment factories to hire up to 30 per cent of their workers under temporary, instead of permanent, contracts. If this law is passed, those who are shifted to temporary employment would lose the benefits of paid leave, social security and an annual bonus and see their earnings decline (Oxfam International 2004; Kidder and Raworth 2004).[3]

In today's global world, as economic insecurity and volatility are on the rise, the associated risks are increasingly being borne by ordinary workers and working communities rather than by large corporations and their owners (ILO 2004a).[4] This is due not only to labour market deregulation but also to the global system of production that involves dispersed production coordinated through networks or chains of firms. In the name of global competition, private corporations are hiring workers under insecure employment contracts of various kinds or otherwise passing economic risk onto others down the global production chain. Authority and power tend to get concentrated in the top links of value chains or diffused across firms in complex networks, making it difficult for micro-entrepreneurs to gain access and compete and for wage workers to bargain for better wages and working conditions (see Chapter 4). Lead corporations often do not know how their subsidiaries or suppliers hire workers. This means that many of the newly employed in developing countries and a growing share of the workforce in developed countries are not covered by employment-based social and legal protections, thus joining the ranks of those who have always been informally employed in developing countries.

From the 1960s through the early 1980s, it was widely assumed that in developing countries, with economic growth, workers in the informal economy would be absorbed into the modern industrial economy, as had happened historically in the industrialized countries. However, over the past two decades, the informal economy has persisted and grown both in developing and developed countries, appearing in new places and guises.

This has led to a renewal of interest in the informal economy accompanied by considerable rethinking on its size, composition and significance. A group of scholars and activists, including SEWA, HomeNet and other members of the Women in Informal Employment: Globalizing and Organizing (WIEGO) network, have worked with the ILO to broaden the concept and definition of the informal economy to include all forms of informal wage employment and informal self-employment (see Chapter 3). They have also been part of a broader effort with the ILO, UNIFEM, and UNDP to work with both governments and civil society partners to advocate for recognition and protection for people working in the informal economy.

In developing countries, informal employment as defined above represents one half to three quarters of non-agricultural employment (ILO 2002b). The share of informal employment in *total* employment is higher still, given that most of the agricultural workforce is informal: notably, small farmers and casual day labourers or seasonal workers. Even on plantations and large commercial farms, only part of the workforce is hired under formal permanent

---

3 As of April 2005, the law had not been passed in Honduras (Lynda Yanz, Maquila Solidarity Network, personal communication).
4 ILO 2004a presents summary findings from People's Security Surveys in 15 countries and Enterprise Labour Flexibility and Security Surveys in 11 countries.

Box 1.1
NAFTA's Impact on the Female Work Force in Mexico

Several studies of the impact of the 1994 North American Free Trade Agreement (NAFTA) on Mexico looked at the processes of liberalization and structural reform on the labour force, and especially on the female labour force. These have shown that, as a result of changing economic and social conditions during the years prior to and following the signing of NAFTA, women joined the labour force at a faster rate than men. However, women's jobs tended to be low paid and informal. The growth in women's employment did not necessarily lead to an improvement in their living standards. Women found more jobs in the vegetable and fruit export sector in agriculture but, with an increase in working hours and in employment on a piecework basis, their general labour conditions often worsened.

In addition, while women's employment in the *maquiladoras* (assembly and processing for export) grew in absolute terms, it fell in relative terms. Men took many of the new manufacturing jobs created in the *maquiladoras* due both to push factors, as employment opportunities were limited outside the sector, and to pull factors, as the industry and companies began to value higher-skilled workers. Between 1998 and 2004 women's share of the jobs in the *maquiladoras* fell from 63 per cent to a little under 54 per cent.*

Since 2000, the *maquiladoras* have shed almost 200,000 jobs. Women have been consistently shed at a faster rate then men as the composition of the sector has shifted towards electronics and transportation equipment, which have a higher proportion of male employees than textile manufactures (Fleck 2001).

As *maquiladora* employment contracted and the Mexican economy faltered, women were forced to look for other types of employment, often accepting lower wages and poorer labour conditions. Jobs in the informal economy increased greatly, with a larger share of the female workforce (41%) than the male workforce (37%) in informal employment. White et al. (2003) calculate that between 1995 and 2000 the informal economy expanded by almost 930,000 workers, more than half (56%) of which were women.

Real wages in Mexico are lower today than when NAFTA was implemented. In 1997, three monthly minimum wages were needed to purchase a basic food basket. By 2000, the average household needed four times the monthly minimum wage to purchase a basic food basket. The numbers of households with three or more income-earners almost doubled between 1992 and 2000 – reflecting the need to earn more money to secure the same consumption items. These declines in real wages have occurred in a labour market that is highly sex-segregated. The percentage of employed women earning less than twice the minimum wage is greater than that for employed men. Women with a basic education are segregated in jobs that pay far less than is earned by men with a basic education. Furthermore, three out of every four rural women in 2002 worked without receiving any kind of payment. White et al. (2003) calculate that the gender difference in wages in 2000 is more than two weeks wages for a woman with a basic education, meaning that a woman must work 2 weeks more than a man to make up the difference in wages.

Source: UNIFEM, 2000; White, Salas and Gammage 2003; Polaski 2004; ECLAC 2004a.
*Data for 2000-2004 from INEGI, Statistics of Maquiladora Export Industry.

---

contracts. In developed countries, three categories of non-standard work – own account self-employment, part-time work (in which women predominate) and temporary work – comprise 30 per cent of overall employment in 15 European countries and 25 per cent of total employment in the United States (ILO 2002b). [5]

Over the past two decades, as employment in the informal economy has increased, women have entered the labour force in large numbers. The connection between these two trends is not clear. Are women taking over 'men's jobs' that, in the process, are being informalized? Are women entering informalized types of work that men now avoid? Or are women being actively recruited for new forms of employment that are, by design, informal? Whatever processes are at work, women tend to be over-represented in informal employment and, more so, in the lower-paid, lower-status and more precarious forms of informal employment (see Chapter 3).

Trade liberalization has created many employment opportunities for women, particularly in export-oriented light manufacturing. In fact, wherever export-oriented manufacturing industries have grown, women have been drawn into this work (UNRISD 2005). But such growth has happened in only a few countries, including Bangladesh, China, Malaysia, Mexico and Thailand (ibid.) In any particular industry, women in one country may experience a job increase (garments in China) while in another they experience a job loss (garments in South Africa). Employment opportunities may move quickly from country to country so that gains experienced in any country can be relatively short-lived.

In addition, the jobs created in export-oriented manufacturing—whether industrial outwork or factory work— are not necessarily 'good' jobs, as they generally are not covered by labour or social protections (see Chapter 4). Moreover, over time, as these industries have upgraded or matured and need a more skilled workforce, men often take over the jobs that women secured when the country first opened its economy. Box 1.1 describes the impact of the North American Free Trade Agreement (NAFTA) on the female work force in Mexico. It shows that women's employment first grew in absolute numbers, but over time fell relative to men's employment, forcing women to seek even more precarious forms of employment. Real wages for women are lower, the percentage of female-headed households has doubled and there is a marked gender gap in earnings.

These workers and others who lose their jobs when companies mechanize, retrench or shift locations get left behind in the process of economic growth and trade liberalization. So do smallest-scale

---

[5] Not all non-standard work in developed countries can be equated with informal work in developing countries, as some of it is covered by formal contractual arrangements and legal protections (ILO 2002b).

producers and traders who have little (if any) access to government subsidies, tax rebates or promotional measures to help them compete with imported goods or in export markets. These 'losers' in the global economy have to find ways to survive in the local economy, many resorting to such occupations as waste picking or low-end street trading.

Some observers paint rather idealistic pictures of the informal economy: people 'volunteer' or 'choose' to work in the informal economy to avoid the costs of formality (Maloney 2004); informal operators are 'plucky entrepreneurs' (de Soto 1989); the informal economy provides a 'cushion' during economic crises (World Bank 1998); and ties of solidarity and reciprocity within the informal economy provide 'an element of insurance and risk sharing' (World Bank 1995). Others argue that disadvantaged social groups, especially women within them, lack access to the relevant skills, capital and state resources that would enable them to secure better paid and more secure employment within the informal economy (much less in the formal economy). Still others argue that firms choose to hire workers under low-paid and unprotected contractual arrangements and that, within specific sectors of the economy, larger and more dominant firms construct barriers to exclude the self-employed from better and more secure opportunities (Breman 1996). As this report will illustrate, the informal economy is highly segmented, so that there is some truth to each of these perspectives depending which group of informal workers the observers focus on. This report will focus on the place of the working poor, especially women, in the informal economy.

A related theme is that working does not necessarily lead to poverty reduction. Many of those who work are not able to work their way out of poverty. In fact, labour market arrangements can serve to perpetuate poverty and disadvantage. In addition to more employment opportunities, the poor need higher *returns to their labour*: this depends, in turn, on their portfolio of assets (physical, human and social), their ability to compete in markets and the terms under which they compete (Osmani 2005). What is needed to reduce poverty, therefore, is a mix of policies to create a favourable environment and increase the assets and competitiveness of the poor along with organizing strategies and institutional changes to increase their bargaining power.

Employment in the MDGs and PRSPs

Work and employment have been the central concerns of the International Labour Organization (ILO), which recently has championed the notion of 'decent work' as a path out of poverty as well as a basic human right (ILO 1999). As defined by the ILO, 'decent work' is employment with sufficient income and opportunities, rights at work, social protection, as well as social dialogue (i.e., negotiation and consultation between representatives of governments, employers and workers on issues of common interest relating to economic and social policies). As such, employment has also been part of the broader development agenda within the UN system, including that of UNDP, UNIFEM, and other development organizations.

Employment is also relatively high on the development agenda of the European Union, reflecting the historical interest of European policy makers in employment and labour markets as central to economic prosperity. Employment also features in many of the regional and national debates on poverty reduction. For example, the 2004 Extraordinary Summit of Heads of State and Government of the African Union in Burkino Faso adopted a declaration and plan of action calling for employment to be placed at the centre of poverty reduction strategies.

Perhaps not surprisingly, therefore, employment is also mentioned in the mission statements of the international financial agencies. But when it comes to policy prescriptions and practice, these institutions are typically more concerned with high rates of economic growth than with high levels of employment. In large part this is because mainstream economists and policy makers, as well as the Bretton Woods Institutions treat employment as an outcome rather than a target of macroeconomic policies and view interventions in labour markets as creating distortions in market operations that can interfere with expectations of economic growth (Säve-Soderbergh 2005).

The UN Millennium Declaration, adopted at the Summit, outlines a vision of a world based on freedom from want and freedom from fear. This broad vision was translated into eight time-bound Millennium Development Goals, each with quantifiable targets and indicators (see Box 1.2). The year for meeting the targets for most of these goals is 2015.

Employment creation is not one of the eight MDGs, and employment is neither a target nor an indicator under the first major goal of eradicating extreme poverty and hunger.[6] It is included as an indicator under Goal 3 of gender equality but, as currently specified, it is at best a crude measure of gender equality (see Chapter 3). There is also an indicator on youth employment under Goal 8, reflecting international concern about the large and growing number of unemployed youth around the world. The ILO (2003a) estimates that unemployment among the young was at least twice as high as unemployment in the total labour force in all regions around the world in 2003, and that there will be over 500 million new entrants into the global labour force between 2003 and 2015.

---

6 "Productive employment and decent work" have been added as priority goals in the draft Output Document of the UN General Assembly's President for the MDG Summit in September 2005.

Box 1.2

Millennium Development Goals

Goal 1: to eradicate extreme poverty and hunger
Goal 2: to achieve universal primary education
Goal 3: to promote gender equality and empower women
Goal 4: to reduce child mortality
Goal 5: to promote maternal health
Goal 6: to combat HIV/AIDS, malaria, and other diseases
Goal 7: to ensure environmental sustainability, and
Goal 8: to develop a global partnership for development

In 1999, in response to civil society demands to reduce the unsustainable debt of poor developing countries, the Bretton Woods Institutions agreed that national poverty reduction strategy papers (PRSPs) would provide the basis for concessional lending by the World Bank and IMF and for debt relief to the most heavily-indebted poor countries. The national PRSPs are supposed to be country-owned, expressing not only the perspective of governments but also the needs and interests of people, particularly the poor, solicited through a participatory process (Zuckerman and Garrett 2003). They are meant to represent government-owned, participatory development strategies for reducing poverty.

The employment policy content of PRSPs differs from country to country. However, if we look at the content of the documents, some reasonable generalizations emerge. Most of the PRSPs identify the lack of decent employment opportunities as contributing to high levels of poverty. And many of them single out the low quality and precarious nature of informal and agricultural employment as needing to be addressed. In promoting sustainable 'pro-poor' growth, the role of employment simply cannot be ignored.

The PRSPs' record on recognizing the importance of women's labour – both paid and unpaid – is far spottier. Some are silent on the issue; others give it a token mention. Still others explicitly recognize the connections among women's paid employment, informalization and the feminization of poverty: for example, Chad's 2003 PRSP acknowledges that women frequently face a higher risk of poverty due to the low quality and instability of informal employment.

Although employment features prominently in PRSP diagnosis of the poverty problem, the prescriptive policy content is weaker. As mentioned, much more attention is devoted to the supply side of the employment problem – that is, human capital, education and vocational training – than to the demand side, namely, insuring adequate employment opportunities. Often, demand for labour is seen as a by-product of productive activities. Many PRSPs assume that growth will automatically generate job opportunities that will reduce poverty. Some of the strategies do emphasize the need to invest in labour-intensive production practices and small- and medium-sized enterprises (SMEs). However, little attention is paid to the quantity and quality of employment generated. The primary focus is either the enterprise (e.g., SMEs), a specific sector (e.g., tourism or agro-processing) or the amount produced, not the employment outcomes themselves.

UNIFEM reviewed 41 PRSPs, of which 23 incorporated some form of employment indicator as part of the monitoring and evaluation process.[7] The unemployment rate, total employment or number of small and microenterprises were the most common indicators included. However, these indicators are not the best for monitoring the well-being of workers in the informal economy, where underemployment, low earnings and unstable incomes are particularly important.[8] Furthermore, many of the countries lack timely data resources to effectively monitor the employment indicators they have identified.

Only five of the PRSPs reviewed set any kind of explicit target for employment. For example, Kenya's framework targets 500,000 new employment opportunities a year. Only Viet Nam's strategy includes an explicit target for women's employment: by 2010, half of all new jobs in Viet Nam should be held by women.

A recent UNIFEM study found that the gender content of the PRSPs is inadequate in much the same way as is the employment content: the prescriptive recommendations are far weaker than the diagnostics; gender-specific recommendations are frequently limited to a handful of issues or interventions (e.g., reproductive health or girls' education); and gender-specific targets and indicators are insufficient or absent altogether. In addition, the PRSPs contain little or no analysis of women's unpaid care work (UNIFEM 2005b). This has broad implications for the strategies' ability to address feminized poverty, and particularly severe consequences for the PRSPs' ability to address issues of women's access to employment and independent sources of income.

Finally, the PRSPs treat the question of employment in general, and women's paid work in particular, in a piecemeal way. None of them present a coherent, integrated strategy for tackling the problems of employment that the papers identified. For example, all the PRSPs stressed the importance of

---

7 The PRSPs included Albania (2001), Armenia (2003), Azerbaijan (2003), Benin (2003), Bhutan (2004), Bolivia (2001), Burkina Faso (2004), Cambodia (2003), Cameroon (2002), Chad (2003), Djibouti (2004), Ethiopia (2002), Gambia (2002), Georgia (2003), Ghana (2003), Guinea (2002), Guyana (2002), Honduras (2001), Kenya (2004), Kyrgyzstan (2003), Lao People's Democratic Republic (2004), Malawi (2002), Mali (2003), Mauritania (2000), Moldova (2004), Mongolia (2003), Mozambique (2001), Nepal (2003), Nicaragua (2001), Niger (2002), Pakistan (2004), Rwanda (2002), Senegal (2002), Serbia and Montenegro (2004), Sri Lanka (2003a), Tajikistan (2002), Uganda (2000), United Republic of Tanzania (2000), Viet Nam (2003), Yemen (2002) and Zambia (2002).
8 The focus on unemployment represents a developed country bias among policy makers; in developing countries, underemployment and low-quality employment are more widespread than is open unemployment. The ILO (2003a) estimates that worldwide, in 2003, there were nearly three times as many working poor earning less than US$1 per day (550 million) as unemployed persons (186 million).

macroeconomic stability. However, they did not go the extra step to explore what types of macroeconomic policies would facilitate improvement of employment opportunities, what trade-offs might exist between macroeconomic policies and employment outcomes, and what the impact of economic stabilization would be on different segments of the labour force.

A draft of a 2004 UNDP review of 78 national Millennium Development Goals reports found minimal and inconsistent coverage of gender issues in employment in any of the goals. Of the reports reviewed, eight (10%) highlighted increased access to employment for women as a strategy for poverty reduction under Goal 1, 25 (32%) reported on wage gaps and income differentials and 15 (19%) mentioned domestic work and unpaid work under Goal 3. In addition, five mentioned unemployment and its consequences for young women under Goal 8. The review did not indicate that any report highlighted women's participation in the informal economy under any goal. UNDP noted, however, that overall reporting on gender equality had improved, compared to a review of a smaller number of reports (13) undertaken in 2003: 54 per cent of the reports from 2004 specifically mentioned women's vulnerability to poverty under Goal 1, compared to less than half in 2003 (UNDP 2005b).

Organization of this Report

This report makes the case for an increased focus on informal employment, particularly that of working poor women, in efforts to reduce poverty and promote gender equality. Chapter 2 argues that understanding why women end up in the most insecure types of informal employment requires understanding the totality of women's work and the linkages among the different types of women's work: paid and unpaid, formal and informal. It begins with a brief overview of efforts by women's rights advocates and feminist economists to improve understanding and measurement of the different types of women's work. It then looks at the current context of women's paid and unpaid care work, including demographic trends, state social spending patterns and life-cycle concerns. A third section considers the linkages – temporal, spatial, segmentation and valuation of work – between women's paid and unpaid work, using case studies to illustrate. The final section again uses case studies to consider the intersection of gender and other sources of disadvantage (class, race, ethnicity, religion and geography) in the realm of work, and traces out the links between occupational mobility and recent trends in women's migration between developed and developing countries.

Chapter 3 provides recent statistical evidence on the size and composition of formal and informal employment in both developing and developed countries and reviews recent efforts to include in Millennium Development Goal 3 more relevant indicators for gender equality in employment, namely, employment by type and by earnings. The bulk of the chapter presents an analysis of specially-tabulated data from one developed country (Canada) and six developing countries (Costa Rica, Egypt, El Salvador, Ghana, India and South Africa) on the size and segmentation of the total workforce (formal/ informal, agricultural/non-agricultural, men/women); on the average earnings across these different segments by sector and by sex; and on the poverty risk (i.e., the likelihood of being from a poor household) of working in these various segments by sector and sex. It concludes with a call for improved labour force statistics and a better understanding of labour markets.

Chapter 4 investigates the costs and benefits of informal employment for women and men. It begins with an analysis of the work arrangements of informal workers characterized by place of work, employment relationship and production system, all key determinants of the costs and benefits of informal employment. It then presents a new perspective on the assumed costs and benefits of informal work; offers a causal model of who ends up in informal employment and why; and provides evidence from field studies in India and South Africa and case studies of occupational groups among informal women workers that illustrate the costs and benefits associated with different work arrangements. It concludes with new ways of thinking about income poverty and the other dimensions of poverty from the perspective of the working poor; about gender and other sources of disadvantage for working poor women; and about the operation of informal labour markets.

Unless informal workers become organized, in whatever form works best for them, they will not be able to negotiate effectively for supportive policy responses. Chapter 5 presents an overview of the ways in which women workers in the informal economy are organizing, emphasizing the critical need for women to organize around their identity as workers and to have their own organizations or play leadership roles in organizations of women and men workers. Support to women's organizing as workers in the informal economy represents an essential component of the future agenda for everyone concerned about reducing both poverty and gender inequality.

Chapter 6 presents a framework for policy and action in support of the working poor, especially women, in the informal economy. It presents good practice examples, drawn from a wide range of countries. It concludes with a call for concerted action on four priority areas.

CHAPTER 2: The Totality of Women's Work

Basket weaver and child, Eritrea.
Photo: Giacomo Pirozzi/UNICEF/HQ97-1091

"When I had to go to work, I used to worry about my child. I would take him with me to the tobacco field. But my employer objected. Then I would leave him at home, but I still worried about him. But what could I do? I had to earn, and I had no option."

Agricultural labourer, India (cited in Dasgupta 2002)

To understand the role of employment in perpetuating or reducing poverty, including feminized poverty, we need to look at where working women and men are located in the global workforce and at the nature of work in today's global economy. First, however, it is important to look at the totality of women's work. Women's ability to participate in the labour market is contingent on other demands on their time, especially for unpaid work in the household and community. Understanding the relationship between women's work and poverty therefore requires a comprehensive view of formal and informal paid work, subsistence production, unpaid work in family enterprises, unpaid care work for household members and community volunteer work.

Studies of women's work generally focus on different aspects of their work rather than the whole. Analyses of women's paid employment range from an examination of the 'glass ceiling' that constrains highly skilled women from advancing as far as men, to a focus on job segregation and the relegation of working class women to pink collar jobs, lacking the same pay levels or job security as men in blue collar employment. Another focus is 'the care economy' and women's role in unpaid care work, inside households and in communities. With some exceptions, however, the literature has tended to underestimate the importance of women's informal work, especially in developing countries.[1]

At the same time, increased attention to the gender dimensions of HIV/AIDS has highlighted the fact that women in many countries are being pulled out of productive work, especially in agriculture, to take care of the ill and the dying (Heyzer 2004; UNAIDS et al. 2004; Budlender 2003). This has provoked a new look at the ways in which women's unpaid care work in the household and community constrains their ability to access or continue in paid employment, and illuminates the hidden costs of shifting the provision of health and welfare services to women's unpaid care work.

This chapter looks at the ways in which women's unpaid care work constrains their access to or participation in paid employment, focusing on women's low-paid informal work. It highlights global patterns of stratification between women and men, and between richer women and poorer women. Four cases illustrate the links between the different types of work, looking at four inter-linked dimensions: temporal and spatial and the segmentation and valuation of work. A further selection of cases illustrates the intersection of gender with class, ethnicity, caste and geography, and how these all combine to locate the working poor, particularly women, in precarious forms of informal employment and thus to perpetuate poverty.

Understanding and Measuring Women's Work

Since the 1970s a number of women's organizations and feminist scholars have focused on improving the way in which women's work is conceptualized and measured, highlighting five distinct types of work: *formal market work*, *informal market work*, *subsistence production*, *unpaid care work* and *volunteer work* (Benería 1993; UNIFEM 2000). Only *formal market work* is adequately measured by conventional data collection methods; the others all require the design of better methods of data collection or, at an even more basic level, new conceptual frameworks and definitions.

In official statistics, the measurement of work and production hinges on the boundary set by the System of National Accounts (SNA) (UN 1995, 2000). Work that falls within the boundary is considered 'economic' while work that falls outside the boundary is considered 'non-economic'. Those who perform only 'non-economic' activities are considered 'economically inactive'. *Formal market work* falls clearly and neatly within the production boundary. *Informal market work* and a large part of *subsistence production* (i.e., production and processing of food crops) have always

---

1 Exceptions include early work on specific regions (e.g., Heyzer 1986; Benería and Roldán 1987) as well as more recent work on the global labour force (see, e.g., Pearson 2004).

Box 2.1 Unpaid Care Work

The term 'unpaid care work' is used to refer to the provision of services within households for other household and community members. It avoids the ambiguities of other terms, including 'domestic labour', which can refer both to unpaid care work and to the work of paid domestic workers; 'unpaid labour', which can also refer to unpaid care work as well as unpaid work in the family business; 'reproductive work', which can refer to unpaid care work as well as giving birth and breastfeeding; and 'home work', which can also refer to paid work done in the home on subcontract from an employer.

Each word in the term 'unpaid care work' is important:

- 'unpaid' meaning that the person doing the activity does not receive a wage for it.
- 'care' meaning that the activity serves people and their well-being.
- 'work' meaning that the activity has a cost in terms of time and energy and arises out of a social or contractual obligation, such as marriage or less formal social relationships.

Source: UNIFEM 2000.

---

fallen within the production boundary, in principle, but conceptual and methodological challenges to fully measuring and properly classifying women's informal activities remain. Other parts of *subsistence production* and *unpaid housework and family services* were excluded from the production boundary until 1993.

As part of the 1993 revision of the System of National Accounts, the production boundary was extended to encompass the production of *all goods* for household consumption, including the processing and storage of all agricultural products; the production of other primary products, such as mining salt, carrying water and collecting firewood; and other kinds of processing, such as weaving cloth and making garments, pottery, utensils, furniture and furnishings (UN 2000). The recognition of subsistence production of goods as 'economic' activities was in great part due to the efforts of women's rights advocates working at both the national and international levels. Despite their efforts, however, the provision of domestic and personal *services* by household members for consumption within the household, such as cooking and cleaning plus care for children and the elderly, continued to be left outside the production boundary. Again in an effort to improve data on the full contribution of women to the economy, the 1993 SNA recommended that valuation of activities outside the SNA boundary be undertaken in 'satellite accounts' outside the national accounts (UN 1995, 2000).

For many years the women's movement in general and feminist economists in particular have advocated that social and economic policies take into account their impact on women's unpaid care work. *Progress of the World's Women 2000* used the term 'unpaid care work' to refer to "women's provision of services within households and communities" (see Box 2.1). As that report pointed out, not all care work is unpaid and not all unpaid work involves care. Much care work is done by paid workers (e.g., domestic workers, nursing assistants, social workers), while the unpaid work that many women do for subsistence production and family enterprises does not involve care.

One way to measure unpaid care work is through time-use surveys. These surveys gather data on what women, men and children do over the course of the day, and provide information on all types of work. They also form the basis for satellite accounts. In response to the recommendation of the Beijing Platform for Action, the United Nations Statistics Division (UNSD) developed an international classification of activities for time-use statistics that is sensitive to the differences between women and men, and between girl children and boy children, in remunerated and unremunerated work.[2]

In 1993, largely due to concern with the need for improved measurement of women's economic activity, the International Conference of Labour Statisticians (ICLS) agreed on a definition of the informal sector (UN 1995). Subsequently the ILO, the International Expert Group on Informal Sector Statistics (the Delhi Group) and the WIEGO network have worked together to broaden the concept to cover certain types of informal employment that had not been included. The expanded definition includes self-employment in informal enterprises (i.e., small and unregistered enterprises) and wage employment in informal jobs (i.e., unregulated and unprotected jobs) for informal enterprises, formal enterprises, households or for no fixed employer (see Chapter 3). Guidelines to implement this definition were endorsed by the ICLS in 2003.

While pressing for change in statistical concepts and definitions, women's advocates have also requested new methods of data collection that can capture more fully women's subsistence and informal production, which tend to be undercounted in national censuses and surveys. For example, beginning in the early 1990s UNIFEM supported work in countries in Asia to improve data collected in national censuses on women's work. And in 1995, the Fourth World Conference on Women, in its recommendations to improve and disseminate sex-disaggregated data, proposed several actions to develop a more comprehensive knowledge of all forms of work and employment.

Despite this progress, we are still a long way from adequately measuring different types of

---

2 For details see http://www.un.org/dept3/unsd/timeuse/inter.htm

women's work. What is primarily needed is for national statistical systems to incorporate in their regular labour force surveys and in periodic time-use surveys the new concepts and measurement strategies, including the expanded definition of informal employment and suggested new employment indicators for Millennium Development Goal 3 detailed in Chapter 3.

Mapping Women's Paid and Unpaid Work

Over the past three decades women's labour force participation rates have been increasing in most parts of the world. This is not true of the transitional economies of Eastern and Central Europe, where employment rates for both men and women have dropped since 1990 (UNRISD 2005). Also, in the Middle East and North Africa, women's labour force participation rates remain very low. However, the general trend has been towards an increase in the numbers of women working. What does this mean in terms of women's economic security and rights? What does it imply for gender inequality and poverty? To answer these questions we first need to look at the impact of wider forces on women's work as a whole, both paid and unpaid. These forces are both macro, including the wider economic trends mentioned in Chapter 1 as well as state-level social spending and broad demographic trends, and micro, including the different relationships individuals have to the labour market at different periods of their lives and the daily reality of balancing competing demands on their time.

State social spending, the labour market and care work

As noted in Chapter 1, international financial institutions as part of their free market policy prescriptions have encouraged governments to adopt a set of economic policies designed to control inflation and enhance growth. These include trade liberalization, market deregulation, reductions in government employment and privatization of services (e.g., health, education, welfare, housing) formerly paid for by the state. All of these policies impact on gender relations, women's work and the provision of care.

In addition to household size and composition, and the division of labour within the household, women's ability to engage in paid employment is dependent on state policies that encourage or constrain their participation (e.g., through the provision of affordable child care). The state is also a provider of employment in health, education and welfare service sectors, and as such helps shape the labour market; in many countries women make up most of the state-employed teachers, nurses and social workers. These service sectors are located at the nexus between public and private sectors, formal and informal care, and low-paid and unpaid care, and are thus critical in understanding women's paid and unpaid labour. Changes in state social provision, combined with changes in women's participation in the labour market, shift the boundaries between paid formal and informal care work, and between these and unpaid care work. While this is true in both developed and developing countries, the meagre supply of state services in many developing countries means that women are bearing a heavy burden of unpaid care work, often impeding their ability to earn a livelihood.

With regard to health-care provision, countries in the global North have moved away from universal health services towards various types of fee-based care, or public-private partnerships, sometimes with a residual free (and usually poorer quality) public service for those who cannot afford to pay. It is widely recognized that it is women who pay the costs of this individualization of care, as the increased time spent taking care of family members limits both their participation in paid employment and their leisure (Pascall and Lewis 2004). Wealthier families can buy health care for themselves, and/or pay someone else to provide care. After bearing children, better educated women can pay for childcare and keep their careers; less well educated women are likely to return to poorly paid, part-time jobs in an effort to balance unpaid care work with earning an income.

In Europe, many countries have shifted the way in which they fund paid care work. In the past, the typical pattern was that the state or municipality either provided care-givers or funded other organizations to provide care. Now the tendency is to provide cash funds directly to those needing care so that they can purchase their own care from others. In France, this shift was "part of a more general policy to stimulate low paid employment for women" (Ungerson 2003: 394). In the Netherlands, it was intended to convert unpaid care work to formal paid work, and was "specifically directed towards pulling informal economic activity into the formal labour market, and workers into the social security system" (ibid: 384).

In addition to these job-creation and employment regulation outcomes, this shift in funding could also result in greater empowerment of those cared for, giving them more choice about whom to employ and on what terms. However, those being cared for may have difficulty getting the information about care workers they need to make an informed choice. And, importantly for this report, the care worker who used to be employed full-time by the local welfare office may find that her or his work as the direct employee of the person needing care is now more precarious, with less security and fewer benefits.

In broad terms, the advanced welfare states were built on the idea of stable nuclear families that include a male breadwinner in permanent employment. The man's income would support the family; his receipt of the so-called 'social wage' – including health insurance for him and his dependents, pension benefits and insurance against unemployment and disability – would provide security for the entire family. This 'male breadwinner model' has been replaced by the 'adult worker model', which assumes that both women and men are employed. What is not recognized, however, is that women's decisions about work are still largely dependent on 'the unarticulated dimension' of the male breadwinner model: unpaid care work. Without state support for this work, "women are being asked to bear the main burden of welfare state restructuring" (Lewis 2002: 333).

In former communist countries, governments encouraged women to participate in the labour market on equal terms with men. This involved extremely high rates of state social spending, especially on childcare, while little attention was given to finding ways of changing the gendered division of care work (Pascall and Lewis 2004). In contrast, some European countries have provided incentives to working men to engage in parenting by, for example, providing relatively generous paternity leave. However, paternity leave is not taken up as extensively as it could be (Orloff 2000), and it is noteworthy that policy initiatives for greater involvement of men have focused on men's role as fathers rather than as general care providers.

In most developing countries, in contrast, the reality for most people is that state provision of education, health, welfare and childcare services has always been limited. Following structural adjustment, even those limited services have been curtailed. In education and in health, user-fees are now widespread and health care is designed to target those who can pay rather than the population as a whole. The cuts in state service provision were meant to encourage greater market provision, but markets do not readily respond to poor people and their need for social services. In some countries, international aid has compensated for cuts in state provision, but this leaves social service provision vulnerable to changes in donor thinking about what services should be supported. And while faith-based and community-based organizations, as well as more formal local welfare organizations, may make an important contribution to health, education and welfare, they are few and far between in rural areas, where the greatest poverty may be found and where it is more difficult to leverage access to other forms of support.

At the same time that the state has cut childcare provision and privatized its health and welfare services, women have entered the labour force in larger numbers in both developed and developing countries, partly due to the inability of households to survive on a single worker income. Yet with few exceptions, there is little evidence of men taking on substantially more care-giving responsibilities, and insufficient attention is given to policies that encourage men to do so. As a result, women are paying the costs of free market economic policy prescriptions. And the changes in women's patterns of paid work seem to have little impact on "the most ubiquitous and long-lasting conception of the woman (which) in virtually all countries and traditions of the world, is as a giver of care: homemaker, mother, wife, tender of the needs of the elderly – in general, a supporter of the needs and ends of others" (Nussbaum 2005: 3).

Demographic trends and paid and unpaid work

A number of demographic trends also affect women's work. While the best known is fertility, and its link to women's labour force participation, also important are population ageing and migration. The impact of these trends on both employment opportunities and unpaid care work for different groups of women are particularly relevant.

The world's population is ageing. The more developed regions have led this process, as fertility is still relatively high in the less developed regions. However, even in the less developed regions more rapid population ageing is anticipated. Trends in the number of persons of working age (15 to 59 years) are especially important. In developed regions, while the proportion of the working age population increased slightly between 1950 and 2005 from 61 per cent to 63 per cent, a decline to 52 per cent is expected by 2050 (UN 2005). In less developed regions the proportion of the working age population is expected to decline slightly, from 61 per cent in 2005 to 59 per cent in 2050. However, among the least developed countries the proportion is projected to rise from 53 per cent in 2005 to 61 per cent in 2050. These trends have implications for employment, for the provision of paid and unpaid health and welfare services, and for unpaid care work. Developing regions must somehow create jobs for the growing working age population, while developed regions must find a way to support the care needs of growing numbers of older persons. Yet developing regions will also face this challenge in the not too distant future.

Looking at the relationship between demographic changes and the increase in paid domestic work in Latin America, Barrientos (2004) offers some possible explanations about supply and demand that may be generalized to other regions. He notes that population ageing may be creating a demand for long-term care of elderly people, or the entry of more women into the labour market may be creating a market in household services. Alternatively, the supply of women in domestic work could be a response to their own need for more household income, related to the decline in

Women carrying grass used for fodder and fuel, Nepal. Photo: Martha Chen

men's incomes associated with labour informalization and rising unemployment.

China, with 1 billion people (one sixth of the world's population), is undergoing rapid demographic change (Cook 2003) marked by a rapidly ageing population as well as exceptionally low fertility. The transition to a market economy has occasioned both rapid economic growth and widespread unemployment. The 'one child' policy means that the unemployed older generations have a limited number of children to support them. There is a marked gender imbalance in the children who are currently being born, based on a preference for sons, with boys significantly outnumbering girls. Among other problems, this will place great strain on the care-giving responsibilities of decreasing numbers of women – unless men become more active providers of care.

Some developing countries have experienced reverses in the demographic transition, mainly due to the HIV/AIDS pandemic. Over the last two decades, life expectancy has decreased dramatically in some sub-Saharan Africa countries: in South Africa, for example, life expectancy at birth fell from over 60 years in the mid-1990s to slightly over 40 years by 2010 (Dorrington and Johnson 2002). This has increased the amount of unpaid care work and voluntary community work that falls on women, as the formal health-care system in many countries is breaking down. At the same time, in sub-Saharan Africa, the HIV/AIDS virus affects women in greater numbers and at a younger age than it does men (UNAIDS et al. 2004).

Worldwide, the growing number of young people also has implications for employment creation. The ILO estimates that unemployment among the young was twice as high or more as unemployment in the total labour force in all regions in 2003. It also estimates that there will be over 500 million new entrants into the global labour force between 2003 and 2015 – the MDG target year for reducing extreme poverty and hunger by half (ILO 2003a). About 50 per cent of these new entrants will be young women. Recognizing this, Millennium Development Goal 8 includes an indicator on youth employment.

With regard to migration, employment has been a major factor in the movement of persons between regions, countries and rural and urban areas within countries. Women are increasingly entering the migration stream, both within their own countries as well as to other countries (UN 2000). While initially women migrated mainly to join their male family members, increasingly they are moving as autonomous individuals. This has effects on the labour market in the countries they move to, as well as on labour markets and care responsibilities in the countries, communities and households they leave behind (ILO 2004b).

Life course changes

Work and employment are a source of as well as a response to risk and vulnerability, which people experience differently over the course of their lives. Life course analysis helps to identify risks arising from a person's relationship to the labour market, even where this relationship is indirect, as

Table 2.1 — Risks and Vulnerabilities Associated with Employment at Different Stages of the Life Cycle

Life cycle stage	Types of associated risks and vulnerabilities
Very young children 0 to 4	Nutritional risks to children of working and non-working mothers, with lifelong developmental deficits Delays in early cognitive development if left with an inappropriate care-giver Acute vulnerability to disease and infection with poor access to health services due to parents' low income Exposure to toxic fumes, dust, extreme heat and cold, chemicals and pesticides (in homework and/or when infants accompany mothers who engage in street trading, agriculture, small-scale mining)
Children 5 to 12	Risk of not attending school because of domestic or income earning responsibilities for girls vs. boys Invisibility of young children's work, whether as 'normal' household responsibilities or in non-family enterprises when it is tied to parents' employment For working children, the triple burden of jobs, unpaid care work and schooling and its long-term impacts on opportunities and productivity, and the differing effects on girls and boys Lower access to school associated with parents' low income and the differing impact on girls and boys
Adolescents 13 to 19	Vulnerability of (especially girl) children to early withdrawal from school Triple burden of job, unpaid care and schooling and the long-term impact on opportunities and productivity and differing effects on girls and boys Entry into high risk employment categories, hazardous industries, prostitution, etc.
Young adults in their 20s and 30s	Lack of access to financial institutions/asset building opportunities Loss of employment or employment insecurity for women through pregnancy and childcare Move from double to single-income family through pregnancy; men may have to work harder or take additional work
Middle adults	Loss of employment, or employment insecurity through care for both younger and older family members Costs of illness and death, especially in context of HIV/AIDS Expectation that women in this age group do unpaid volunteer care work
Older people	Loss of income when work is lost, in absence of work-related provision for retirement and/or state support Continuing to work due to income insecurity and/or to support dependents Widows' loss of access to late husband's family resources Onerous child care responsibilities in countries where AIDS or military destabilization has resulted in few middle age adults and high numbers of children in stress

Source: Adopted from Lund and Srinivas (2000: 37, 38).

in the case of infant needs. Table 2.1 gives an overview of work-related risks and vulnerabilities at different stages of the life cycle.

Periods in a life cycle are demographically, physically and culturally dependent, and change over time. There are overlaps between the different stages, and some people may not go through all of the stages. Not all men and women marry or have children. There are pressures for or against the use of child labour in different countries, and different demands on girls compared to boys with regard to household and other tasks. Societies in which girls get married and have their first children in their early teens contrast with those where childbearing is generally much later, and where the decision to have children at a later age is connected to decisions about employment. 'Old age' has a different meaning in a country such as Japan, where life expectancy is now over 80, compared to Botswana, where until recently it was around 70 but where it is now less than 40.

Bearing these differences in mind, Table 2.1 highlights the risks and vulnerabilities inherent in the relationship between women's employment and responsibility for care work at different stages of the life cycle, setting up conditions for the gender specific transmission of poverty to the next generation. Cuts in state provided child care services, for example, may lead to girls being pulled out of school to fill the care gap – with lifelong effects on their ability to enter the labour market and earn a decent income.

The gendered nature of these life cycle risks and vulnerabilities can be seen clearly in patterns of widowhood and remarriage. Older men who are widowed are far more likely to re-marry than older women. In India, for example, 38 per cent of women over age 50 are widowed compared to 10 per cent of men over 50 (Government of India 2001). Elderly widows cannot count on their late husband's kin or their own kin to maintain them, so many of them have to work well into their seventies, doing whatever work they can find and are able to do (Chen 2000).

In general the greater longevity of women and men means more years of responsibility for the care of older parents by their sons and daughters. Where increased longevity coincides with high fertility, a woman of the middle generation comes to be responsible for the care of her parents as well as for her own children and grandchildren.

The Dynamics of Women's Paid and Unpaid Work

Understanding the relationship between different types of women's paid and unpaid work helps shed light on the dynamics of poverty and gender inequality. If job creation programmes are to benefit women, for example they must take into account the impact of expectations about women's role in unpaid care work, in terms of women's ability to access or sustain paid market work. Four dimensions help to illuminate these relationships.

The first dimension is *temporal*. Time-use studies have shown that women spend more time in work overall, spend fewer hours in paid work and in general have less discretionary time than men do (UN 1995, 2000). Women spend more time than men doing unpaid care work and housework, with multiple and overlapping activities, such as childcare, cooking and cleaning. At the same time they also engage in paid and unpaid activities, for example, doing piece-rate paid work while cooking and childminding. In developed countries, a high percentage of part-time workers are women, who combine paid market work and unpaid care work. In developing countries, women spend a good deal of time in unpaid food production and processing, and fuel and water collection, which limits their time for both paid market work and unpaid care work.

A second dimension is *spatial*. The location of an individual's work may be in his or her own home, in somebody else's home, on a farm, in a forest, on a street or in an office. Women's obligations to do unpaid care work often oblige them to work at home, while their decision to migrate in search of work has implications for their own unpaid work for their families. Migration may be internal, usually from rural to urban areas, cross-border or further afield; it can be temporary, permanent or alternate between the two. In all cases, women migrants with dependents have to find substitute care-givers. In their receiving countries, being without their dependents may enable them to do more than one paid job (perhaps a full-time job that carries secure status and social protection benefits). The temporal dimension may also come into play, with an interruption in income earning between leaving work in the home country and taking up new work after migrating.

A third dimension is that of *employment segmentation*. Women's role in unpaid care work tends to channel them into similar occupations and sectors in the paid economy: notably, the clothing and textile industries, teaching, childcare, health care and domestic services. It also channels them into certain types of employment that are more precarious in terms of earnings and benefits such as part-time work or informal wage work.

Employment segmentation is closely related to the fourth dimension, the *valuation* of different types of work. The fact that women's unpaid care work is given a low value means that even when these activities are monetized or commodified, the work is still undervalued:

> The fact that these types of work – sewing, child care, and housework – are done 'free' by so many women within their own households, suggests (a) that there are few skills involved – it is something that women, at least, can do 'naturally'; and (b) that the work has low value, because it can be obtained free in other circumstances. The result is low wages and low status (Budlender 2002).

In market or employment transactions, this under-valuation is implicit and unplanned, reflected in low wages and low status. Furthermore, when efforts to estimate the value of unpaid care work are based on a comparison with the wages of under-paid care workers, the resulting valuation will also be low.

These four dimensions are closely linked, especially the temporal with the spatial, and employment segmentation with the valuation of different types of work. They are used here, singly and in combination, to show the linkages between different types of work, and the effects of these linkages on women's disadvantage in the labour market. They are also a means of identifying the trade-offs that must be made between different types of work, and the costs to those who make them in terms of job and income security.

Hidden costs of combining employment, paid and unpaid care work

Part-time employment may be formal in status, as in the case below, and may enable women to care for family members while earning an income. The costs for women of reconciling paid work and unpaid care work, however, are usually hidden. The case of Lucy and Jack illustrates the trade-offs between full-time and part-time employment, and between paid work and unpaid care work – and the costs of these trade-offs in terms of men's and women's present and future security.

Caring for an elderly relative in South Africa: Lucy and Jack

Lucy is 38 years old, and is a full-time manager of the cashiers at a supermarket. Her job carries health insurance and a retirement savings scheme. She is in line for promotion to middle management. Her husband Jack works for a security firm; the job is relatively secure, but with low earnings (lower than Lucy's), long hours and no retirement benefits. They are financially stable, but not well-off, and have to budget carefully. They employ a domestic worker two days a week.

Their three children are 16, 14 and 8 years old and are all in school. Lucy would prefer to work part-time, as she would like to be at home when the children get back from school each day. However, she and Jack are anxious to provide their children with tertiary education, as they see this as the key to more secure and better-paid futures for the children. What makes it possible to save for this is Lucy's full-time salary. They deposit what they estimate to be the difference between this and what she would earn if she worked part time into a special 'education account', as a way of managing savings.

Then Jack's widowed mother has a stroke, is hospitalized and cannot live independently. Lucy and Jack are her only family support; there is no affordable accommodation in old age homes; besides, they feel obliged to look after her. She comes to live with them. She does not need full-time nursing care, but does require intensive care at certain times of the day – when dressing, toileting and eating. Lucy shifts from full-time to part-time work, and the hours of the domestic worker are increased so that she is always in the home when Lucy is not. Jack's mother lives with them for 10 years before she dies.

What do we learn from this case? First is the degree to which care work is assigned along gender lines. There was no consideration that Jack should move from full-time work to part-time work to take over any care-giving, despite the fact that it was his mother who required care. Second is the amount of income loss that accompanied Lucy's shift to part-time work in order to do the care work. Costs were calculated of her direct loss of earnings, or what the savings in the education account would have been had Lucy kept the full-time job and continued to bank the difference. The savings over 10 years would comfortably have seen the three children through expensive tertiary education.

Third are the costs of the 'temporary' 10-year interruption in Lucy's career in terms of her own job satisfaction and the loss of a pension to support her own and Jack's retirement. There is also the reduced education of their children, which leaves them less likely in future to be able to take care of their ageing parents.

Finally, we see the relationship between shifts in the employment status of professional women and that of less skilled women workers. The domestic worker was asked to work additional hours, that meshed with Lucy's reduced hours, to help take care of Jack's mother. She was also required to shift her role from domestic work to care work. This was purely an informal arrangement, and the domestic worker's wage did not change as a result of the new nursing skills she had to learn and practice. She 'added value', but received no recognition for this.

Low income, poor working conditions and quality of unpaid care

Most women are confronted at some stage of their lives with having to balance work and child or elder care. Better-off women can afford to pay others to look after their children or elderly relatives. For poorer women, if paid care is not available or not affordable, then the ability to work depends on whether there are dependable (usually female) household members to assist with care.

Working from one's own home, whether as an unpaid contributing family member, an industrial outworker or in self-employment, enables caring for children or elderly relatives to continue alongside this work. Where a woman has to rely on paid or unpaid care-givers while she is away at work, the mere presence of such care-givers does not necessarily guarantee an appropriate quality of care, as the following case illustrates.

Low paid employment and child care: mothers in the clothing industry in Lesotho

Trade liberalization has led to the rapid growth of the garment industry in Lesotho, opening up new employment opportunities for young women in this extremely poor country. A study of women workers in these factories looked at the relationship between their working conditions and their capacity to care for their children (Sekhamane 2004). The author interviewed a sample of working mothers, along with the women who took care of their young children, and observed how the care was managed. Her sample was drawn from women with a malnourished child under three years old who had applied to a programme for nutrition supplements. The findings, while limited to the sample, allow insights into the ways in which women's low paid employment affects their ability to secure good quality paid and unpaid care for their young children.

The major obstacle mothers faced were long and inflexible work hours, between 10 and 12 hours a day during the week and up to 10 hours a day at weekends. During periods when hours were even longer, women reported never seeing their children awake. They were allowed no time off to care for or get health care for their children. Workers seeking medical care for themselves had to produce a medical certificate simply to protect their jobs, but their wages were still deducted for the time off. Some women thus avoided both pre-natal and post-natal clinics, risking their own health as well as that of their children.

Economic need and low wages meant that most mothers had returned to work one week after giving birth, thus limiting or stopping breast-feeding. Infant formula is expensive, so often their infants received severely diluted milk and/or sugar solutions. Yet some of the women spent their money on socializing and drinking after work, placing the nutritional and health status of their children even more at risk. Their low wages also limited their choice of paid care-givers, relying on unpaid relatives, who were usually very young or much older. Young care-givers often behaved as one might expect: neglecting their duties, becoming easily distracted and occasionally even eating the child's food.

This study, while small, shows the impact of low paid work on poverty and parenting, feeding into a generational cycle. New employment opportunities often entail low wages and working conditions that compromise workers' health and constrain their ability to seek care, limit their choice of care-givers, and lead to poor feeding routines for infant children. This cycle will transmit poverty and poor employment possibilities to the next generation. Yet despite the poor working conditions, employment in the foreign-owned factories represented a step up for the majority of the working mothers, either due to their previous lack of employment or compared to their former employment.

The costs of women's volunteer work in the community

Across the world, volunteer work is promoted as a social and public good, as a sign of social solidarity and as having benefits for both the giver and the receiver. In developed countries, volunteer work is usually viewed as supplementary to other forms of social services or support. In many poor countries, however, where health and welfare services are scarce or non-existent, voluntary care work may be the only form of support there is. The kind of volunteer work that takes place as part of an organized programme is usually subject to gender role expectations and comes at a cost to volunteers (Benería 2003).

A number of studies are investigating the costs of voluntary and unpaid work by family members in the context of HIV/AIDS (Ogden et al. 2004; Akintola 2004). The scale of this pandemic has made more visible the care work that is needed for other common chronic diseases such as tuberculosis and malaria. It is largely women who do the care-giving, and this detracts from time available to do other work. In the rural context, this especially refers to subsistence production.

A comparative study of home-based care schemes for people with AIDS was carried out in South Africa and Uganda. The schemes used both unpaid family members and non-kin volunteers, with different levels of support from and interaction with non-governmental organizations (NGOs) and government. In Uganda, the organized community volunteer work reduced the capacity of care-givers to grow their own food. As one volunteer said: "The patient is hungry and we are hungry too" (Akintola 2004: 25-26). HIV/AIDS meant lowered household incomes along with greater health-related expenditures. Volunteers had similar needs to those for whom they provided care and also needed material support. In the South African initiatives, there was a high rate of attrition among volunteers owing to the lack of financial compensation and the high stress levels.

A further gendered dynamic in home-based volunteer care of people with AIDS was revealed in a UNIFEM initiative in Botswana, Mozambique and Zimbabwe. The great majority of volunteer care-givers were women. Women have higher AIDS prevalence rates than men in this region, but the disproportionate numbers of women receiving care was higher than the sex-prevalence AIDS rates would suggest. This could be because when men become ill, female family members take care of them. In contrast, when women become ill, it is most often volunteers, mostly women, from outside the kin group that are called on (Budlender 2003).

Both gender and class need to be inscribed into the analysis of 'volunteer work' and 'community care'. A community is not a formal entity: a group of people sharing geographical space, as the term is generally used, may or may not have the necessary structure, or the material resources, required to undertake 'community care' in a way that does not make further demands on already scarce time. Calls for volunteer and community care work also conceal the serious emotional and psychological stress experienced by volunteers, and the hard physical work involved in trying to provide competent care in the presence of chronic diarrhoea and an insufficient water supply. Throughout the world, the promotion of unsupported home-based care by women not only impedes greater gender equality (Akintola 2004), but also impacts on poverty, especially where women are pulled out of production to take care of the ill and dying.

In Lesotho, for example, a joint ILO-UNIFEM delegation to review the link between employment and unpaid care in the context of HIV/AIDS found that absenteeism among garment factory workers – most of whom are women – is rising

Carpet sellers at a street market, Kosovo. Photo: Hans Madej/Bilderberg/Aurora

dramatically (UNIFEM 2002a). One factory manager reported that out of 6,500 workers (virtually all women), each month, nearly half visit the factory health clinic. Absenteeism is due not only to worker illness, but also to care for family or community members. It is costly not only for factories but also for their workers, whose pay is deducted for each day lost. At the same time, employers are beginning to cut back on benefits to workers affected by HIV/AIDS, arguing that these costs have become untenable. A manager of a factory with 5,000 workers used to provide free transport to funerals of employees or family members when there was only about one funeral per month, but stopped when these increased to about one a week (ibid.).

Chains of paid and unpaid care

Appreciation of the linkages between formal and informal productive work has been enhanced by the application of value chain analysis to local or international chains of production and distribution. Work in paid and unpaid care can be viewed through this same value chain lens. Care work takes place on a continuum, from a full-time paid nurse with a secure employment contract to a part-time and probably low-paid formal or informal worker, to unpaid work by a family member or neighbour, or as part of a voluntary scheme. Through this lens we can see the links between formal and informal work, and between paid and unpaid work, as well as the changing spatial boundaries of care-giving – between the health facility and the home.

Chains of care in the global south: a doctor in South Africa

A doctor brought up a family of five children, then returned to pursue her professional career in a public hospital for some 30 years before retiring. Through her civil service job, she had medical insurance and a pension, which added to her widow's pension enabled her to live independently until she had a stroke.

While medical insurance provided short-term residential health care, after her stroke she required full-time care at home. She contracted a private nursing service, owned by two professional nurses who had left government to be their own bosses. The agency hired two assistants to care for the client on a rotating basis. Both were paid only when they worked and received no social benefits. Both had sick family members, for whom they had to make private care arrangements while they were on duty. One gave her cousin a month's rent-free accommodation in exchange for two weeks care each month for her ailing husband. The other paid a neighbour to come in occasionally to care for her son who was in advanced stages of AIDS but had been discharged from hospital in line with the new health policy of encouraging home-based care.

While the contracting firm was responsible for the formal management of the client-assistant part of this chain of care, the supervision was inadequate for the kind of support the assistants needed in developing a relationship with the increasingly demanding client. The client's daughter was the informal manager of the chain, a role made possible by her own well-paid, part-time and flexible employment. She in turn employed a part-time domestic worker.

What can be learned from this case? First, the financing of this chain of care was anchored in the full-time secure work of the client and her husband who had over a lifetime built up a contributory medical insurance and pensions plan. Second, and by contrast, the nursing assistants were sub-contracted wage workers, working on terms that were precarious and insecure – in common with many workers in the informal economy. Although they had contracts, they did not qualify for work-related benefits such as paid holidays or sick leave. Work was their only source of income.

Third, the assistants had to make arrangements to cover their own unpaid care-giving responsibilities at home. Either they paid for such help, at a direct cost to themselves, or they relied on another woman's unpaid or very low paid care time. Fourth, in the South African context from which this case is drawn, sub-contracted assistants get limited work-related benefits, but they will become eligible for the means-tested old age pension when they turn 60. This monthly non-contributory cash transfer will go some way to meeting their material needs. They also have access to a limited range of free health services. This is quite different to the situation of people in most developing countries, where there is little state support for the retirement years and fees are charged for state health services.

These cases show the links between different types of work, and how the costs of paid work are obscured by the failure to value the unpaid work on which it depends. They also show why many forms of work do not by themselves provide a pathway out of poverty. Women are expected to reconcile paid and unpaid work, receiving little state support, with the result that the kinds of paid work that they most often find themselves in are precisely those that fail to enable them to escape from poverty. The concepts of 'volunteer work' and 'community care' conceal the real costs involved in care work as well as the gender bias that ensures that it is women who perform it.

Gender and Other Sources of Disadvantage: Implications for Poverty Reduction

In every economic system, women face constraints in the realm of paid work by reason of their gender. As detailed in this chapter, women face greater demands on their time, notably for unpaid care work and domestic chores, than men. Child rearing and other forms of unpaid care work always interrupt women's work more than they do men's work. Furthermore, women's access to property is typically less than that of men and often mediated through their relationship to men; and women face greater social constraints than men on their physical mobility. Perhaps not surprisingly, unpaid work in the family enterprise is also consistently done by women more than by men.

However, understanding the links between women's employment and their poverty status requires integrating an analysis of gender with that of other relationships. Class, religion, race/ethnicity and space intersect with gender to position many women in precarious forms of work. Wealth is frequently distributed along ethnic and racial lines. In many Latin American countries, for instance, indigenous communities and communities of African descent have the lowest levels of education, are concentrated in precarious and poorly remunerated work and are the most impoverished (Heyzer 2002; ILO 2004a). Women in these communities are doubly disadvantaged by reason of their gender and of their wider social identity.

In India, on the other hand, religion, caste and ethnic identity all play a role in what work people do. Among Hindus, many individuals and families– particularly those from artisan and service castes - continue in hereditary caste occupations even today. If and when individuals leave the hereditary occupation, their caste also determines what kind of alternative work they can take up. Gender norms impose limits on women's physical mobility and what work they can do. Both high-caste Hindus, particularly in North India, and Muslims practice purdah (the veiling and/or seclusion of women) which imposes restrictions on women's physical and work mobility. If and when these women work for pay, they are likely to do so from their homes—with the result that a large share of all women workers in India are home-based (Chen 2000; Unni and Rani 2005).

The inadequacy of 'gender' alone to explain women's poverty and lack of empowerment is also illustrated by the phenomenon of paid domestic work. Millions of domestic workers worldwide, most of whom are women, are employed by other women or have their chief interaction at work with their male employer's wife. Typically this is a 'master-servant' relationship, with the class difference often coinciding with differences in ethnicity and language between employer and employee.

The relationship between (woman) employer and (woman) domestic worker is complex. As women, they have shared interests in, for example, child development and education. Where the woman employer works, her career prospects are contingent on the (typically poorly paid) work of the domestic worker. The day-to-day security of the employer's children depends on the employee, who has to be away from her own children to do this work. The subordinate domestic worker has little autonomy or voice, but may receive some measures of assistance such as with health costs, children's school fees or the handing on of second-hand clothes. However, these are not contractual obligations, cannot be anticipated or planned for and depend on the whim of the employer.

The subordination in class terms is very often reflected in and compounded by a racial or ethnic dimension. In South Africa, most white families, even poor ones, employ live-in African or coloured domestic workers, though over the last three decades or so there has been a trend towards part-time domestic work. The employment of domestic workers by African, Indian and coloured elites is also widespread. Given urban housing shortages, the boundary between paid and unpaid domestic work is often blurred, with labour done by extended family members in exchange for board and lodging.

Patterns of international migration also show how gender intersects with class, with demographic trends and with changes in the demand and supply side of the labour market between women in developed and developing countries, and between men and women. In the last two decades women have made up an increasing proportion of all migrants to more affluent countries. It is generally noted that some economic migrants, both within and across borders, are not the poorest of the poor. Many come from upwardly mobile families, or use migration in a step to upward mobility. Relative to the status of women in the sending country, women migrants may be better off. But relative to women in the receiving country, they are likely to be much worse off, and they may take employment requiring a much lower level of skill than they possess.[3]

Chile's economic growth in the 1990s provided domestic work opportunities in the capital city, Santiago, for Peruvian women displaced by unemployment resulting from economic restructuring. Traditionally, domestic work for Santiago's middle class had been supplied by young Chilean women from rural areas. Improvements in the labour law with regard to domestic work, however, led to greater awareness of their rights among Chilean domestic workers, who became better able to defend these rights despite their dispersed workplaces. Many Chileans now favour employing Peruvian women (who are often better educated than the rural women they are displacing). Although they generally pay the same wages to both native and migrant workers, employers favour the Peruvians because their precarious political and legal circumstances make them less likely to protest the traditional master-servant relationship (Maher and Staab 2005).

In health work, too, a global shortage of labour in health care has led to changing global patterns of mobility (Flyn and Kofman 2004). In developed countries, as wages for nursing have not kept pace with inflation, fewer people are entering the field, and the existing nursing population is ageing. The demand is being met by women migrants from developing countries as well as from developed countries such as Australia and New Zealand. A number of northern countries run aggressive recruiting campaigns, and find a ready response in countries where working conditions and pay structures in the health services are poor, and where migration offers the chance of career mobility. In Ghana, for example, the number of nurses who left the country in 2000 to work in developed countries was twice the number of new nurses who graduated from nursing programmes within the country; in the United Kingdom, between 2001 and 2002, more nurses from overseas than nationals were added to the nursing register (Buchan and Sochalski 2004). AIDS gives an added impetus to the migration of health professionals, when work in the health services in their own countries becomes intolerable.

This migration from poorer to richer countries provides opportunities to individual women, and remittances sent home assist their families. Remittances also contribute to domestic savings in their home countries. In global terms, however, the migration of skilled personnel represents a significant subsidization of developed countries by developing countries, as the latter carry the costs of expensive education and training. It also leaves behind a deficit in health personnel, which in turn feeds the development of a two-tier healthcare system in developing countries – a good private system for the rich and a poor public one for the poor – as well as, more generally, the erosion of whatever health service there is. This has a direct impact on the unpaid care work of women.

For the society as a whole, this migration may contribute to class differentiation. It may open up employment opportunities for some women in the sending countries in low paid domestic or care work in the migrants' homes; on the other hand, it may simply add to the workload of the existing unpaid care workers and volunteers. From the perspective of the migrating health worker, migration raises the question of who looks after her family in her absence. Skilled health professionals in the North, whether native or migrant, employ domestic and care workers, some of whom may be migrants, at wages low relative to their own, to see to their household and personal domestic needs.

Although gender is only one source of disadvantage faced by women, it is important to

---

3   See Kofman 2004 on stratification in women's global migration patterns; Esim and Smith 2004 on Asian domestic workers who migrate to the Arab States; Zambrano and Basante 2005 on Ecuadorian domestic workers in Spain and Italy; Constable 1997 for Filipina domestic workers in Hong Kong.

underscore the fact that in virtually all countries and traditions of the world women bear the primary responsibility for providing care (Nussbaum 2005), which poses constraints on the kind of employment they can take up. This, in turn, has direct implications not only for their own economic security but also for the economic security of the next generation. The case of Lucy and Jack illustrated the impact on the future of children when a mother has to shift from full-time to part-time work. The Lesotho case showed how the low incomes and working conditions of mothers reduced the time they spent on breastfeeding and left them dependent on untrained care-givers; their long hours and rigid work regulations reduced their ability to tend to the health and other care needs of their children, and they lost wages if they sought health care for themselves. The forced neglect of children in their earliest years has life-long repercussions and cannot be remedied in later years. The reliance on women's unpaid care work to provide social services contributes directly to the cross-generational transmission of poverty.

In sum, under free market policies the state's role, in both developed and developing countries, has served to extend both the power and security of capital, while working against support for women's unpaid care work. There are hidden costs of transferring service provision to women's unpaid work, including stagnant productivity, the deskilling of the workforce and the transmission of poverty to the next generation. The policies that combine to increase the demands on women's paid and unpaid time simultaneously limit women's ability to secure a decent livelihood and to engage in wider struggles to gain economic and social security.

Professional women's mobility is often dependent on the role of a subordinate woman providing both household and care work. And the combination of ageing populations and smaller families suggests that the demand for unpaid care work and domestic work will increase (Benería 2003). Women will shift to part-time work in order to solve a present problem of, say, care of an older relative. This will lower current income and have permanent long-term impacts on the financial security of the whole family.

In developing countries, more calls for volunteer work can be expected, to compensate for scarce state health and welfare services and expressive private services. HIV/AIDS has greatly increased the demand for unpaid care work and volunteer work. It has also shifted inter-generational responsibilities: when those in the adult generation get ill or die, older people as well as younger children have to work if households are to survive. It is important to look at volunteer work from the perspective of the care-giver and to recognized the gendered aspects of 'community', especially when it is used in calls for voluntary work in community-based care programmes. And it critical to explore ways of encouraging men to increase their participation in unpaid care work.

Not only does women's responsibility for unpaid care work help determine where they are situated in the labour market, but gendered notions of 'women's work' and 'men's work' help shape the structure of the labour market. As Chapters 3 and 4 will show, the segmentation of labour markets by gender and the gender gaps in earnings and benefits across and within these segments contribute to the relative poverty and disadvantage of women compared to men, regardless of class, religion or ethnicity. Most of the world's working poor, especially women, are concentrated in informal employment, and for most, the benefits are not sufficient and the costs too high to enable them to have an adequate standard of living over their working lives. To be successful, therefore, efforts to eliminate poverty must break the link between women's location in the global labour force and their disproportionate exposure to poverty and insecurity.

3 Employment, Gender and Poverty

Goat herder, Rajasthan state, India.
Photo: Martha Chen

"Statistics have power.... When statistics are in the hands of activists, then struggles are strengthened."

Ela Bhatt, founder of SEWA

Over the past three decades, there has been a marked increase in women's share of employment in both developed and developing countries – a trend often referred to as the *feminization of the labour force*. Simultaneously, there has also been an increase in certain types of informal and non-standard employment that have high degrees of insecurity – often referred to as the *informalization of the labour force*. This has given rise to the idea that the trends are inter-linked. However, while no one disputes that women are entering the labour force in growing numbers, there is ongoing debate about the processes underlying this phenomenon. Are women entering jobs that were previously occupied by men, or are some forms of work being converted into the type of arrangements traditionally associated with women? Or both?

Feminist scholars question the suggestion of any causal link between these two trends. They point out that shifts in social reproduction, not just in labour markets, contribute to the coincidence of feminization and informalization. Some have also noted that informalization affects both women and men: that there is a general insecurity in the labour market and that this insecurity is often shaped not only by gender but by ethnicity, religion, age and migration status (see, e.g., Standing 1989, 1999; Armstrong 1996; Bakker 1996; Vosko 2002, 2003).

A parallel observation is that the burden of poverty borne by women, especially in developing countries, is different from that of men, a phenomenon often referred to as the *feminization of poverty.* During the UN Decade for Women (1975-1985) researchers and advocates drew attention to the disadvantaged position of women economically and socially, especially those in female-headed households, and called for a gender perspective in the whole field of poverty research.

Since the basic unit of poverty analysis is the household, not the individual, the only straightforward way to analyse gender and poverty is to compare the poverty levels of female-headed and male-headed households (Kabeer 1996; Burn 2004). Recently, the idea that the social and economic inequalities that women experience can automatically be associated with female-headed households has come into question (see e.g., Chant 2003). However, the idea of the feminization of poverty has been a powerful advocacy tool for women's rights advocates, expressing as it does an observed reality in many places. This makes it particularly important to improve the measurements. Several recent frameworks have been advanced to improve the understanding of poverty from a gender perspective that also attends to social relations of race, migration status and disability (Chant 2003; UNIFEM 2005b; Vosko et al. 2003). Collectively these frameworks suggest that a multi-dimensional approach is critical to assessing issues of gender and poverty.

Women's share of the labour force has increased in almost all regions of the world. By 1997, women comprised over 40 per cent of the labour force in Eastern and South-Eastern Asia, sub-Saharan Africa, the Caribbean and the developed regions, approaching that of men (UN 2000:110). The largest increase occurred in Latin America, where women constituted little more than a quarter of the labour force in 1980 but made up a third of the labour force in Central America and nearly two fifths in South America by 1997. From 1980 to 1997 the proportion of women in the labour force also grew in Western Europe and the other developed regions but remained the same in Eastern Europe. More recent data show that women's share of the labour force has generally continued to increase.[1] However, women still represent a third or less of the labour force in Northern Africa, Western Asia, Southern Asia and Central America, and recent data available for four countries of Northern Africa show that women's share of the labour force in this region may be decreasing.

With the growth in women's employment, attention has turned to the quality of their employment: the types of jobs, earnings and benefits. This concern is especially relevant now as global eco-

---

1 The most recent data are based on the United Nations Statistics Division, "Statistics and indicators on women and men," table 5d. http://unstats.un.org/unsd/demographic/products/indwm/ww2003. Given the small number of countries with data in some regions, they are interpreted here with caution.

Box 3.1

The Story Behind the Numbers: Women and Employment in Central and Eastern Europe and the Commonwealth of Independent States*

What is the impact of the collapse of state socialism on women's labour market position? Two major reports examined this question and arrived at different conclusions – even while using similar data. The World Bank's *Gender in Transition* found "no empirical evidence that the treatment of women in the labour market has systematically deteriorated across the region" (World Bank 2003: xi). By contrast, a report prepared for the European Foundation for the Improvement of Living and Working Conditions concluded that "…women's advanced gender-equality legacy in the international ranking order has been seriously damaged, leaving only vestiges, such as high education, and female presence in many professions" (Pollert and Fodor 2005:62).

A UNIFEM analysis of harmonized data for 19 countries in Central and Eastern Europe and the CIS region from the Gender Statistics Database of the United Nations Economic Commission for Europe showed that these different evaluations of women's situation in great part reflect a difference in the questions asked. The World Bank report focused on women's labour force position relative to men's. The labour market position of the majority of women had declined but so had that of many men; therefore women's relative disadvantage barely grew. Further, the standard indicators of gender inequality in work – the wage gap or relative levels of horizontal job segregation – had not deteriorated.

The second comparison focused on the trends for women over time. Here the UNIFEM analysis showed that millions of women lost their jobs, and either became unemployed or dropped out of the labour market altogether. Already high levels of job segregation have remained stable and women are still being crowded into less prestigious, underpaid and public service jobs. Only a handful of women could take advantage of the new opportunities offered by international companies or domestic private sector firms. Poverty rates increased greatly as the scope and real value of social protection and services declined simultaneously with the disappearance of jobs. Overt discrimination increased, especially towards older women, women with young children and Roma women.

The UNIFEM study also showed the importance of exploring the social and cultural contexts behind the typical indicators of gender equality. For example, a 20 per cent wage gap between women and men is more tolerable in a centrally planned, state socialist economy when income differences are small and people can make ends meet on average wages, especially as these are supplemented by a relatively large number of benefits in kind (such as housing subsidies, subsidies on certain food stuff, etc.). Today a wage gap of a similar size may mean the difference between economic self-sufficiency and dependence.

The findings of this UNIFEM study are supported by recent ILO research in the Czech Republic, Hungary and Poland (Fultz et al. 2003). In these countries the transition has brought greater losses of social protection to women as compared to men. In particular, in two of the three countries large cuts in family benefits left working parents, mostly women, with considerably less support for efforts to balance family and professional responsibilities.

* Based on UNIFEM 2005a.

---

nomic trends are changing the nature of employment opportunities for women and men everywhere (see Chapter 4). In developing and transition countries particularly, the segmentation of labour markets for women and men and the impact this has on earnings, benefits and poverty status need to be examined more closely. A recent study of the changing economic well-being of women and men in the transition countries of Eastern and Central Europe and the Commonwealth of Independent States (CIS) looks at a wide range of data related to labour force participation, earnings and social protection to provide new insights on the impact of the political, economic and social changes occurring in these countries (see Box 3.1).

This chapter presents new ways of conceptualizing and measuring the feminization of the labour force, the informalization of the labour force and the feminization of poverty – and the links among them. Following a look at the recently expanded definition of informal employment, which focuses on the terms and conditions of work in addition to the characteristics of enterprises, it presents the recommended employment indicator for MDG Goal 3. The bulk of the chapter then presents new data from statistical analyses commissioned for this report in seven countries on segmentation of the labour force and average earnings and poverty risk across the different employment segments. These findings show both the feasibility of this type of statistical analysis and the importance of such findings for understanding the links between employment, gender and poverty

Informal Employment: Definition and Recent Data

Informal employment and the related concept of the informal sector are relatively new concepts in labour force statistics. In 1993 the International Conference of Labour Statisticians (ICLS) adopted an international statistical definition of the 'informal sector' to refer to employment and production that takes place in small and/or unregistered enterprises. In 2003 the ICLS broadened the definition to include certain types of informal wage employment outside informal enterprises: this larger concept is referred to as informal employment.

So defined, informal employment is a large and heterogeneous category. For purposes of analysis and policy-making it is useful to divide formal and informal employment into more homogeneous sub-sectors according to status in employment, as follows:[2]

Informal self-employment including:
- employers in informal enterprises;
- own account workers in informal enterprises;
- unpaid family workers (in informal and formal enterprises);

---

2 Status in employment is used to delineate two key aspects of labour contractual arrangements: the allocation of authority over the work process and the outcome of the work done; and the allocation of economic risks involved (ILO 2002a).

- members of informal producers' cooperatives (where these exist).³

Informal wage employment: employees without formal contracts, worker benefits or social protection employed by formal or informal enterprises or as paid domestic workers by households. Depending on the scope of labour regulations and the extent to which they are enforced and complied with, informal jobs can exist in almost any type of wage employment. However, certain types of wage work are more likely than others to be informal. These include:

- employees of informal enterprises;
- casual or day labourers;
- temporary or part-time workers;
- paid domestic workers;
- unregistered or undeclared workers;
- industrial outworkers (also called homeworkers).

Informal employment is particularly important in developing countries, where it comprises one half to three quarters of non-agricultural employment: specifically, 48 per cent in Northern Africa; 51 per cent in Latin America; 65 per cent in Asia; and 72 per cent in sub-Saharan Africa. If South Africa is excluded, the share of informal employment in non-agricultural employment rises to 78 per cent in sub-Saharan Africa.⁴ If comparable data were available for other countries in Southern Asia in addition to India, the regional average would likely be much higher. If informal employment in agriculture is included, as is done in some countries, the proportion of informal employment greatly increases: from 83 per cent of *non-agricultural* employment to 93 per cent of *total* employment in India; from 55 to 62 per cent in Mexico; and from 28 to 34 per cent in South Africa.

Throughout the developing world, informal employment is generally a larger source of employment for women than formal employment and generally a larger source of employment for women than for men. Other than in Northern Africa, where 43 per cent of women workers are in informal employment, 60 per cent or more of women workers in the developing world are in informal employment (outside agriculture). In sub-Saharan Africa, 84 per cent of women non-agricultural workers are informally employed compared to 63 per cent of men; and in Latin America the figures are 58 per cent of women in comparison to 48 per cent of men. In Asia, the proportion is 65 per cent for both women and men.

Self-employment comprises a greater share of informal employment (outside of agriculture) than does wage employment, ranging from 60 to 70 per cent of informal employment, depending on the region. In most countries for which data are available, women (as well as men) in informal employment are more likely to be in self-employment than in wage employment (see Table 3.1). In Northern Africa and Asia and in at least half of the countries of sub-Saharan Africa and Latin America, more women in informal employment (outside agriculture) are in self-employment than in wage employment. By contrast informal wage employment is more important for women in Kenya, South Africa and four countries in South America – Brazil, Chile, Columbia and Costa Rica. In these countries more than half of women in informal employment are wage workers. Moreover, in all but one of these countries – South Africa – women are more likely to be informal wage workers than are men. In explaining these patterns, it is important to recognize that paid domestic work is an important category of informal employment for women in all Latin American countries as well as in South Africa.

Millennium Development Goal 3: Recommended Employment Indicators

As noted in Chapter 1, the Millennium Development Goals (MDGs) have become a driving force for international development, setting development priorities as well as time-bound targets and indicators for measuring progress in implementation. While employment is one of the indicators to monitor progress under Goal 3, both women's rights advocates and statisticians have questioned the value of the current indicator – the share of women in non-agricultural wage employment – as a measure of women's economic status. The Millennium Project Task Force on Education and Gender Equality mentions two problems in particular: (i) an increase in women's share of paid employment adds to women's total workload, so that what women may gain in terms of cash they lose in terms of time, and (ii) the indicator measures only the presence or absence of work and not the quality of work (Grown et al. 2003).

The indicator has additional limitations when it is used as the sole indicator to monitor changes in women's economic situation. For one thing, in many countries, especially developing countries, non-agricultural wage employment represents only a small portion of total employment. In addition, the indicator

- is difficult to interpret unless additional information is available on the share of women in total employment, which would allow assessment of whether women are under- or over-represented in non-agricultural wage employment; and
- does not reveal that there are different types of non-agricultural wage employment. Some of them are better than others in terms of the earning and/or the legal and social protection that they offer (Antrobus 2005; Hussmanns 2004).

---

3 The guidelines also include production for own final use (i.e., subsistence production) as informal. In many countries this is not considered an important category and is not included in employment statistics.
4 Data in this section from ILO 2002b.

Table 3.1: Wage and Self Employment in Non-agricultural Informal Employment by Sex, 1994/2000

Country/Region	Self-employment as a percentage of non-agricultural informal employment			Wage employment as a percentage of non-agricultural informal employment		
	Total	Women	Men	Total	Women	Men
Northern Africa	**62**	**72**	**60**	**38**	**28**	**40**
Algeria	67	81	64	33	19	36
Egypt	50	67	47	50	33	53
Morocco	81	89	78	19	11	22
Tunisia	52	51	52	48	49	48
Sub-Saharan Africa	**70**	**71**	**70**	**30**	**29**	**30**
Benin	95	98	91	5	2	9
Chad	93	99	86	7	1	14
Guinea	95	98	94	5	2	6
Kenya	42	33	56	58	67	44
South Africa	25	27	23	75	73	77
Latin America	**60**	**58**	**61**	**40**	**42**	**39**
Bolivia	81	91	71	19	9	29
Brazil	41	32	50	59	68	50
Chile	52	39	64	48	61	36
Colombia	38	36	40	62	64	60
Costa Rica	55	49	59	45	51	41
Dominican Rep.	74	63	80	26	37	20
El Salvador	65	71	57	35	29	43
Guatemala	60	65	55	40	35	45
Honduras	72	77	65	28	23	35
Mexico	54	53	54	46	47	46
Venezuela	69	66	70	31	34	30
Asia	**59**	**63**	**55**	**41**	**37**	**45**
India	52	57	51	48	43	49
Indonesia	63	70	59	37	30	41
Philippines	48	63	36	52	37	64
Syria	65	57	67	35	43	33
Thailand	66	68	64	34	32	36

Source: ILO 2002b. Data prepared by Jacques Charmes from official national statistics.

In view of these problems, the Sub-Group on Gender Indicators of the Inter-Agency and Expert Group (IAEG) on MDG Indicators discussed the feasibility of a new indicator that would include both agricultural and non-agricultural employment and distinguish between formal and informal employment. An indicator that builds on the current one but frames it in a more comprehensive way – employment by type – was proposed by the ILO (see Box 3.2). It was recommended for Goal 3 by the IAEG Sub-Group on Gender Indicators and by the Task Force on Education and Gender Equality (Grown et al. 2005). This new indicator provides a more complete picture of where women are situated relative to men in a multi-segmented labour force.

The task force also recommended the addition of an indicator on gender gaps in earnings in wage employment and self employment, noting that this remains among the most persistent forms of inequality in the labour market (Grown et al. 2005). It recognized the need for new methodological work as well as the collection of new data in order to generate statistics on sex differentials in earnings from employment, especially earnings from self-employment, and recommended that priority be given to the development of these data (ibid.). Ideally, data on average earnings by sex for all categories of the employment by type indicator should be developed.[5]

The studies commissioned for this report utilize the basic categories or types of employment in the proposed employment indicator. Each country case study tabulates data in terms of formal and informal employment, agricultural and non-agricultural employment, wage and self-employment and related employment status categories and by sex. Data for earnings are presented for each of the categories. Taken overall, the case studies provide a test for the feasibility

---

5 A basis for such work would be the factors that determine discrimination in earnings, including not just wage data but also job segregation, social valuation of skills and other issues (see ILO 2003c: 44-47).

and desirability of the recommended employment by type and earnings indicators for Goal 3.

While improving women's opportunities in the labour market and earnings are central to the eradication of poverty, Goal 1 to reduce poverty and hunger was not framed in terms of either employment or gender. However, the Task Force on Education and Gender Equality concluded that unless improving women's earnings is seen as central to increasing the incomes of poor households, it will be difficult to meet this goal.

Households receive income from a variety of sources – employment, remittances, transfers from government or other households and, in some cases, rents and profits. Poor households are likely to depend more on earned income than on other types of income. Although poverty is multifaceted (see Chapters 1 and 4), income remains a crucial factor influencing how poverty is experienced and how poor families are able to cope. Therefore, access to employment and the quality of the opportunities available matter a great deal in determining who is poor and who is not.

The links between working in the informal economy, being a man or women and being poor can be formulated as a series of questions. Are those who work in the informal economy poorer than those who work in the formal economy? Are female informal workers poorer than male informal workers? What are the differences in earnings and poverty status among women and men workers in the various types of employment that make up the informal economy, and how do these compare with workers in similar types of work in the formal economy where they exist?

Unfortunately, data have not been readily available to answer these questions. While increasing numbers of countries are collecting data on employment in the informal sector and a few countries are collecting data even on the broader concept of informal employment, this topic is not yet a well-established part of national programmes of data collection and tabulation. Official data from national surveys still do not permit extensive comparisons of employment in terms of formal and informal employment, status in employment within each, the distribution of women and men workers across these categories or the wages or poverty status associated with them.

However, in some of the countries that have collected the required data, researchers have begun to do the kind of statistical analysis that answers these questions. Building on these efforts, UNIFEM commissioned research for this report in seven countries to look more closely at labour force segmentation by employment status, earnings and poverty. A common tabulation framework was developed and analysis was carried out in five developing countries: Costa Rica, Egypt, El Salvador, Ghana and South Africa. A similar study was prepared for India based on city-specific data and an earlier national study. The framework was also used to examine the links between employment, earnings and poverty in one developed country: Canada.

Box 3.2

Proposed Indicator on Employment (Goal 3): Share of Women in Employment by Type

EMPLOYMENT BY TYPE	WOMEN AS % OF EMPLOYED PERSONS (BOTH SEXES)
Total employment (all types)	X
1. Agricultural employment (1)	X
2. Non-agricultural wage employment (2)	X
of which 2.1: Informal wage employment (3)	X
3. Non-agricultural self-employment (4)	X
of which 3.1: Informal self-employment (5)	X

(1) No further subdivision, as most agricultural employment is self-employment and informal.
(2) Current MDG indicator.
(3) Employees holding informal jobs in formal sector enterprises, informal sector enterprises or as paid domestic workers employed by households. Direct measurement (LFS data) or use of residual method.
(4) Own-account workers, employers, contributing family workers and, where relevant, members of producers' cooperatives.
(5) Contributing family workers and informal sector entrepreneurs, including members of informal producers' cooperatives. When data on informal sector entrepreneurs are not available, missing data may be estimated by using the share of informal sector entrepreneurs in total non-agricultural self-employment (own-account workers, employers, members of producers' cooperatives) of countries in the same region or sub-region.

Labour Force Segmentation, Earnings, and Poverty: Developed Country Data

In developed countries, many women and men work in forms of employment and arrangements that differ from the full-time, full year job with benefits and with labour and social protections (Cranford and Vosko 2005; Pocock et al. 2004; Fudge and Vosko 2001; Carré et al. 2001). Such non-standard forms of employment are significant and even growing in many of the countries, although comprehensive data are not available because of differing definitions and the fact that few countries collect data on all categories (Campbell and Burgess 2001; Vosko 2005). For instance, there is very limited data on inter-firm contracting, a new form of non-standard employment that is emerging in the fast growing sectors that provide labour-intensive services to other businesses or public institutions (e.g., janitorial services).

Forms of employment commonly classified as non-standard work – namely, part-time and temporary wage employment and own account self-employment – are a more important source of employment for women than for men in developed countries. This is shown in comparing both the numbers of women and men employed and non-standard employment as a proportion of total women's and total men's employment:

- There are generally more women than men in part-time employment (both wage and self-employment) and temporary jobs. In 28 developed countries (including all OECD countries) in the 1990s, women comprised the majority of part-time workers (Carré and Herranz 2002). Women's share of part-time employment ranged from 60 per cent in Turkey to 97 per cent in Sweden.
- In many European countries the majority of workers in temporary employment are women. In nine of fifteen European Union (EU) countries, women account for about half or more of temporary employed workers, and a solid majority in six of these (ibid.): Sweden (59%), Ireland (58%), Belgium (57%), United Kingdom (55%), Netherlands (54%) and Denmark (52%). EU countries where women are the minority of temporary employees are Spain (38%), Austria (43%), Greece (44%), and Germany (45%).
- In Australia, Canada and the United States in 2000, there were more women than men in several forms of non-standard employment that are particularly precarious, including own-account self-employment, temporary employment and part-time permanent employment (Vosko 2004).

Thus in each of the three countries a higher proportion of the female workforce (about 30-50%) than the male workforce (about 20-35%) is engaged in forms of employment differing from the norm of the full-time permanent job (ibid.).

For women, the so-called flexibility associated with non-standard work is often cast in positive terms, allowing them to combine paid work with unpaid care responsibilities. Chapter 2 considers the impact of unpaid care work on paid work, particularly informal paid work, and Chapter 4 looks at the costs and benefits of informal work more generally. The example below looks more closely at the precariousness associated with non-standard jobs in developed countries that are subject to a process of informalization and, therefore, resemble informal wage work in developing countries.[6]

Temporary employment as precarious employment: the example of Canada

Temporary jobs – including fixed term/contract, casual, seasonal and on-call work as well as work through a temporary agency – have been one of the driving forces behind the growth of non-standard employment since the 1990s in Canada. Wages and household income of persons in temporary and permanent jobs were compared using Statistics Canada's 2002 Survey of Labour and Income Dynamics. Results are summarized below:

Numbers working as temporary/permanent employees: Temporary jobs in Canada grew from 7 to 10 per cent of employment from the early 1990s to 2002 and now represent the major form of non-standard work. In 2002, more women than men were employed in temporary work: 1.14 million women compared to 1.09 million men. Temporary jobs are slightly more important as a source of employment for women (18%) than for men (16%) To capture ethic/racial identity, statistical surveys in Canada ask all respondents to identify themselves as "visible-minority" or "nonvisible-minority." [7] Among women, visible minorities are more likely to be employed in temporary jobs (21%) than non-visible minorities (18%). But among men visible minorities are only slightly less likely to work in temporary jobs (15 % vs.17%).

Hourly wages: As expected, hourly wages are lower for temporary than for permanent workers and for women than for men. Differences in hourly wages (both mean and median) between temporary and permanent employees are greater for men (ranging from $6.00 to $7.00 Cdn) than for women ($3.00 to $4.00 Cdn). A similar pattern appears when wages are viewed in terms of education: wage differences between permanent and

---

6 The data analysis for Canada was done by Sylvia Fuller and Leah F. Vosko, York University, Toronto.
7 The Employment Equity Act mandates the application of equity measures to visible minorities, people with disabilities, aboriginal people and women. It defines visible minorities as persons other than aboriginal people, who are non-caucasian in race or non-white in colour.

temporary jobs are generally higher among more educated workers. The contrast in earnings between temporary and permanent workers is greater among men than among women at all educational levels. Additional factors that affect earnings comparisons include the fact that younger workers, whose wages are always lower than those of older workers, are more likely than older workers to have temporary jobs; the occupational structure of temporary jobs differs from permanent jobs; and the percentage of part-time work tends to be higher for temporary jobs than for permanent.

Low annual earnings: Almost 80 per cent of women and 65 per cent of men in temporary work have low overall annual earnings (less than $20,000 Cdn/yr) compared to 39 per cent of women and 19 per cent of men in permanent jobs. There is little difference between visible minority and non-visible minority women workers in their incidence of low annual earnings, but male visible minority temporary workers fare worse than their non-visible counterparts (75% to 63%). Still the incidence of low annual earnings for visible minority men in temporary jobs is slightly lower than for visible minority women (75% in contrast to 80%).

Multi-variate model: The earnings penalty associated with temporary employment was tested by controlling for individual demographic variables (age, immigrant status, household demographic, race, education and years of work experience) and for job characteristics (occupation, industry, part-time, firm size, industry and unionization). Even after accounting for these differences between temporary and permanent workers, there remained a substantial and statically significant wage penalty associated with temporary employment for both women and men. When controlling for individual demographic variables, women in temporary jobs earn 8 per cent lower hourly wages and men earn 11 per cent lower hourly wages than their permanent counterparts. In other words, the earnings penalty is higher for men than for women. When controlling for job characteristics, the penalty for temporary employment increases somewhat to 9 per cent for women and 12 per cent for men, although the difference in women's and men's coefficients is no longer statistically significant.

Low household income: Canada's Low Income Cutoff is defined as levels at which families or unattached individuals spend 20 per cent more than average on food, shelter and clothing. Although low household income is not a direct measure of wages and earnings penalties related to temporary work, it helps illustrate the degree to which the household characteristics of temporary workers offset their wage and earnings disadvantage and the extent to which the country's tax and income transfer system also has an effect. These data show that temporary workers have a higher incidence of low household income after taxes than permanent workers: 9 per cent of temporary male workers and 10 per cent of temporary female workers have low household incomes compared to 3 per cent of permanently employed men and 4 per cent of permanently employed women. Visible minority temporary workers have a higher incidence of low household income. The differences between women and men are not great, but visible minority women in temporary jobs have the highest incidence of living in low-income households (18% of women versus 16% of men.)

Summary: earnings penalty of temporary jobs

The analysis shows that there is a clear earnings disadvantage to persons who work in temporary jobs. While most persons in temporary jobs have low earnings, the proportion of women with low annual earnings is much higher than for men: almost 80 per cent of women in comparison to 65 per cent of men. When viewed in terms of household income, to some degree household characteristics and the country's tax and income transfer policies offset the earnings disadvantage of temporary work because fewer women than men lived in households with low earnings. However, visible minorities employed in temporary jobs have a higher incidence of living in low-income households.

The analysis also shows that the earnings penalty for working in temporary jobs is greater for men than for women. Underlying this pattern is the general segmentation of the labour force by sex. Because more men (than women) are employed in high-earning permanent jobs, there is a greater contrast for men in lower-earning temporary work. Furthermore, temporary work itself is stratified by gender. The forms of temporary employment that are highly precarious – temporary agency work and casual work – are generally those in which women predominate.

Labour Market Segmentation, Earnings and Poverty: New Data from Developing Countries

The developing countries selected for this pilot research are diverse in size, geographical location, demographic history and culture (see Box 3.3). In all of the countries, informal employment is widespread.

Each of the country case studies was based on national data sets that offered the possibility of identifying workers according to the main employment status categories – formal and informal, and agricultural and non-agricultural. The distinction between informal and formal self-employment, including employers and own-account workers, was based on whether an enterprise was registered with a government agency and/or its size. In line with the definition adopted by the 17th ICLS, social protection criteria were primary in distinguishing formal from informal wage employment – specifically the

Box 3.3

The Labour Force and Related Characteristics of the Six Countries

POPULATION SIZE:
Relatively small: Costa Rica and El Salvador
Moderate: Egypt, Ghana and South Africa
Large: India

ECONOMY:
Low-income: Ghana, El Salvador and India
Middle-income: Costa Rica, Egypt and South Africa

WOMEN AND MEN IN EMPLOYMENT AND UNEMPLOYMENT:
Employment rates for women range from 40 to 50 per cent in Costa Rica, Egypt, El Salvador and South Africa to a high of 87 per cent in Ghana; the rate for India is much lower (26%)*: men's rates are consistently higher and show less variation from country to country.
In part this could be due to poor enumeration of women's employment.

FORMAL/INFORMAL EMPLOYMENT:
Informal employment is widespread in all the countries studied. In some cases – notably India and Ghana – informal jobs and activities represent over 90 per cent of all employment opportunities. Even in Costa Rica, the county with the highest shares of formal opportunities, informal employment accounts for nearly half of all employment. In all the countries except El Salvador (where shares are virtually equal), informal employment represents a larger share of women's than of men's employment.

AGRICULTURAL/NON-AGRICULTURAL EMPLOYMENT:
In Costa Rica, El Salvador and Ghana, women tend to be concentrated in non-agricultural informal employment. However, in Egypt and India informal agriculture is a larger share of women's total employment relative to men's. In these countries, a large number of women are employed informally as unpaid workers on family farms and agricultural enterprises. This shifts the overall balance of the gender division of informal employment in these two countries toward agricultural and away from non-agricultural employment.

* The low employment rate for India may be due in part to its definition of the working age population, which begins at age 5. For other countries it begins at age 15. Employment rates for both women and men are lower in India than in the other countries.

However, analysts are beginning to recognize that a dual labour market model is not sufficient to capture the increasingly multi-faceted employment dynamics in developing economies. Moreover, this model lacks the amount of detail needed to fully understand the relationships among gender, employment and poverty in a globally integrated world.

Dual labour market theory currently treats the informal labour market as a single undifferentiated whole. However, as noted earlier, many types of employment belong under the broad umbrella 'informal': informal employers, own-account workers, informal employees, casual wage workers, domestic workers, unpaid workers in family enterprises and industrial outworkers (also called homeworkers). The importance of these distinctions becomes apparent in the statistical analysis from six developing countries examined below.[8] The labour forces of these countries are highly segmented in terms of gender and employment status and this in turn has an important impact on relative earnings and the risk of poverty.

Table 3.2 presents information on the composition of informal employment – agricultural and non-agricultural – for women and men in the six developing countries. With respect to non-agricultural informal employment, women are more likely to work as own-account workers, domestic workers and unpaid contributing workers in family enterprises than are men. In contrast, men are more likely to work as employers and wage workers. In general, women are concentrated in the more precarious and lower quality forms of non-agricultural, informal employment, a point to which we will return later.

Own-account workers in non-agricultural employment frequently are a large, if not the largest, percentage of women's informal employment. For example, in El Salvador, own-account workers represent 52 per cent of women's informal employment. In Ghana, non-agricultural own-account activities represent 39 per cent of women's informal employment – and approximately a fifth of all employment, formal and informal, in the country. Among the countries portrayed here, only in Egypt and India, where informal agricultural activities (especially as unpaid family workers) are a particularly important source of employment for women, are men more likely to be represented in non-agricultural own-account employment. However, even in these countries, own-account

existence of social security contributions, paid leave and/or employer contributions to a pension. Wage employment without at least one such social protection was considered to be informal. This may differ from the definition used by countries' official statistical agencies. For example, official estimates of informal employment in South Africa reflect employment in non-registered business enterprises (with or without social protection), with domestic and agricultural workers enumerated separately. Details on classification scheme for each country are included in table notes at the end of the chapter.

Segmentation of the informal workforce

Labour markets in developing countries have, in the past, been characterized as dualistic. A dual labour market is thought to include (i) a formal, regulated segment in which there are few high-quality jobs, and (ii) a large, unregulated segment in which workers excluded from formal jobs are employed.

---

8 Countries studied did not distinguish industrial outwork in their labour force statistics. For data on relative wages of industrial outworkers compared to other categories of informal workers, see Chen et al. 2004.

Table 3.2 Percentage Distribution of Women's and Men's Informal Employment by Employment Status

		Non-agricultural					Agricultural					
		Employer	Own-Account	Wage worker	Domestic	Unpaid Family	Employer	Own-Account	Wage worker	Domestic	Unpaid Family	**TOTAL**
Costa Rica	W	8	37	20	25	6	1	1	1	0	1	100
	M	14	27	26	10	1	5	11	13	0	3	100
Egypt	W	0	4	6	n.a.	3	0	0	2	n.a.	85	100
	M	3	7	45	n.a.	5	11	4	15	n.a.	10	100
El Salvador	W	4	52	16	14	10	0	1	2	n.a.	1	100
	M	5	19	34	1	3	2	14	16	n.a.	6	100
Ghana	W	n.a.	39	5	n.a.	3	n.a.	33	0	n.a.	20	100
	M	n.a.	16	15	n.a.	1	n.a.	55	3	n.a.	10	100
India	W	0	6	8	n.a.	6	0	11	35	n.a.	34	100
	M	0	19	16	n.a.	4	0	24	26	n.a.	11	100
South Africa	W	3	16	43	26	2	1	2	7	n.a.	0	100
	M	6	9	58	1	1	2	3	20	n.a.	0	100

n.a.= data not available or insufficient observations to derive statistically significant estimates.
Source: Prepared by James Heintz for this report. See table notes at end of chapter.

employment remains a significant source of income for a large number of women.

Domestic work, a form of wage employment that is often informal, also accounts for a large proportion of the informal employment opportunities available to women (although not all countries in this analysis had detailed data on domestic workers).[9] Paid domestic work represents what is often called the 'commodification' of women's traditional unpaid care work. In Costa Rica and South Africa domestic work represents about a quarter of women's informal employment. However, not all domestic workers are informal. In South Africa, for example, a small but growing number of domestic workers have unemployment insurance and are thus considered as formal workers (see Chapter 6). Labour legislation in countries such as Chile and Peru also recently extended some aspects of social protection benefits to domestic workers. While this represents an important step, enforcing the legislation may be difficult.

Even though not all the data for the countries studied separate domestic labour from other types of wage employment, informal wage employment tends to be a more important source of employment for men than for women. For example, informal wage employment is 31 per cent of men's informal employment in Egypt, but only 6 per cent of women's. In South Africa as many as 78 per cent of men in informal employment are in wage employment – including agriculture but especially in non-agricultural labour (58%); the comparable figure for women is still high (50%) but much less (the South Africa figures exclude domestic employment).

In the countries studied, men generally predominate in informal employment in agriculture – except as unpaid family workers and except in India, where there are more women than men in agricultural wage employment. Nevertheless, informal agricultural employment remains an important source of income-generating work for women, particularly in low-income countries. Informal agricultural activities represent over 53 per cent of women's informal employment in Ghana and over 80 per cent in India.

Women often contribute to income-generating activities – both agricultural and non-agricultural – without controlling the income they generate. Unpaid work on family agricultural enterprises accounts for 20 per cent of women's informal employment in Ghana, 34 per cent in India and an astounding 85 per cent in Egypt. Overall, agricultural employment accounts for 54 per cent of all employment in Ghana and 40 per cent in Egypt. Rural employment comprises 76 per cent of all employment in India. Since most labour force and living standards surveys do not collect specific information on industrial outwork (or homework), a cross-country comparison is not possible. However, a recent study of employment in Ahmedabad City which collected information on different types of informal employment found that homeworkers accounted for nearly 25 per cent of women's informal employment but less than 10 per cent of men's (Unni 2000: Table 5.1).

Formal employment

In general, formal employment is of much better quality than informal employment. Earnings are significantly higher, incomes are more stable, social protections exist and the risk of poverty is lower. However, labour force segmentation is also apparent with respect to formal employment – with men and women having differential access to the

---

9 The lack of data on domestic work likely reflects the absence of a separate category under status in employment. All labour force surveys, but not all living standard surveys, enumerate domestic work separately through the classification of employment by industry.

various kinds of formal employment. A global report from the ILO following up the Declaration on Fundamental Principles and Rights at Work explores the reasons for this and offers policy suggestions to address it (ILO 2003c). Table 3.3 summarizes patterns of formal employment for five of the six developing countries considered here.

As shown, the vast majority of formal employment is non-agricultural. This is less an indication of the relative importance of agriculture for rural worker livelihoods than a result of the high degree of informality among agricultural employment opportunities. In most of the countries studied, wage employment arrangements dominate formal employment. The exception is Ghana where for women (but not for men) formal own-account employment is more important than formal wage employment.

Women have less access to private formal wage employment than men in all country case studies except El Salvador. This could be due to the high level of international labour migration among male workers in El Salvador who send income back home. The remittances, but not the employment statuses of the overseas migrants, are captured by the household surveys. In all the countries studied, public employment is a critical source of formal job opportunities for women. In Costa Rica, Egypt, El Salvador and South Africa, women in formal jobs are more likely than men to be employed in the public sector. Ghana is an exception, but mostly because of the relative importance of own-account workers in women's formal employment. Still, in Ghana, women are six times more likely to have a formal public sector job than a formal private sector job.

Other variations in the type of wage employment are apparent. Often, casual wage employment is best classified as a form of informal wage employment, but this is not always the case. Some casual workers in Costa Rica have access to social protections similar to formal, regular employees.

In sum, the labour forces of the six countries are highly segmented in terms of sex and employment status. There is a clear distinction between formal and informal employment, with women more likely to work in informal activities. The public sector is important in providing women access to formal wage employment. However, segmentation is also apparent within the informal labour force. Outside of agriculture, women are more likely to be own account workers, domestic workers and unpaid contributing workers on family enterprises. Within agriculture, men tend to be disproportionately represented among own-account workers in the countries investigated. To the extent that women are concentrated in low-quality employment, their risk of poverty will be exacerbated, all other factors being equal.

Earnings and hours of work

Patterns of labour force segmentation by themselves say little about the average quality of remunerative work. While a standardized estimate of earnings, such as hourly earnings, can illustrate differences in the quality of employment opportunities available to men and women, it is hard to estimate these across countries because of different currencies, fluctuations in exchange rates and variations in price levels. When comparisons are possible, they can show the multiple dimensions of gender inequality in employment. Women are not only in different and more precarious types of employment than men but within a given category women's earnings are generally lower than men's.

Patterns in hourly earnings can be more easily compared using *relative hourly earnings,* that is, average earnings expressed as a percentage of a common baseline. Table 3.4 shows relative hourly earnings by employment status category. Hourly earnings for formal, private non-agricultural wage

Table 3.3 Percentage Distribution of Women's and Men's Formal Employment by Type

		Non-agricultural				Agricultural				TOTAL
		Employer	Own-account	Wage worker/private	Wage worker/public	Employer	Own-account	Wage worker/private	Wage worker/public	
Costa Rica	W	2	3	51	40	0	0	4	0	100
	M	3	5	60	19	1	0	12	0	100
Egypt	W	2	1	7	89	0	0	0	1	100
	M	10	7	15	65	1	0	0	2	100
El Salvador	W	1	0	73	26	0	0	0	n.a.	100
	M	3	0	69	25	1	0	2	n.a.	100
Ghana	W	n.a.	60	5	33	n.a.	0	2	n.a.	100
	M	n.a.	29	12	55	n.a.	0	4	0	100
South Africa	W	6	1	57	33	1	0	2	n.a.	100
	M	10	2	61	21	2	0	4	n.a.	100

n.a. = data not available or observations insufficient to derive statistically significant estimates.
Source: Prepared by James Heintz for this report. See table notes at end of chapter.
Note: Summaries of formal employment for the India case study are not strictly comparable to the categories prepared for the five others

Table 3.4: Hourly Earnings as a Percentage of the Hourly Earnings of Formal, Private Non-agricultural Wage Workers by Employment Status Category

	Costa Rica	Egypt	El Salvador	Ghana	South Africa
Formal					
Non-agricultural					
Employers	257.0	n.a.	544.0	n.a.	n.a.
Own-account	141.8	n.a.	654.2	89.6	255.5
Private wage	100.0	100.0	100.0	100.0	100.0
Public wage	146.1	80.2	174.1	116.1	140.8
Agricultural					
Private wage	62.8	n.a.	78.0	n.a.	38.2
Informal					
Non-agricultural					
Employers	138.2	n.a.	249.9	n.a.	43.7
Own-account	56.3	n.a.	78.5	66.6	29.4
All wage	n.a.	75.6	n.a.	97.1	53.8
Private wage	60.0	77.4	62.7	n.a.	49.6
Public wage	n.a.	49.3	90.7	106.9	117.2
Domestic	28.7	n.a.	27.7	n.a.	16.8
Agricultural					
Own-account	35.2	n.a.	79.2	48.8	n.a.
Private wage	34.5	55.3	40.1	49.6	17.2
Public wage	n.a.	n.a.	53.8	n.a.	n.a.

n.a.= data not available or insufficient observations to derive statistically significant estimates.
Source: Prepared by James Heintz for this report. See table notes at end of chapter.

workers are used as the basis of comparison, with relative hourly earnings for other categories expressed as a percentage of this baseline.

In all countries, hourly earnings in most forms of informal and agricultural employment fall well below earnings for formal, non-agricultural employment. Two exceptions are informal employers and, in some cases, informal public wage workers. In both Costa Rica and El Salvador, hourly earnings for informal employers are equal to or higher than earnings in formal employment. In Ghana and South Africa, estimated hourly earnings of informal public wage workers are higher on average than earnings in formal, private non-agricultural employment.[10] In general, public wage employment, both formal and informal, has higher average earnings than private wage employment, Egypt being an exception. This unexpected finding may reflect the diversity of public employment as the public sector encompasses both government and public enterprises. In many countries, public enterprises are concentrated in utilities, transportation and communication services where earnings may be higher relative to average earnings in the private sector.

Domestic work and informal non-agricultural own-account employment – employment categories with large numbers of women – have significantly lower hourly earnings compared to all forms of formal employment and lower earnings relative to all categories of informal employment shown here. Average informal earnings in agriculture are also among the lowest in all the countries featured. However, informal agricultural employment accounts for a larger share of men's employment than women's employment for every country in Table 3.4 except Egypt.

How do earnings of informal, own-account workers measure up to those of informal wage workers?[11] Except for El Salvador, hourly earnings in informal private wage employment are higher than those for own-account workers. These earnings also tend to be highly unstable. However, it is important to note that the quality of wage employment varies with the type of employment, a distinction that can be lost in aggregate categories. Although own-account employment is a precarious type of informal employment, it can be better in terms of the returns to labour than other types of informal employment, such as domestic work or informal casual wage employment.

For workers in small and microenterprises, which include enterprises operating in the informal economy, earnings depend on the size of the firm. Table 3.5 presents estimates compiled from a 2003 small and microenterprise survey for Egypt.

---

10 In both countries, the higher earnings of informal public sector workers reflect the high quality and desirability of public employment, even without full social protections. These earnings estimates could change if alternative criteria were used to distinguish formal from informal employment.
11 Earnings estimates for own-account workers tend to be inflated due to the presence of unpaid contributing workers in family enterprises, with the exception of Ghana, for which estimates were adjusted to reflect these contributions. Unpaid workers generate income that is attributed to another household member so that estimates of average individual self-employment earnings will tend to be overstated.

Table 3.5 — Average Wages per Worker and Women's Share of Employment for Small and Microenterprises by Size, Egypt, 2003 (expressed in 2002 Egyptian pounds)

Size of Firm	Average Wages	Women as % of Total Employment
1 worker	112.8	17.1
2 to 4 workers	172.1	9.4
5 to 9 workers	290.1	7.9
10 to 24 workers	1,073.4	5.9
Total (firms of all sizes)	160.1	14.3

Source: Data prepared by Alia El-Mahd for this report. See table notes at end of chapter.
Note: There were insufficient observations to determine statistically significant wages for workers in informal enterprises with 25 or more workers.

Average workers' wages increase with firm size. However, women account for a decreasing share of total employment as the size of the firm increases. In Egypt, women tend to work in smaller enterprises and therefore earn less relative to men.

Gender differentials in hourly earnings are apparent in all the countries and in most of the employment status categories. Table 3.6 presents women's hourly earnings as a percentage of men's by employment status for Costa Rica, Egypt, El Salvador, Ghana and South Africa. Women's hourly earnings fall below those of men in identical employment categories with the notable exception of Egypt. The earnings gap is particularly pronounced among own-account workers – both agricultural and non-agricultural – and is narrowest in public wage employment. In El Salvador, women's hourly earnings in public employment even exceed those of men on average. Women there tend to be concentrated in secretarial and administrative and professional employment, while fewer women than men are temporary employees and hold lower paying jobs. As a result there is less variance in women's earnings than in men's.

The case of Egypt is unique among the countries examined here. However, it should be remembered that unpaid work in family enterprises (both agriculture and non-agriculture) accounts for 88 per cent of women's employment in Egypt (Table 3.2). These women are not represented in the earnings estimates in Table 3.6. The relatively small number of women who work in paid wage employment tend to be highly educated – more so on average than the much larger numbers of men in paid wage employment. This helps explain their unusually high wages relative to men.

Estimates of earnings can be problematic when unpaid household members work, and generate income, in family enterprises. As unpaid workers, their earnings should be zero, but their labour has

Table 3.6 — Women's Hourly Earnings as a Percentage of Men's Hourly Earnings

	Costa Rica	Egypt	El Salvador	Ghana	South Africa
Formal					
Non-agricultural					
Employers	56.6	n.a.	78.9	n.a.	n.a.
Own-account	62.1	n.a.	45.1	54.6	n.a.
Private wage	84.6	151.9	87.5	n.a.	89.5
Public wage	87.7	107.6	116.2	84.2	95.6
Agricultural					
Private wage	85.1	n.a.	105.4	n.a.	66.3
Informal					
Non-agricultural					
Employers	97.6	n.a.	83.8	n.a.	83.6
Own-account	50.6	n.a.	65.1	80.2	59.6
All wage	n.a.	263.3	n.a.	69.8	n.a.
Private wage	79.5	317.1	75.4	n.a.	107.0
Public wage	n.a.	n.a.	135.2	88.0	99.2
Domestic	57.4	n.a.	56.2	n.a.	100.0
Agricultural					
Own-account	53.3	n.a.	56.9	65.0	n.a.
Private wage	n.a.	n.a.	86.4	n.a.	98.5
Public wage	n.a.	n.a.	177.6	n.a.	n.a.

n.a.=data not available or insufficient observations to derive statistically significant estimates.
Source: Prepared by James Heintz for this report. See table notes at end of chapter.

Table 3.7

Hourly Earnings in Selected Employment Status Categories, Ghana
(in cedis and purchasing power parity adjusted U.S. dollars)

	Women	Men	Total
Non-agricultural			
Formal, self-employed	588 ($1.11)	1,077 ($2.04)	1,052 ($1.98)
Informal, own-account	568 ($1.08)	708 ($1.34)	604 ($1.14)
Unpaid family (imputed)	472 ($0.89)	293 ($0.55)	409 ($0.77)
Agricultural			
Informal, own-account	336 ($0.64)	517 ($0.98)	442 ($0.84)
Unpaid family (imputed)	420 ($0.80)	421 ($0.80)	421 ($0.80)

Source: Data prepared by James Heintz for this report. See table notes at end of chapter.

real monetary value; it contributes to household income either explicitly (if products are sold) or implicitly (if households consume what they produce). The fact that, in many countries, women are disproportionately represented among unpaid workers in family enterprises means that their contributions to income generation are often undervalued.

It is important to impute the contribution of unpaid workers on family enterprise using household survey data, as recommended by the 16th ICLS (1998). Unless this is done the earnings of the self-employed in a household enterprise will be over-stated. Table 3.7 shows imputed hourly earnings for these workers in Ghana. To impute earnings for unpaid workers on family enterprises, an average hourly rate is computed for all work – paid and unpaid – performed in a particular household enterprise. This rate is then used to estimate the contribution of the unpaid family members. In Ghana, unpaid work in family enterprises accounts for 23 per cent of women's employment. The imputed hourly earnings in Table 3.7 suggest that these women make a significant contribution to household income. More generally, this is an important correction to make in estimating the earnings of those persons who are self-employed in household enterprises.

Employment income depends on hours of work as well as on hourly earnings. Table 3.8 summarizes estimated weekly hours of work for employed men and women by employment status. With some exceptions, women tend to work fewer hours than men in income-generating employment.[12] Since women also have lower hourly earnings, their employment income is less than that of men – often by a significant amount.

Time spent working in unpaid care work could account for some of the gender disparities in average hours of work in income-generating activities.

Table 3.9 shows estimates of hours worked in income-generating employment and unpaid care work in Ghana. Employed women spend, on average, over four times as many hours in unpaid care work as do employed men. Moreover, self-employed women spend considerably more time working in unpaid care work than do women in wage employment. Similar patterns can also be seen for men. In addition, women employed in agriculture spend more time in unpaid care work than women employed outside of agriculture. However, the same is not true for men employed in agriculture.

One reason why women employed as own-account workers spend longer hours in both unpaid care work and employment relative to women in wage employment may be labour supply constraints, as self-employed women are more likely to work at home than those who are wage-employed. If self-employment provides women with the flexibility to combine unpaid and remunerative work more easily, this could help explain the significantly longer hours worked by self-employed women.

Both below-average and above-average hours of employment can be symptomatic of *underemployment* of informal workers. Unstable incomes, sporadic production and inadequate demand often characterize informal work, so that informal workers might not be able to work as many hours as they would like. However, since many informal activities are also characterized by low productivity and low earnings, those in very low-productivity informal employment might need to work longer hours in order to earn a basic income. Moreover, the skills of informal workers may not be fully utilized, despite their long hours. Underemployment can take many different forms, and hours of work, by themselves, are not always a good indicator of underemployment.

---

12 Exceptions include women informal own-account workers in El Salvador, unpaid family agricultural workers in Egypt and domestic workers in South Africa.

Table 3.8

Average Weekly Hours of Work by Sex and Employment Status

		Formal				Informal						
		Non-agricultural			Agric.	Non-agricultural				Agricultural		
		Own-account	Private wage	Public wage	Private wage	Own-account	Private wage	Public wage	Domestic	Own-account	Private wage	Unpaid
Costa Rica	W	28.6	45.3	43.8	49.8	30.9	42.7	34.9	36.6	24.6	n.a.	32.8
	M	45.7	53.3	49.5	54.2	49.3	49.1	42.9	45.3	40.4	40.4	40.2
Egypt	W	n.a.	44.3	39.4	n.a.	41.6	51.4	n.a.	n.a.	n.a.	n.a.	84.1
	M	58.9	54.8	45.1	n.a.	44.1	51.3	47.5	n.a.	51.2	40.0	51.0
El Salvador	W	52.0	46.0	39.0	44.0	41.0	46.0	39.0	58.0	31.0	41.0	33.0
	M	37.0	49.0	45.0	51.0	43.0	45.0	44.0	51.0	37.0	38.0	36.0
Ghana	W	57.9	n.a.	43.4	n.a.	54.6	n.a.	43.1	n.a.	37.0	n.a.	22.7
	M	61.5	47.8	47.4	50.7	58.9	n.a.	50.8	n.a.	41.1	51.7	28.6
South Africa	W	47.6	44.0	42.2	48.5	43.3	44.2	38.3	40.8	14.2	46.1	26.3
	M	49.7	46.9	43.9	48.2	45.2	48.8	44.2	39.1	25.3	47.6	57.5

n.a.=data not available or insufficient observations to derive statistically significant estimates.
Source: Prepared by James Heintz for this report. See table notes at end of chapter.

Summary: gender segmentation and gender gaps

This discussion underscores the multiple dimensions of gender inequalities among workers. First, the labour force is segmented in terms of both formal and informal employment and women are concentrated in more precarious and lower quality employment. Access to formal employment is restricted and public employment is often the best source of decent, formal jobs for women. Average earnings also vary across segments of the informal labour force. A hierarchy exists in which women are disproportionately represented in segments with low earnings. In general, informal employers have the highest average earnings followed by their employees, then own-account workers and then casual wage workers and domestic workers.

Second, within a given employment status category, women's earnings are lower than men's. Only in exceptional cases, such as where only highly educated women participate in certain forms of employment, does this fail to hold. Third, women spend fewer hours in remunerative labour on average than men, in part due to the hours they spend in unpaid care work. Responsibilities for unpaid care work also reinforce labour force segmentation – women can be restricted to own-account or home-based employment, even if total hours worked are longer and incomes lower.

Taken together, fewer and less rewarding employment opportunities, lower wages and fewer hours of work mean that employed women earn much smaller incomes. All of these factors influence the risk of poverty women face.

Poverty rates and the working poor

Demonstrating a relationship between women's work and poverty requires that the analysis of labour force segmentation, earnings and hours of work be complemented with an examination of poverty rates among employed women and men.

Table 3.9

Total Hours Worked per Week in Employment and Unpaid Care Work, Employed Population (15+), Ghana, 1998/1999

	Women			Men		
	Unpaid care work	Employment	Total	Unpaid care work	Employment	Total
Formal employment, non-agricultural						
Private wage employment	n.a.	n.a.	n.a.	7.6	47.8	55.4
Public wage employment	30.0	43.4	73.4	8.8	47.4	56.2
Self-employed	33.8	57.9	91.7	9.7	61.5	71.2
Informal employment, non-agricultural						
Own-account	39.8	54.6	94.4	11.0	58.9	69.9
Wage employment	31.5	52.9	84.4	9.4	55.8	65.2
Unpaid family	33.7	n.a.	n.a.	17.9	n.a.	n.a.
Informal employment, agricultural						
Own-account	46.7	37.0	83.7	9.2	41.1	50.3
Wage employment	n.a	n.a.	n.a.	9.7	51.7	61.4
Unpaid family	46.4	22.7	69.1	9.6	28.6	38.2
TOTAL	42.4	46.3	88.7	9.7	47.9	57.6

Source: Prepared by James Heintz for this report. See table notes at end of chapter.

Table 3.10

Working Poor as a Percentage of Employment (15+) in Selected Employment Statuses by Sex, 2003, El Salvador

	Women	Men
Formal, non-agricultural		
Private wage employees	15	17
Public wage employees	5	13
Formal, agricultural		
Private wage employees	n.a.	30
Informal, non-agricultural		
Employers	17	13
Own-account workers	35	30
Private wage employees	31	33
Public wage employees	22	26
Domestic workers	29	35
Unpaid family workers	31	35
Informal, agricultural		
Own-account workers	57	65
Private wage employees	51	55
Unpaid family workers	61	62

n.a. =data not available or insufficient observations to derive statistically significant estimates.
Source: Prepared by FUNDE for this report. See table notes at end of chapter.

One way to measure the poverty rates of employed persons is to define the proportion of all employed persons in different employment statuses that are from poor households as the 'working poor'. This definition allows us to analyse the link between employment status and the risk of poverty that individuals face. As used here, individuals are considered to be 'working poor' if they were both employed and living in households whose incomes place them below the poverty line.[13] This definition of 'working poor' represents one technique for connecting the characteristics of employment, measured at the *individual* level, to the risk of poverty, measured at the *household* level. What this method allows us to do is to explore the links between gender, employment and poverty and not – as in many studies of feminized poverty – argue that the relationship between women and poverty is articulated primarily in terms of the sex of the household head.[14]

Table 3.10 shows how the working poor measurement of poverty rates has been applied in the case of El Salvador. Not surprisingly, many of the patterns already observed with respect to earnings are also apparent in the estimated poverty rates. The lowest risks of poverty are found among formal, non-agricultural workers, while poverty is more prevalent among agricultural workers. Moreover, workers in public employment, both formal and informal, have some of the lowest poverty rates among the relevant comparison group – all formal workers or all informal workers.

Similar patterns can be observed for the other countries examined here. However, comparing poverty rates across countries is problematic. Poverty standards, household composition, prices and consumption baskets all vary from country to country. To avoid this problem, we can apply the same methodology that we applied earlier to comparisons of hourly earnings in order to compare poverty rates – that is, use *relative poverty rates* among the working poor. By relative poverty rates we mean the average poverty rate expressed as a percentage of a common baseline. This allows us to use a similar baseline as was used earlier to calculate relative hourly earnings: the working poor poverty rate for non-agricultural, private formal wage employees. However, the definition differs from other usages that refer to the extent of inequality within a given income distribution.

For example, if the poverty rate among non-agricultural, private formal wage employees were 15 per cent and the poverty rate among informal domestic workers were 45 per cent, then the relative poverty rate for informal domestic workers would be 300 per cent (or three times the poverty rate of non-agricultural, private formal wage employees).

Relative poverty rates of male and female workers in Costa Rica, Egypt, El Salvador and Ghana (Table 3.11) show the same patterns emerging as in El Salvador: relative poverty rates among informal workers are higher than those among formal workers and informal agricultural workers have the highest risk for poverty. Poverty rates among women working in non-agricultural

---

13 The working poor poverty rates described here represent income poverty estimates, not consumption or expenditure-based measurements of poverty.
14 The data for household income may include earnings from children. But as labour force data generally refer to age 15 and above, the links between children's work and household poverty are not analysed here.

Table 3.11

Relative Poverty Rates: Working Poor Poverty Rates by Sex and Employment Status Category and Formal and Informal Employment, as a Percentage of the Poverty Rate for Formal Private Non-agricultural Wage Workers

		Formal				Informal							
		Non-agricultural			Agric.	Non-agricultural					Agricultural		
		Own-account	Private wage	Public wage	Private wage	Own-account	Private wage	Public wage	Domestic	Unpaid	Own-account	Private wage	Unpaid
Costa Rica	W	n.a.	100	n.a.	n.a.	735	330	n.a.	678	757	n.a.	n.a.	n.a.
	M	n.a.	100	51	244	249	205	n.a.	n.a.	158	644	598	57
Egypt	W	n.a.	100	64	n.a.	416	293	n.a.	n.a.	219	n.a.	n.a.	28
	M	69	100	100	n.a.	218	200	n.a.	n.a.	86	192	263	205
El Salvador	W	n.a.	100	30	n.a.	233	207	145	193	206	372	338	398
	M	197	100	80	184	179	197	155	210	214	573	161	370
Ghana	W	233	100	164	n.a.	257	n.a.	177	n.a.	314	334	n.a.	394
	M	173	100	166	n.a.	146	n.a.	174	n.a.	226	275	215	305

n.a.=data not available or insufficient observations to derive statistically significant estimates.
Source: Prepared by James Heintz for this report. See table notes at end of chapter.

---

informal activities – particularly as own-account workers, or unpaid workers on family enterprises – are also substantially higher.

The working poor poverty rates estimated for the country studies indicate that gender-based differences in poverty rates among working women and men are complex. Clearly, women are concentrated in forms of employment with high rates of poverty. However, no systematic pattern emerged in the country case studies in terms of differences between men's and women's poverty rates *within* a particular employment status category. This is striking since there was a clear gap between women's and men's earnings in the same employment category, as documented in the previous section.

The complexity in analysing gender-based differences in poverty among working people results from the need to combine poverty measurements (made at the household level) with employment data (collected at the individual level). Other variables – such as the factors that determine women's labour force participation, reproductive choices and household composition – influence the correlation between poverty rates and employment status along gender lines.

For example, in households with two or more adults, at least one of whom is male and employed, women's labour supply responds to pressures on household resources and intra-household gender dynamics. These factors influence the allocation of women's time between market and non-market activities. As a result, households in which women are engaged in remunerative work might have lower poverty rates relative to households in which women do not allocate time to income-generating activities – that is, women's employment income makes a significant difference in the poverty status of families with multiple earners. Therefore, a household's poverty status can be determined by women's access to paid employment, which itself is influenced by income constraints and gender power dynamics within the family. Similarly, the composition of households – e.g., the number of children – influences both poverty rates and women's labour supply decisions.

Because of the complexities associated with differences in poverty rates among working men and women, it helps to supplement the estimates of the working poor poverty rates with an analysis of poverty rates at the household level in order to take into account such factors as the number of earners per household. Table 3.12 presents estimates of poverty rates among South African households with different sources of employment income. Households are categorized by (1) number of earners, (2) sex of the head of household, (3) sex of the primary earner and (4) whether the majority of the household's income was derived from formal or informal sources.

The table reveals some striking patterns. Households that depend primarily on informal employment income have significantly higher poverty rates than households with a majority of income coming from formal employment. The gender differentials in poverty become much more evident at the household level. Female-headed households have significantly higher poverty rates than male-headed household. However, this differential is much less pronounced when households have access to formal employment. A similar pattern can be observed when comparing households whose primary earner is female compared to households whose primary earner is male.

A few words of caution are necessary, however, in drawing conclusions from this example. The link between female headship and poverty varies from country to country. Statistical analysis of large, national data sets for developing countries show that while female-headed households are poorer in some of them, the evidence is by no means conclusive (UN 1995:129). One important factor is that female-headed house-

Table 3.12

Poverty Rates by Household Type, South Africa, 2003*

	Head of Household** (identified in the Labour Force Survey)		Primary Earner (largest share of HH earnings)	
	Female-headed	Male-headed	Female	Male
Majority of earned income from informal employment				
One earner (age 15 years +)	63.7	48.3	58.5	40.9
Two earners (age 15 years +)	49.1	35.4	44.2	33.5
More than two earners	43.0	28.4	n.a.	25.4
Majority of earned income from formal employment				
One earner (age 15 years +)	18.0	13.7	13.1	11.8
Two earners (age 15 years +)	11.0	5.0	n.a.	4.4
More than two earners	n.a.	n.a.	n.a.	n.a.

Source: Prepared by D. Casale, C. Muller and D. Posel for this report. See table notes at end of chapter.
* Estimates based on employment income only since information on other income sources is not available in the South African Labour Force Survey.
**The definition of head of household is de facto, rather than de jure.

holds are not a homogeneous category. It is important to understand the different social processes (i.e., migration, widowhood, divorce, separation, staying single) that lead to female headedness; as well as the number, sex and age of the children and adult persons in the household (Folbre 1990). There are many types of female-headed households and this analysis disaggregates them by only two additional criteria: the primary source of employment income (formal and informal) and number of earners. Even so, the example illustrates the importance of the type of employment income and number of earners in determining women's risk of poverty.

As expected, poverty rates decline as the number of earners increases, suggesting that labour supply decisions can have a significant impact on household poverty. Again, caution is needed when interpreting gender-based differences in individual working poor poverty rates within a given employment status category.

The risk of poverty also varies from industry to industry and with the type of informal employment. Table 3.13 presents estimates from a recent study of informal employment and poverty in India. It shows poverty rates for households that sustain themselves on informal employment income by broad industrial sector and employment type. In this case, households classified as sustaining themselves on informal employment income are households with at least one person employed as an informal worker and no other household member employed outside of the informal economy.

The table shows the importance of the type of informal wage employment. Households with incomes below the poverty line are classified as 'poor' while those with incomes less than 75 per cent of the poverty line are classified as 'very poor'. Households that depend on informal, regular wage employment have lower poverty rates relative to households that rely on self-employment or casual wage income. The highest poverty rates are among households that sustain themselves on casual wage employment. For example, over one-fifth of such households are very poor while 47 per cent – nearly half – are poor. This hierarchy of poverty risk – regular wage employment having the lowest, self-employment the next highest and casual wage employment the highest risk – is robust across industrial sectors in urban India.

A hierarchy of poverty risk

Just as there is a hierarchy of earnings, there is a hierarchy of poverty risk associated with the segmentation of the labour force. Figures 3.1-3.3 illustrate the hierarchies of earnings and poverty

Table 3.13

Poverty Rates Among Persons in Households Sustaining Themselves on Informal Income, Urban India, 1999/2000

Industrial Sector	Household Employment Income Type					
	Self-employed		Regular wage employment		Casual wage employment	
	Very poor	Poor	Very poor	Poor	Very Poor	Poor
Manufacturing	8.90	25.89	6.76	21.30	18.52	41.55
Construction	6.76	20.28	5.91	14.70	19.48	43.35
Trade	8.27	21.01	7.24	19.11	17.20	36.99
All urban employment	**9.53**	**24.71**	**7.42**	**21.57**	**22.86**	**47.06**

Source: Sastry 2004. See table notes at end of chapter.

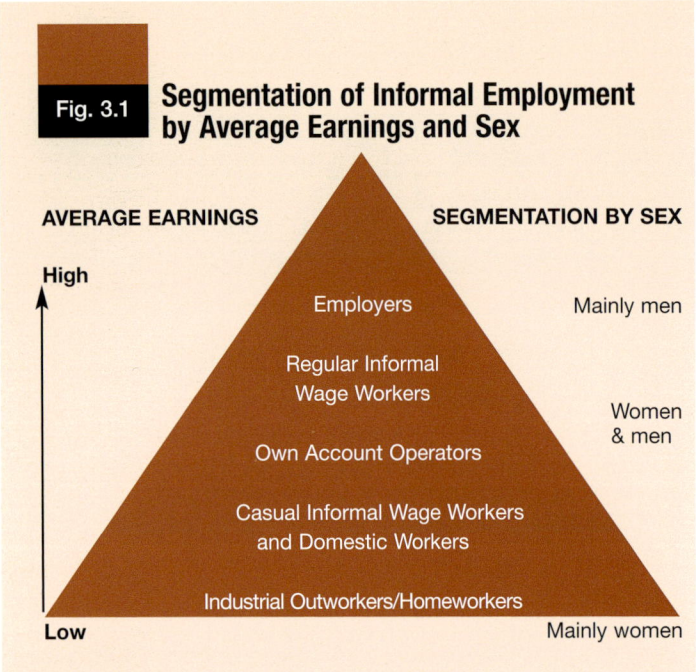

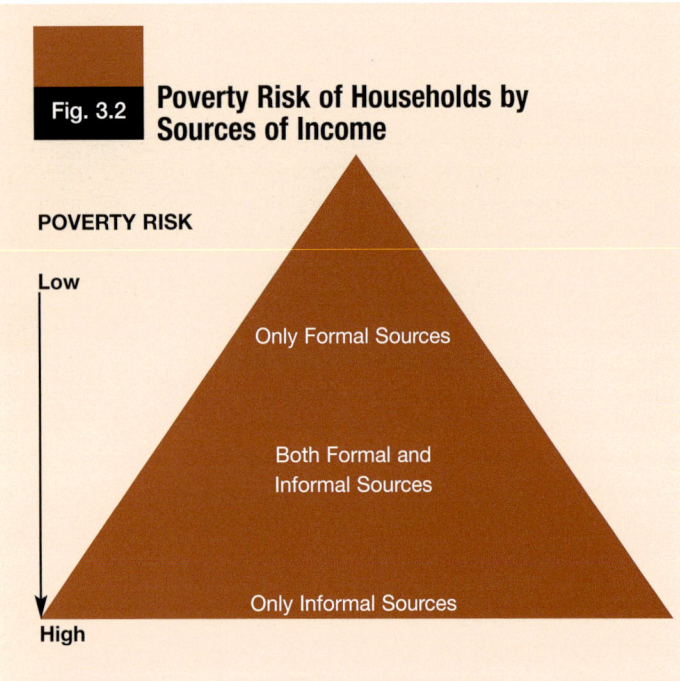

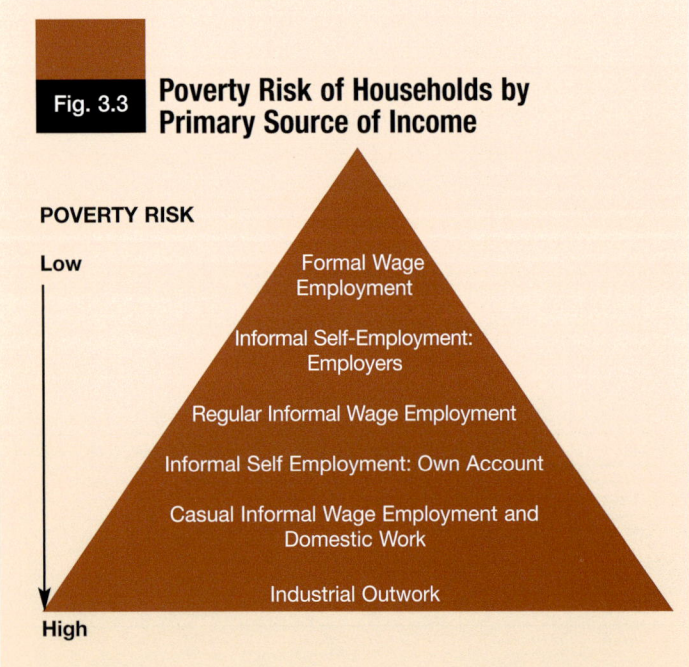

risk based on the evidence presented here and in other studies. These diagrams provide a succinct summary of the lessons of this chapter and can be used as advocacy tools to underscore the critical importance of the intersection of gender, employment, and poverty. They also provide a structure for framing further research on these interrelationships.

Figure 3.1 shows the hierarchy of earnings within the informal labour force suggested by the case studies presented here and other country-specific studies of industrial outworkers and casual informal wage employment. Earnings are highest among informal employers and regular informal wage workers, dominated by men's employment, and lowest among casual wage workers and industrial outworkers, dominated by women's employment. In earlier statistical analyses, industrial outworkers were found to have the lowest average earnings of all (Charmes and Lekehal n.d.; Chen and Snodgrass 2001).

This chapter also presented evidence of the hierarchy of poverty risk among households that depend on different sources of employment income (Figure 3.2). Households that rely primarily on income from informal employment face higher poverty rates than those that rely on income from formal employment. These patterns suggest a general hierarchy of household poverty risk rooted in a multi-segmented labour force (Figure 3.3). Households that depend on the most precarious forms of informal employment are likely to have substantially higher poverty rates than those that have access to more stable and better quality employment.

In developing countries many working women face a disproportionate risk of poverty compared to working men. Labour force segmentation means that women tend to be confined to activities in which earnings are low and poverty rates are high. However, the risk of poverty among women engaged in remunerative work is directly linked to dynamics within the household. Women's labour force participation can help keep a family out of poverty. However, in households with multiple earners – at least one being male – women still earn less income than men, although women's earnings contribute to lower household poverty rates and can thus improve human development outcomes.

Women's risk of poverty can be much more pronounced in female-headed households or in households in which a woman is the primary earner. Access to formal employment attenuates this risk dramatically. However, decent formal employment for women tends to be predominantly in the public sector, now being cut severely in developing countries. As employment opportunities become less and less formal (and more and more accessible to women), the risk of poverty increases dramatically.

Labour Markets and Labour Force Statistics

The findings presented in this chapter point to the important effects of the structure of the workforce on poverty and equality outcomes. In developing countries, employment growth for women has been largely in low-wage manufacturing, informal trading (e.g., working as street vendors) and low-productivity services in which high levels of formal skills are relatively unimportant, where on-the-job training is brief (if it exists at all) and there are few (if any) benefits or legal protection. In developed countries, much of the job growth for women has been in part-time and temporary jobs of various kinds. Whatever the causal factors, this pattern of feminization of the labour force is not conducive to reducing poverty or enhancing equality.

The findings presented here also have important implications for how we think about labour markets. Labour economists often focus on the supply and demand of wage labour and model the institutional setting in which labour is exchanged for a wage. In this framework, workers supply labour power and firms demand it. Unemployment is simply a situation in which such labour markets, narrowly defined, are unable to adjust wages so that those wanting employment (labour supply) match those offering employment (labour demand). As noted earlier, dual labour market theories assume that those who cannot find work in the formal labour market, but are still willing to work, are seamlessly absorbed into the informal economy.

This view of labour markets as the interaction between the supply of and demand for waged labour excludes important categories of the labour force – particularly in developing countries. First, it leaves out significant numbers of self-employed persons, including those who hire others, those who work on their own account and those who are unpaid workers in family enterprises. Second, it tends to conflate the various types of waged workers: formal salaried workers in both private and public enterprises, employees of informal enterprises, contracted or sub-contracted workers of various kinds, domestic workers and casual day labourers. Third, it fails to estimate or account for the extent of *underemployment*, including among the self-employed, which often more accurately captures the employment problem in developing countries than does unemployment.

To reflect the reality of the global labour force in today's world, an expanded definition of labour markets is needed. James Heintz, one of the authors of this report, proposes the following: "All production and exchange activities that impact employment, conditions of work and returns to labour." Clearly, not all members of the labour force sell their labour or *only* their labour.

A seller of traditional breads, Uzbekistan. Photo: Nick Coleman/AFP/Getty

Some sell goods or specialized services. Some of those who sell goods first buy them from others. Many of those who sell goods also produce them: by investing their capital and hiring others, or by investing their capital and their labour and, often, the labour of other family members. The self-employed workers who both produce and sell often have to source raw materials or intermediate goods from suppliers. Others, such as domestic workers, sell their labour directly to the final consumer. In many of these transactions, prices – other than wages – are the market mechanism.

Only when economists and development planners operate with a model of the labour market that includes rather than omits the majority of working people in the global economy will they be able to understand the links between poverty and employment, and how these links are determined by class, gender and other sources of disadvantage. Such an understanding is essential to combating poverty and gender inequality.

This chapter has provided a framework for analysing the gendered segmentation of the labour force – both formal and informal—and has presented country data to illustrate the distribution of the male and female workforce across these segments, average earnings by sex across the segments and poverty risk by sex across the segments. This framework suggests one way to simultaneously measure the feminization of the workforce, the informalization of the workforce and the feminization of poverty. Our hope is that it has shown the usefulness and importance of these data and this kind of analysis.

Much more needs to be done to improve employment and earnings data before an analysis such as this can be undertaken on a wider scale. More countries need to collect statistics on the informal employment, and countries that already do so need to improve the quality of the statistics that they collect. The development of statistics on earnings and working conditions in informal employment presents special problems. Methodological work needs to be undertaken to prepare guidelines for both the collection and compilation of these data. In addition, in order to undertake an analysis of employment and poverty, attention needs to be given at the national level to linking labour force and income and expenditure surveys. Moreover, allocating resources for establishing a crucial foundation of relevant employment statistics must be a priority within the poverty reduction strategies developed by individual countries. This chapter has also shown the need to develop an overarching framework that allows the classification and analysis of the full set of employment statuses that exist in both developed and developing countries.

It is to be hoped that the recommended employment indicator for Goal 3 of the MDGs will provide an impetus for furthering the required work in statistics. Its adoption for international monitoring and its use for monitoring at the regional and national levels would stimulate additional resources and work by statisticians in developing these data, researchers in analysing them and advocates in using them.

In conclusion, the quantity and quality of employment available to women, men and households matter a great deal in determining who is poor and who is not – not only in terms of income poverty but also in terms of other dimensions of poverty. Only when these issues are fully integrated into economic policies and development strategies will sustainable solutions to gender inequalities, poverty and other human development deficits be realized. The conceptual tools and the pioneering data analysis presented in this chapter, and the cost-benefit analysis of informal work presented in the next chapter, point the way for future data analysis and policy research to underscore this reality.

Table Notes: General

The format for the country studies was developed by James Heintz, Joann Vanek and Marty Chen in consultation with Ralf Hussmanns and Marie Thérèse Dupré at ILO. Funding for country case studies was provided by UNIFEM. ILO supported preparation of the report by James Heintz, "Summary of country case-studies and tabulations for 2005 Progress of the World's Women."

Tables 3.2 through 3.13 are based on research commissioned for this report, although several of the tables incorporate estimates for India drawn from an earlier report. The estimates presented in the tables were compiled from the following sources:

Costa Rica. Estimates based on the 2003 *Encuesta Permanente de Hogares de Propósitos Múltiples*, administered by the Costa Rican national statistics institute (Instituto Nacional de Estadística y Censos, INEC). Research led by Jesper Venema, ILO Regional Office, Panama.

Egypt. Two sets of estimates for Egypt were compiled, one based on household survey data and the other based on a survey of small and microenterprises. The household survey estimates were used for all tables except Table 3.5. For the estimates based on household survey data, the 1998 *Egyptian Labour Market Survey* (ELMS) was used. This survey was carried out by the Central Agency for Public Mobilization and Statistics (CAPMAS) with the cooperation of the Economic Research Forum (ERF) in Cairo. Researcher: Mona Amer, University of Cairo. For the estimates based on enterprise survey data, the 2003 *Micro- and Small Enterprise Survey* was used. The survey was carried out by the Cairo Demographic Center. Researcher: Alia El-Mahdi, University of Cairo.

El Salvador. Estimates based on the 2003 *Encuesta de Hogares de Propósitos Múltiples*, (EHPM) administered by the General Office of Statistics and the Census (Dirección Generalde Estadistica y Censos). Researchers: Edgar Lara López and Reinaldo Chanchán, FUNDE (Fundación Nacional para el Desarrollo), with the assistance of Sarah Gammage.

Ghana. Estimates based on the 1998/1999 *Ghana Living Standards Survey* (GLSS 4) administered by the Ghana Statistical Service. Researcher: James Heintz.

India. Estimates based on the 55th round of the *National Sample Survey*, 1999-2000 and drawn from the 2000 "Report on Statistical Studies Relating to Informal Economy in India" by Prof. N.S. Sastry (National Council for Applied Economic Research). The report was funded by UNDP, India.

South Africa. Estimates based on the September 2003 *Labour Force Survey* administered by Statistics South Africa. Researchers: Daniela Casale, Colette Muller and Dorrit Posel, University of KwaZulu Natal, Durban.

Unless otherwise noted, the tabulations are of employed individuals, 15 years of age or older. No upper age limit is placed on the estimates with the exception of South Africa, where women become eligible for pensions at 60 and men at 65 and the estimates are therefore for women aged 15-60 and men aged 15-65.

Table Notes: Specific

Tables 3.2 and 3.3. Employment status classifications are based on an individual's primary occupation for persons engaged in multiple employment activities.

Informal employers and own-account workers are distinguished from formal employers and own-account workers using one of two criteria: (1) whether the enterprise is registered with a government agency or (2) the size of the enterprise. Registration is used for the studies of Egypt, Ghana, India and South Africa. Size of the enterprise was used for Costa Rica and El Salvador. In both cases, an enterprise was deemed informal if it had five or fewer people working in it.

Informal wage employment was distinguished from formal wage employment using one or more of the following criteria: existence of paid leave, a pension scheme and/or contributions to the social security system. The exact set of criteria varied from country to country depending on available data: Costa Rica (social security), Egypt (social security), El Salvador (social security), Ghana (paid leave and pension), India (social security) and South Africa (paid leave, pension and social security). In addition, for the Indian estimates only, casual and part-time employees are also counted as informal wage employees.

Several countries do not provide disaggregated data for the category domestic workers. In these cases, domestic workers would be included as private wage employees and classified as formal or informal using the above classification criteria.

Table 3.4. There is not a one-to-one correspondence between the employment status categories listed under 'formal' and 'informal' employment. Employment status categories for which there was no data, too little data for statistical comparisons or no meaningful interpretation across all countries were excluded (e.g., 'formal domestic workers' or 'formal unpaid workers on family enterprises'). In addition, there are uncertainties to measuring earnings that should be kept in mind when interpreting these results. Earnings from formal employment are likely to be underestimated, as people frequently do not know the value of non-monetary earnings. Also, employment at the lower end of the distribution may be underrepresented in these earnings estimations, since a significant number of workers report no earnings and thus are not included in the calculations. Therefore, the 'n.a.' in Table 3.4 might represent a lack of adequate information rather than limited employment in low-income activities.

Tables 3.4 and 3.6. Hourly earnings include all reported employment income. Usual hours worked were used to compute a standard hourly rate. Individuals reporting excessive hours worked (generally, more than 140 per week) were dropped. The value of non-wage benefits and in-kind payments were included in earnings calculations. However, there is a tendency to underestimate these contributions. Also, only employed persons who reported their income are included in the estimations. The computation of self-employment income varies from country to country. For the Egyptian household data, no information on self-employment income is provided. In most cases, self-employment earnings included the value of goods produced in a family enterprise. The following are specific notes on earnings estimations by country.

Costa Rica: Earnings of waged employees are adjusted for non-wage payments. Estimates of self-employment income are based on reported profits and adjusted for the value of household consumption of goods produced.

Egypt: Earnings available only for wage employees and comprise the basic wage, supplemental wage, allowances, bonuses, incentives, overtime, profit sharing and other monetary earnings.

El Salvador: Reported earnings are used for all categories of employment. Only employed individuals reporting positive earnings are included in these estimates.

Ghana: Earnings of waged employees are adjusted for non-wage payments. Estimates of self-employment income are based on respondents' estimates of net employment earnings of the enterprise and adjusted for the value of household consumption of goods produced.

South Africa: Earnings reported represent gross earnings including overtime, allowances and bonuses and before deductions. Respondents are able to provide their earnings as either an absolute value or in an earnings bracket. Where information on earnings brackets only was provided, the value of the midpoint of the bracket was used. Estimates of self-employment income are based on respondents' estimates of net employment earnings. In-kind and non-monetary income is likely not included in these estimates.

Table 3.5. Estimates of wages by enterprise size in Egypt are based on enterprise survey data, not household survey data (see above).

Table 3.7. See notes for Ghana above. To impute average hourly earnings, the self-employment income for individuals working on family enterprises was redistributed among family members reporting that they were self-employed or were unpaid family workers. Total self-employment income from the family enterprise was divided by total hours worked on the enterprise – including the hours worked by unpaid family members. This average hourly rate was then multiplied by each individual's working hours to re-estimate each individual's self-employment income. Earnings in cedis were converted to dollars using the average market exchange rate over the sample period. Purchasing power parity (PPP) conversions were made using the 1999 PPP conversion factor reported by the World Bank's *World Development Indicators* database.

Table 3.8. Usual hours worked were used to compute a standard hourly rate. Only employed persons who reported hours of paid work were used in compiling these estimates.

Table 3.9. Usual hours worked were used to compute a standard hourly rate. Only employed persons who reported hours of paid employment and unpaid (non-market) caring labour were used in compiling these estimates.

Table 3.10. Individuals are considered to be 'working poor' if they live in households whose total income – employment and non-employment – falls below a national poverty line. Therefore, the poverty rates in this table are a measure of income poverty, not consumption poverty. For El Salvador, a per capita poverty line is used, multiplied by the number of household members without adjustments based on an adult equivalence scale.

Table 3.11. Individuals are considered to be 'working poor' if they live in households whose total income – employment and non-employment – falls below a national poverty line. Therefore, the poverty rates in this table are a measure of income poverty, not consumption poverty. For Costa Rica and Ghana, the poverty line is adjusted for household size using an adult equivalency scale. For Egypt, poverty rates were calculated on the basis of a wealth asset index as the 1998 ELMS data does not include information on household expenditures. This wealth asset index was calculated using a factor analysis. Households defined as poor are households belonging to the two lowest quintiles of the wealth index. For El Salvador, a per capita poverty line is used, multiplied by the number of household members to determine the household poverty line.

Table 3.12. Poor households are those whose incomes fall below a poverty line. Poverty lines are set and adjusted for household size and composition. The poverty line used for this table equals 494 rands per adult equivalent per month in 2003 prices. The poverty line represents the per adult equivalent household subsistence level (HSL) set by the Institute for Development Planning Research at the University of Port Elizabeth, South Africa (see Woolard and Leibbrandt, 2001:49). For these estimates, only employment income was used to determine an individual's poverty status, since the South African Labour Force Survey does not contain data on all sources of income. The survey also does not distinguish between formal and acting heads of households.

Table 3.13. Households classified as sustaining themselves on informal employment income are households with at least one person employed as an informal worker and no other household member employed outside of the informal economy. All households with income below the poverty line are classified as poor. Households with income below 75 per cent of the poverty line are classified as very poor.

CHAPTER 4
The Reality of Women's Informal Work

A vendor carrying birds for sale, Manila, the Philippines.
Photo: Joel Nito/AFP/Getty

"Risk is the acceptance of endangering one's honour, or safety or future, in order to earn an income or to cover immediate expenses."

Working poor man, Egypt (cited in Narayan 2000)

The poverty and other outcomes of work are a function not only of the level of earnings but also of the period over which earnings are sustained and the arrangements through which they are achieved, including related costs and benefits. A large share of the global workforce, especially in developing countries, is engaged in informal employment – either in traditional forms or in new forms associated with trade liberalization and growing labour market informalization.

This chapter shifts the focus from *how much* women and men earn and *whether* they are poor to *how* women and men earn and *why* they are poor. It focuses on the costs and benefits associated with the different types of informal employment, especially those in which working poor women are concentrated, and suggests new ways of thinking about poverty, gender and informal labour markets based on this analysis.

It is often assumed that many if not most of those who work informally do so because of the advantages it offers compared to working formally (Maloney 2004). But this assumption is made primarily by those who focus on the self-employed – and often on the more entrepreneurial among these – rather than on informal wage workers. It also tends to overlook the negative aspects of informal work and downplay the fact that informal workers do not enjoy many of the positive aspects of formal work because they are not registered and are not recognized by the state. In short, the benefits of informal employment tend to be overstated and the costs understated. For a more realistic picture, we need to look at both the costs and benefits of informal work from the perspective of the working poor, especially women.

Nature of Informal Work

Understanding the full costs and benefits of informal work requires first of all understanding the nature of informal work, which is complex and changing (Chen et al. 2004). In many developing countries especially, different systems of production and exchange operate side-by-side. Manufacturing takes place in modern factories or in small workshops, on sidewalks and at home. Construction is carried out using manual labour and rickety scaffolding as well as modern diggers and cranes. Goods are bought and sold in private homes, street markets, kiosks and small shops, as well as modern supermarkets and shopping plazas. The expanding service sector includes personal services as well as data entry and call centres for airlines, hospitals and other service industries.

Adding to this diversity, production is increasingly global as firms move to or operate through networks or chains of firms in countries all over the world. Computers and related technologies facilitate all aspects of production and exchange from product design to production to marketing. The bar code helps retail firms respond quickly to shifts in consumer demand; and digital graphics technology helps them transfer designs to their suppliers. In order to respond quickly, manufacturing firms seek flexibility in their labour relations by sub-contracting out various tasks, hiring workers on repeat short-term contracts or maintaining a minimum core work force with a reserve labour force mobilized during peak seasons.

Three dimensions of work arrangements are useful in determining the nature, costs and benefits of informal work: place of work, employment relations and production system.

Place of work

The conventional view of the workplace is of a factory, shop or office, as well as formal service outlets such as clinics and schools. But this has always excluded the workplaces of millions of people, more so in developing than developed countries, namely, those in informal employment. Today, as informal employment is rising everywhere, a more inclusive classification of the workplace is critical.

Some informal economic activities are located in conventional workplaces such as registered shops or offices. But, typically, informal activities are located in non-conventional places, including private homes, open spaces and unregistered shops and workshops.

Each place of work is associated with specific risks, and thus different degrees of security or insecurity, for those who work in them. The relevant factors include:

- ownership and security of tenure of the site;
- relationships of control at the work site: with

fellow workers, with an employer, with other interest groups, with public authorities and/or with family members;
- costs of securing the site (and especially entry costs for poorer women);
- the access to infrastructure needed for work, such as electricity (for light and power), water, toilets, garbage removal, storage of goods;
- access to customers and suppliers;
- potential for upgrading the conditions at the worksite;
- ability of informal workers to organize at the site or away from it in order to secure representation of their interests;
- risks and hazards associated with the site.

Private homes – Significant numbers of people work from their own homes, including own account operators, unpaid contributing family members and industrial outworkers.[1] Among the benefits of working at home, often mentioned by women, is the ability to carry out both paid work and housework plus child or elder care. This multi-tasking, which may be seen as a 'benefit' in terms of enabling women to fulfil multiple expectations, also imposes concrete costs. When a home-based worker stops work in order to care for a child or cook a meal, her productivity drops – and so does her income.

In some circumstances, working from home may be more physically safe for women. In others, it can increase their vulnerability – as they are less visible and less likely to be legally recognized as workers – and limit their access to social protection measures, chances to upgrade their skills or opportunities to organize collectively. Also, those who work at home are less likely than those who work in a workplace outside the home to develop social ties outside the family.

Those who work at home may also be limited in the kind of work they can do and how productive they are by such things as the amount of space available for work and storage, or whether there is electricity and water supply. In Ahmedabad City, India, poor women who live in dilapidated shelters on the streets report that no one is willing to give them piece-rated garment work because of the poor conditions of their homes and lack of clean storage space. In spite of having the necessary sewing skills, they have resorted to work as casual labourers or waste pickers (Unni and Rani 2002; Lund and Unni, n.d.).

Finally, home-based workers may work with toxic substances, putting children especially at risk. They may be unable to read warnings about safe handling and storage, or their homes may not be equipped for proper storage or ventilation. In the case of industrial subcontracting, this is one very concrete way in which some firms shift risk to workers and their families.

Public places – Streets, sidewalks and traffic intersections are the place of work for many traders, along with parks, fairgrounds and municipal markets. The same public spot may be used for different purposes at different times of day: in the mornings and afternoons it might be used to trade consumer goods such as cosmetics, while in the evenings it converts to a sidewalk café run as a small family enterprise.

Despite exposure to pollution, noise and weather, the benefit of working in public spaces is evidenced by the demand for them. In the competitive jostle for sites close to transport and commuter nodes, city authorities respond in different ways, ranging from outright prohibition of street trade to regulated and negotiated use. Harassment, confiscation of goods, imposition of fines, physical assault and time spent in court – all of these affect the bottom line for traders. Given these costs of operating informally, some traders may wish to pay site licenses and other levies, but often the costs of regulation in both time and money are too high in relation to the tiny size of their enterprises and incomes.

Other open spaces – Other common places of work are agricultural land, including pastures and forests, and fishing areas, including ponds, rivers and oceans. Construction sites are not only places of work for construction workers but also for suppliers and transporters of materials, and these sites may attract other informal providers of goods and services – such as street food vendors – while building is taking place.

In many countries, there is a marked gender pattern to the place of work. A recent random-sample survey of both formal and informal workers in Ahmedabad City, India found that less than 25 per cent of the female workforce worked in factories, offices or shops compared to nearly 60 per cent of the male workforce, while nearly 70 per cent of the female workforce worked in their own or other homes, compared to less than 10 per cent of the male workforce (Unni 2000).

Employment relationship

The employment relationship is the central legal concept around which labour laws and collective bargaining agreements recognize and protect the rights of workers. The conventional notion of this relationship, thought to be universal, is that between a person, called the employee (frequently referred to as 'the worker'), with another person,

---

1 This discussion is focused on those who work in their own homes. Those who work in other people's homes include paid domestic workers and nurse assistants (mostly female), security guards and gardeners (mostly male), as well as better-paid professionals such as book-keepers who work for home-based consultants.

called the employer, to whom she or he provides labour or services under certain conditions in return for remuneration" (ILO 2005a, 2003b).[2] This excludes those workers who are self-employed along with many kinds of wage employment in which the employer-employee relationship is disguised, ambiguous or not clearly defined.

In some cases, employers disguise the employment relationship by giving it the appearance of a commercial relationship: e.g., when employers 'sell' raw materials to sub-contracted workers who 'sell' finished goods back to them. In other cases, the relationship may be genuinely ambiguous. For example, some wage workers work at a physical distance from the enterprise that employs them while using equipment and/or raw materials provided by the enterprise, following its instructions and being subject to its control (over quality of goods produced and method of payment) but having full autonomy as to how to organize the work. And some ostensibly self-employed workers may be dependent on one or more contractors, including taxi-drivers, newspaper distribution workers and skilled homeworkers using information communication technology. In cases where the employees of one enterprise provide services or labour to another enterprise, it is unclear who the employer is, what rights the worker has and who is responsible for securing these rights. The classic example in developed countries is the temporary worker who gets work through a temp agency (ILO 2003b).

The main categories of informal employment relations are as follows:

- *employers*: owner operators of informal enterprises who hire others;
- *own account workers*: owner operators of single-person units or family businesses or farms who do not hire others;
- *unpaid contributing family workers*: family workers who work in family businesses or farms without pay;
- *employees*: unprotected employees with a known employer: either an informal enterprise, a formal enterprise, a contracting agency or a household;
- *casual labourers*: wage workers with no fixed employer who sell their labour on a daily or seasonal basis;
- *industrial outworkers*: sub-contracted workers who produce from their homes or a small workshop.[3]

Workers within each of these categories can be more or less dependent or independent, depending on the specific contractual arrangement under which they work. Self-employment ranges from fully-dependent arrangements in which the owner operator controls the process and outcomes of work and absorbs the risks, to semi-dependent arrangements in which the operator does not control the entire process or outcome of her work but may still absorb all of the risks involved. And, as noted earlier, some self-employed persons are dependent on one or two clients or on a dominant counterpart. Also, wage employment ranges from fully-dependent employees to fairly independent casual labourers.

Industrial outworkers who work from their homes are neither self-employed nor wage-employed. They work under sub-contracts for a piece rate without secure contracts or any real bargaining power. The small amount and insecurity of their income is exacerbated by the fact that they have to pay for the non-wage costs of production, such as workplace, equipment and utilities. They have little control over the volume or timing of work orders, the quality of raw material supplied to them or when they are paid. Some industrial outworkers produce goods for major firms abroad. In today's global economy, there may be no greater distance – physical and psychological – or greater imbalance in terms of power, profit and life-style than that between the woman who stitches garments or soccer balls from her home in Pakistan for a brand-name retailer in Europe or North America and the chief executive officer (CEO) of that brand-name corporation.

In sum, most informal workers do not fit neatly under the employer-employee relationship as conventionally understood and, therefore, tend to be excluded from legal and social protection as well as from collective bargaining agreements. In devising responses, the problem needs to be correctly diagnosed: is the scope of the legislation too narrow to cover all workers, or is legislation applicable to them not being enforced? (Daza 2005). But to fully understand the nature of informal work today, it is also important to look beyond employment relationships to the underlying system of production and exchange (du Toit and Ewert 2002).[4]

System of production

In most developing economies today, a complex mix of traditional, industrial and global modes of production and exchange co-exist as parallel or linked systems. In many developing countries, artisanal and agricultural modes of production have

---

2 In 2006, the government, employer and worker delegates to the International Labour Conference will consider a draft Recommendation on the Employment Relationship encouraging states to adopt legal reforms aimed at closing the protection gap (ILO 2005a).
3 In labour force statistics, there is another category: paid contributing members of cooperatives.
4 A single conceptual framework is needed for labour statistics, labour law and labour economics that covers all categories of non-standard employment in developed countries, all categories of informal employment in developing countries and all categories of employment (however defined) in transition economies.

not changed significantly over the past century, and industrialization has not expanded as rapidly or as fully as in developed countries. Self-employment remains a large share of total employment and industrial production takes place in micro and small units, in family businesses or in single person units. Smaller units tend to hire workers on a casual or semi-permanent basis with limited job security or workers benefits, no job ladders, and few (if any) labour-management negotiations. Even in larger units, employment relationships may be unstable and unprotected by labour legislation or collective bargaining agreements. And, in labour-intensive manufacturing sectors from garments and footwear to electronic and automobile parts, production is often sub-contracted to microenterprises or to industrial outworkers.

The global system of production – facilitated by digital technologies – involves dispersed production coordinated through networks or chains of firms. Authority and power tend to get concentrated in the top links of value chains or diffused across firms in complex networks, making it difficult for micro-entrepreneurs to gain access, compete and bargain and for wage workers to bargain for better wages and working conditions. Highly competitive conditions among small-scale suppliers and the significant market power of transnational corporations mean that the lion's share of the value produced across these value chains is captured by the most powerful players. Some small and microentrepreneurs become suppliers in these chains or networks, others become subcontractors or subcontracted workers, while yet others lose out all together.

In developing countries, globalization has been associated with two modes of production that provide little if any job security or legal protection to workers: centralized production in large factories or workshops in *export-processing zones*; and dispersed production across a long chain of suppliers, contractors and industrial outworkers in *global value chains*.[5] Export processing zones (EPZs) are industrial enclaves of export-oriented factories set up by many developing countries to attract foreign investors and increase exports. In other countries, such as Mauritius, EPZ incentives and protections have simply been extended to designated export-oriented firms irrespective of their physical location. In a few countries, the EPZ package of incentives and protections still includes exemption from national labour legislation (ILO 2002d). In global value chains, lead foreign firms negotiate directly with the first-tier of their suppliers, while retaining power and control within the chain and excluding those down the chain from direct negotiations and associated benefits. The first-tier of their suppliers may, in turn, be exempt from or choose to ignore national legislation (Chen et al. 2004).

Of course, EPZs and global value chains are not mutually exclusive ways to organize global production. EPZ factories are part of global commodity chains, though they are governed not only by the lead or parent companies to which they supply goods but also by the government regulations covering the EPZ where they are located. In both cases, there is a marked shift from *intra-firm* (employer-employee) relationships that predominate in industrial production. In the case of EPZs the shift is to *firm-government* relationships, and in the case of value chains it is to *inter-firm* relationships. As a consequence, many wage workers have little control or bargaining power over their terms of involvement (ibid). A widespread feature of global production is the volatility and seasonality of demand. To adjust to the peaks and sloughs in their business cycle, many employers prefer to hire a small core workforce and maintain a 'reserve army' of seasonally employed workers. In addition, wage workers in EPZs are often not allowed to join unions, and many sub-contracted workers in global value chains work from their homes, thereby undermining the socialization and solidarity functions of work.

What this complex reality suggests is that the costs and benefits of informal work are a function not just of working conditions but, more fundamentally, of work arrangements. As used here, 'working conditions' is a term associated with whether the workplace is safe or humanely-run and whether the workers enjoy benefits and legal protection; and 'work arrangements' is a broader term that encompasses place of work, employment status and production system – each of which serves to determine the conditions and outcomes of work. Making the link between informal employment, poverty and gender inequality means assessing the costs and benefits associated with different informal work arrangements against the location of women and men within them.

Benefits of Informal Work

The most widely cited benefits of informal work include tax avoidance, illegal occupation of premises and illegal tapping of electricity, all of which are seen to lower the costs of informal enterprises and to give them a competitive advantage over formal firms that pay taxes, rent and utility bills. A second set of benefits, thought to favour women in particular, are the flexibility of work hours and the convenience of working from home or another convenient location. A further derived benefit is the opportunity that might not otherwise be available

---

5 See Gereffi 1994 for a discussion of two types of global value chains: buyer-driven chains (e.g., garments) and producer-driven chains (e.g., automobiles).

for generating wealth (if a person is entrepreneurial) or for making ends meet (if a person is poor). And for those who might not be able to seek a formal job, such as women whose physical mobility is constrained by social norms, informal work is seen to offer a chance to earn an independent income.

Tax avoidance and competitive advantage

Informal entrepreneurs are thought to avoid the various taxes paid by formal enterprises, including registration fees, corporate income tax and payroll taxes. However, the reality is not so straightforward. Although informal enterprises are not formally registered at the national level, they may be registered at a local municipal level and pay registration fees as well as operating fees for the use of urban space. Moreover, they often pay indirect taxes or fees in the form of bribes, fees to recover confiscated goods and relocation costs in cases of eviction. Street vendors are particularly liable to indirect taxes. Some also pay nearby storekeepers for the use of toilets or space to store goods.

With regard to corporate income taxes, many microenterprises and own account operators are not subject to these since they are not incorporated or do not generate enough profit to fall into existing corporate tax brackets. However, they may still pay taxes because of reporting business profits as personal income due to the difficulty of separating household and business accounts. On the other hand, microenterprises and own account units do not benefit when governments lower corporate income tax rates as part of export-promotion incentive packages. There is no parallel tax incentive for microenterprises or own account operators that are not incorporated.

With regard to payroll taxes, microenterprises that hire others are legally liable to submit these but, by not registering, often avoid them. However, own account operators, who represent a large share of informal enterprises in many developing countries, are not subject to payroll taxes as they do not (by definition) hire workers. In India, own account operations represent over 85 per cent of all informal enterprises in manufacturing (Unni 2005).

Finally, with regard to value-added taxes, informal producers and traders often find it difficult to 'pass' these on to their customers because they operate in such highly competitive and price-sensitive markets. And they cannot claim back the VAT that they pay on inputs because they are not legally registered. Further, a flat rate value-added tax – especially on foodstuffs – can prove regressive for informal workers *as consumers*. This is because low-income households spend a larger proportion of their income on food than higher-income households and, as we saw in Chapter 3, informal workers are more likely to be from poor households than are formal workers.

In 2004, the World Bank extended its Investment Climate Surveys in 11 countries to cover micro and informal firms. These extended surveys found that, compared to all sizes of formal firms (small, medium and large), informal firms:

- pay relatively high bribes (using bribe payments as a share of sales as the measure);
- have less access to formal finance;
- experience more frequent electricity outages;
- find government services less efficient.

The surveys also found that non-compliance with taxes and regulations leaves informal firms vulnerable to being evicted or shut down, and makes them easy targets for bribes or bureaucratic harassment from officials (Hallward-Driemeier and Stone 2004).

Flexibility and convenience

Some forms of informal work are associated with flexible work hours and other forms of convenience such as working at or near one's own home. And, undoubtedly, some women 'prefer' flexible work hours and working from home due to competing time pressures owing to their responsibility for both paid and unpaid work. But other women have little choice, are conditioned to prefer or are forced into these arrangements. The flip-side of flexibility is uncertainty, including uncertain volume and quality of production due to flexible work schedules and poor working conditions; and uncertain work orders and payments due to limited market knowledge and bargaining power. This applies in particular to the many home-based producers who are industrial outworkers – also known as homeworkers (see section on industrial outworkers below).

Industrial outworkers are completely dependent on others for the supply of raw materials and the sale of finished goods and remain isolated from other women doing the same type of work. This dependence, combined with the isolation that makes organizing with others difficult if not impossible, undermines their ability to bargain for higher piece-rates, timely payments or overtime pay. Finally, working at home can represent a cost in terms of bargaining power not just in the market but within the household, because it does not provide women with a viable fall-back position.

Costs of Informal Work

While informal work does offer positive opportunities and benefits, the benefits are not sufficient and the costs are often too high for most of those who work informally to achieve an adequate standard of living over their working lives (see Box 4.1). Some costs are *direct* in the form of 'out of pocket' expenses needed to run an informal business or work informally; others are *indirect,* reflecting the more general conditions under which the working poor live and work. Some of these can be rather high over the long-term, such as when a worker

Box 4.1

Costs of Informal Work

Direct Costs

1. High costs of running informal businesses, including direct and indirect taxes
2. High costs of informal wage work
   - long hours and unscheduled overtime
   - occupational health hazards
3. High costs of accessing capital in informal financial markets and high indebtedness
4. High costs associated with periodic 'shocks' to work

Indirect Costs

1. Lack of secure work and income
   - greater insecurity of work
   - variability and volatility of income
2. Lack of worker benefits and social protection
   - few (if any) rights such as paid sick leave, overtime compensation or severance pay
   - no childcare provisions
   - little (if any) employment-based social protection
   - no health, disability, property, unemployment or life insurance
3. Lack of training and career prospects
4. Lack of capital and other assets
   - lack of/vulnerability of productive assets
   - limited (if any) access to formal financial services
5. Lack of legal status, organization and voice
   - uncertain legal status
   - lack of organization and voice

---

has to sacrifice access to health and education (or training) for herself or family members. Also, there are psychological and emotional costs – in terms of a worker's self-esteem and dignity – associated with many forms of informal work.

Many informal workers face significant occupational hazards in the workplace (direct costs) yet are not covered by occupational health and safety (OHS) regulatory and compensatory mechanisms (indirect costs). For unprotected informal workers, exposure to toxic chemicals, repetitive strain and muscular-skeletal injuries, poor sanitation, excessive working hours and structurally unsafe workplaces not only threaten personal health and safety but can also impact on productivity and income (see Box 4.2).

Existing OHS regulatory mechanisms are generally under-resourced and unable to keep pace with the diversifying nature of work today. Mainstream enforcement mechanisms rely on easily identifiable employers and workplaces and, therefore, exclude many informal workers who do not have a standard employment relationship or conventional work space. In many countries, enterprises with fewer than a specified number of workers may be excluded from OSH legislation. Other forms of vulnerability – such as the impermanence and insecurity of the workplace or the need to work excessive hours on piece-rate contracts – may further contribute to the risk of injury and illness for informal workers yet remain unchallenged by existing regulatory systems.

In addition to the costs of working informally, informal workers often have to forego the benefits associated with working formally and being legally recognized by the state. Formal enterprises are more likely to have access to financial resources and market information, and to be able to secure written and enforceable commercial contracts. Formal entrepreneurs are entitled to join registered business associations through which they gain information about market trends and forge market contacts.

In addition, depending on the country, the state may contribute to unemployment funds, workers' compensation, maternity benefits, health insurance and retirement savings, all of which are forms of risk management and means of smoothing incomes over a lifetime.

In some countries, the state also sets up labour courts or other machinery for settling disputes between employers and employees in ways that enable workers to confront employers on a more equal footing. Finally, to promote exports and competitiveness in specific sectors, the state may offer subsidies and incentives to businesses, including tax rebates, business training, export licenses, export promotion through trade fairs, outright subsidies (e.g., agriculture) and other means.[6]

In addition, some states make provisions that are not based on employment but that, nonetheless, impact on the ability of men and women to work. For example:

- in many European countries, state commitment to child care provision directly encourages women to go to and stay in work;
- in Durban, South Africa, a municipal water tariff – the 'lifeline tariff' – charges lower rates to low-income consumers; poor people who work from home who depend on water for work, such as cooking for sale at local outlets and doing laundry, pay less for their water, thus benefiting as workers as well as consumers;
- in Thailand, a local community development fund gives local groups access to loans at low rates of interest for income-generating initiatives.

Finally, as *citizens*, both formal and informal workers are entitled to benefits from the state that can directly and indirectly contribute to their ability to work productively: for example, health, education and welfare services, infrastructure for residential areas and support for care of elderly peo-

---

6 The informal workforce receives few – if any – of these employment-related benefits, at least in their capacity as workers. However, as dependents of a formally-employed spouse or father, many women (whether working or not) and children receive benefits such as health insurance and widows' pensions – providing the formal work includes social protection, which is less and less common.

ple, children and people with disabilities. However, in many countries, there are systematic biases against *poorer people* either in accessing state-provided services such as health and education or in the quality of those services.

What we can see from this review is that some of the costs of informal work are associated with the behaviour of individual firms, others with government policies and still others with social norms and institutions. Firms often decide the nature of employment and commercial contracts, the costs of employment or commercial transactions and the 'rules-of-the-game'. An example is retailers in the food and garment industries who, through sourcing and purchasing practices, "demand low-cost, fast, and flexible production in their supply chains" (Kidder and Raworth 2004:12).

Government policies often fail to generate aggregate demand for the labour, goods and services provided by the informal economy or to provide legal and regulatory protections to informal firms and workers. Finally, social norms and institutions (family, kin and caste) constrain the physical mobility of individual workers as well their access to and ownership of property.

In brief, competitive market pressures and related corporate practices, a decline in state social spending and legal protections and various forms of discrimination in the broader society – by class, gender, race/ethnicity and geography – reinforce each other to generate significant costs for the working poor in the informal economy.

Together these costs take a huge toll on the financial, physical and psychological well-being of many informal workers, eroding the benefits earned through employment. In the short term, the working poor in the informal economy often have to 'over-work' to cover these costs and still make ends meet. In the long-term, the cumulative toll of being over-worked, under-compensated and under-protected on informal workers, their families and their societies undermines human capital and depletes physical capital.[7] All these costs, both direct and indirect – as well as foregone benefits – must be addressed if the poor are to able to work their way out of poverty.

Exposure to risk

How does gender intersect with types of work in determining the risks and insecurities associated with work? A recent UNIFEM-supported study of women in the informal economy in Bulgaria asked women informal workers (through interviews and focus-group discussions) to assess the risks that they face. As ranked by respondents, the greatest risks were becoming impoverished upon retiring from work and the intergenerational transfer of poverty: respondents explained that they could not

---

Box 4.2

Occupational Health and Safety Hazards

Problems associated with poor health and safety in the workplace vary from job to job and are also heavily dependent on the environment in which each job is undertaken. Some of the common problems associated with different types of informal work include:

1. Garment makers
   - neck and back ache
   - pain in limbs and joints
   - poor vision resulting from eye strain
   - headaches, dizziness and fatigue
   - respiratory problems associated with dust and textile fibres
2. Street vendors
   - exposure to weather – extreme temperatures, wind, rain and sun
   - poor access to clean water
   - poor sanitation from dirty streets and poor drainage, as well as waste produce from other vendors
   - diseases transmitted by vermin
   - lead poisoning and respiratory problems from vehicle fumes
   - musculoskeletal problems associated with ergonomic hazards at workstations and static postures
   - risk of physical harm from municipal authorities, members of the public or other traders
3. Waste pickers
   - exposure to weather – extreme temperatures, wind, rain and sun
   - poor sanitation and limited or no access to clean water
   - exposure to dangerous domestic and industrial waste, including toxic substances such as lead and asbestos
   - exposure to other dangerous matter, including blood, faecal matter, broken glass, needles, sharp metal objects and animal carcasses
   - back and limb pain, itchy skin/rashes
   - diseases transmitted by vermin, flies and mosquitoes
   - specific high risk of tuberculosis, bronchitis, asthma, pneumonia, dysentery and parasites

---

afford to bring up their children properly and would have to rely on their children to supplement their meagre social pensions when they retired (Dimova and Radeva 2004).

A UNIFEM-supported study of home-based workers in poor urban communities in Bolivia and Ecuador developed an index of informality (high, medium, low) based on the regularity and stability of employment. Among economically-active persons in their sample, 95 per cent in Bolivia and 79 per cent in Ecuador were in a main occupation that was moderately or highly informal. In both countries, women were more likely than men to be in the most informal employment (Benería and Floro 2004).

This issue was also explored in a recent study in a black township in KwaZulu Natal province, South Africa. Classifying wage workers into *most formal*, *semi-formal* and *most informal*, the study

---

[7] In a recent paper on the hidden costs of 'precarious' employment to women workers, Kidder and Raworth (2004) present a framework for estimating the long-term costs to society of this work.

Woman selling fish in outdoor market, Kisumu, Kenya. Photo: Martha Chen

found that while income levels in general were very low, the median income for the self-employed was around half that for wage workers. However, there were stark differences among wage workers, with the most informal wage workers having a median income well below that of the self-employed. Controlling for age, education and experience, women earned significantly less than men. The average wage gap was estimated to be around 48 per cent; the gender difference was smallest, however, for those in professional ranks (teachers and nurses) in the civil service (see discussion on public sector employment and earnings in Chapter 3).

The study also showed clear differences with regard to risk. Among the self-employed, less than a quarter received a regular income, as opposed to three quarters of wage workers. The consequences of this in terms of health were seen in the fact that nearly three times as many self-employed workers reported poor health status as wage workers. Moreover, fewer of the self-employed than of the wage workers had work-related insurance that could help tide them over hard times.

Among the wage employed, those who are paid in cash rather than through a bank account or post office also face risk, including the possibility of theft, claims on cash income by relatives or friends and ease of spending (rather than saving) earned income. None of the most formal wage workers were paid in cash, compared to nearly two thirds of the most informal wage workers (Lund and Ardington 2005).

Irregularity and seasonality of work

What people earn is a function not just of their level of earnings but also of the period of time over which these earnings are sustained. For example, findings from a random-sample survey of 104 men and 507 women in low-income slums in Ahmedabad City, India suggest, as might be expected, that formal salaried workers enjoy the most days work per year on average. Within the informal workforce, the self-employed enjoy more days of work per year on average than do casual day labourers or homeworkers.

However, these averages disguise marked gender differences in unemployment. Within each employment status category, women reported fewer days of work and more days of unemployment per year than men. Overall, women averaged 124 days of unemployment per year while men averaged only 74 days of unemployment per year. Also, fewer women (83%) than men (92%) reported that their main activity was regular and more than twice as many women (37%) as men (15%) reported that they carried out two economic activities per day (rather than one) (Rani and Unni 2000).

Seasonality helps explain some of the reported unemployment and irregularity of work. In Ahmedabad City, there are marked seasonal fluctuations in the supply and price of different varieties of fruits, vegetables and other fresh produce that street vendors purchase and sell. Also, the demand for fruits and vegetables rises in summer, falls during the monsoon and winter months and peaks during the major festivals and the wedding season. Similarly, the demand for garments typically falls in summer, rises in winter and peaks just before (and drops sharply after) the major annual festivals and the wedding season. During the monsoon season, the lack of sun and dry spells disrupts many occupations in which both men and women are engaged (construction, screen printing, cloth dyeing, laundry services) as well as those in which women are concentrated (pepper or spice drying, incense stick rolling) (Chen and Snodgrass 2001).

Close-up: Occupational Groups

Garment Workers

Women workers are often considered to be among the relative winners of globalization. Many are earning cash incomes for the first time – often more than they would elsewhere (Kidder and Raworth 2004). But at the bottom end of global value chains that supply fresh produce, garments, shoes or electronic goods to major retailers or manufacturers, there are often hidden costs for women resulting from their work arrangements.

For example, the garment industry employs millions of women workers across the world. Conditions are fiercely competitive, with rapid changes in fashion dictating a severe form of just-in-time production, the consequences of which are well known – low wages, long hours of overtime and an increase in the numbers of industrial outworkers, most of whom are women. The ending of the Multi-Fibre Agreement in January 2005 has introduced further volatility to a complex and rapidly changing industry. The case studies that follow illustrate a continuum of locations and statuses within the garment industry drawn from different countries. These include factory work, contracted or agency work within factories, work as a member of a producer group and homework.

Factory Workers in China. In 1980, a Special Economic Zone (SEZ) was set up in Shenzhen, just across the then border from Hong Kong. At the time, Shenzhen was a small city with around 300,000 inhabitants and fewer than 30,000 recognized workers. By the end of 2000, its total population had increased to over 4.3 million and its labour force to over 3 million. Only 30 per cent of the population is categorized as permanent residents. The other 70 per cent – mainly migrant labourers from rural areas – are classified as temporary residents, a status that until recently has meant that they do not have the official household registration that would entitle them to citizenship in Shenzhen (Ngai 2005).

Garment, electronics and toy-making plants predominate in the SEZ. Designed to attract local and foreign investment, the incentive package offered by the SEZ includes low taxes, low management fees and low rents for large factory compounds. In these light manufacturing industries, more than 70 per cent of the total labour force is female and young (usually under 25 years of age). All of the women workers are classified as rural peasant workers (*mingong*) and do not have the status of formal workers. Because they lack citizenship rights and the cost of rent is high, workers mainly live in dormitories provided by their employers. A recent study assessed the set of factors that situate these workers in an especially precarious position: the practices of international buyers that do not seriously apply corporate 'codes of conduct' to worker conditions in their supplier companies; national and provincial Chinese laws that do not provide basic citizenship rights for non-resident rural migrant workers; and the ready supply of willing female workers who are eager to earn in the years of relative 'freedom' before marriage (ibid.).

With accommodation tied to employment, employers in this 'dormitory labour regime' have control over both the working and living conditions of their employees. Most workers, except management staff, are paid on a piece-rate basis, obliging them to work long hours to produce sufficient quantities to earn good wages. In addition, while workers are entitled to an overtime premium for work done beyond normal hours (40 hours a week), companies take advantage of the fact that workers do not know the terms of Chinese labour law to insist that work done on weekends is not overtime and that workers have no right to refuse to take overtime work. Twelve-hour working days are not uncommon. Rest days are provided only if there is a break in production orders.

To restrict the movements of their migrant workers, companies often keep their identity cards and enforce a system whereby newly hired workers are required to deposit RMB 100 with the company. They also exercise strict discipline and supervision in the dormitories – many of which are crowded, lack sufficient ventilation and lighting, and provide no private or personal space. In 2005, labour shortages were reported in several SEZs in China, suggesting that the supposedly endless pool of women workers willing to work in these zones was drying up (Pun Ngai, personal communication, 2005).

Factory Workers in Bangladesh. In Bangladesh, the export-oriented garment industry in 2000 provided jobs to 1.8 million workers of which 1.5 million were women (Kabeer and Mahmud 2004). But the jobs lack social protection, conditions in many of the factories are below international standards and wage levels are generally lower than those in the rest of the domestic manufacturing sector, that is, informal. This is due both to the presence of a large reserve pool of unskilled female labour in the countryside willing to work for low wages in the garment factories (one of the few modern employment opportunities open to them) and to the absence of collective bargaining or other mechanisms for enforcing the national minimum wage and other labour protections (Bhattacharya and Rahman 2002).

Many of the garment workers work overtime. In 2003, local researchers calculated that women workers in seven garment factories in Dhaka, the capital city of Bangladesh, worked an average of 80 hours overtime per month and that their overtime pay was around 60-80 per cent of what they were due. This under-payment was estimated to be the equivalent of 24 hours of uncompensated work per month. In addition, the women workers faced out-of-pocket expenses when forced to work overtime at night. Whereas they could walk home in daylight hours, they had to pay transport costs at night that added up to the equivalent of an additional 17 hours of uncompensated work per month (Barkat et al. 2003, cited in Oxfam International 2004). While the women workers knew that they were being underpaid for their overtime, they had not received written pay slips and were not aware of the extent of their under-payment.

Agency Workers in Thailand. In Thailand, a firm called GFB operates in Bangkok producing garments for export (e.g., for Liz Claiborne, Victoria's Secret, Playtex). In 2001 it employed about 1,500 workers, of which nearly all were women. Some were paid on a monthly basis and some on a daily basis. A local union successfully negotiated to obtain cost of living increases, transport allowances and bonuses for workers, as well as financial support from the firm to the union. However, changing conditions in the industry simultaneously led to substantial layoffs and great insecurity among all workers.

GFB called on the services of an employment agency called BVS to supply labour on short-term contracts. Workers applying for employment (some of whom were laid-off formal workers) now had a contract with BVS, which stipulated payment of the legal minimum wage and of overtime. At the same time, it omitted a range of benefits that normally accrued to formal workers, such as annual wage increase, survivor benefit, cost of living allowance and food allowance (Doane et al. 2003).

Specific and less visible costs of the move to contract-based work included the need for workers to buy their own uniforms, and the demand, totally against Thai law, that they place a deposit worth about six days' wages into a 'guarantee fund', which is repaid in full only if the worker stays for six months or more. Agency workers are prohibited from joining a union, one of the core labour standards of the ILO. Finally, although agency workers pay contributions to the Thai social insurance fund, these are sometimes not forwarded to the Social Security Office, resulting in denial of benefits without recourse through the labour court, which in any event is both expensive and time consuming.

Group-Based Industrial Outwork in Thailand. In another part of Thailand, Lampoon province, a group of 10 women produce garments for the local and export markets, working from the private house of the lead member. They work on a piece-rate basis for less than they could earn if they worked in the nearby factory, and they have to cover the cost in time and transport of securing orders from the firm. These industrial outworkers, all women, are quite clear about the benefits to them of this poorly-paid group work. Flexible time allows them to participate in village activities; additionally, no garment production is done during the farming season, when they all have farm responsibilities. Their working collectively has enabled them to co-invest in their own work-based fund for equipment. It also enables them to access loans for their machines from local government, access assistance from the health services for training on occupational health and safety and contribute to the Thai social insurance fund.

Though these workers are paid less than the agency workers in the factory, in some respects their social relationships and working environment are far better, and they are able to combine different kinds of domestic and income-earning activities. This case represents a variation on industrial outwork that is done as a group rather than as isolated individuals at home and seems to suit the needs of these women workers. There appear to be material and social benefits to working collectively. This group-based industrial outwork seems quite prevalent in Thailand in the garment sector.

Individual Industrial Outworkers or Homeworkers. Industrial outworkers who work from their homes fall into a grey intermediate zone between being fully independent and being fully dependent. In the garment industry, the percentage of homeworkers in the total workforce in the mid-1990s was estimated at 38 per cent in Thailand, between 25-39 per cent in the Philippines, 30 per cent in one region of Mexico, between 30-60 per cent in Chile and 45 per cent in Venezuela (Chen et al. 1999). Homeworkers work under what could be considered either an employment or a commercial contract for a sub-contracting firm or its intermediary. While the firm or its intermediary typically supplies work orders, designs and raw materials and markets the finished goods, the homeworker provides the means of production and the workplace.

The homeworkers also have to absorb many production costs – including utilities as well as the maintenance and depreciation of equipment – and associated risks, often without help from the firm/intermediary. For instance, garment homeworkers commonly have to buy and maintain their own sewing machines, replace needles and thread and pay for the electricity to run their machines and light their workspace. Although not directly supervised by those who contract work to them, they are subject to delivery deadlines and to quality control of the products they deliver. If their work orders are suddenly cancelled, if the firm/intermediary does not accept their goods or if they are not paid for months at a time, homeworkers have little recourse. This is because they operate in a legal limbo in which it is not clear whether they are employees and, if so, which firm or individual in the sub-contracting chain is their employer.

Street Traders
Street Traders in Nairobi, Kenya. An estimated 15,000 street traders compete for space and customers in the Central Business District (CBD) of Nairobi, the capital city of Kenya. They sell a range

of goods, from vegetables and fruits to electrical equipments and accessories, and provide services such as shoe shining, catering and selling of drinks, and art or design services such as designing rubber stamps. The gender divide is marked in the type of goods being sold and services offered: women tend to dominate in the less lucrative trading activities such as the sale of fruits and vegetables, while men dominate in the sale of higher-value non-perishable goods such as electrical equipment and accessories. Trade in old clothes (*mitumba*), which is comparatively lucrative, attracts both women and men, though men tend to have a higher volume of stock. The gender divide in type of goods being sold and volume of stock is partly explained by the differential level of access to capital and economic networks by women and men. Most men who sell electrical equipment either sell on commission or have some form of credit arrangement with their suppliers.

Vendors use different structures including hand carts and different materials for displaying their goods. The materials include cardboards, carton boxes, gunny bags, shawls, plastic sheets and clothes hangers, which allow street vendors to quickly and easily conceal their commodities whenever the city enforcement officers are sighted. Most vendors operate on open grounds without any protective covering, while a few others have makeshift covers using polythene, canvas, corrugated iron sheets and carton sheets, which are not allowed by the city authorities. The vendors operating without any cover or shelter are exposed to harsh weather conditions – sun, rain and dust. This affects not only the traders' health but also the conditions of the goods they sell.

The income or value of sales of street vendors varies according to what they sell. Those who sell electronic goods and accessories earn more than those who sell fruits and vegetables. Most traders purchase their goods on a daily cash basis; most have no access to formal credit and have to borrow from relatives and friends, join Revolving Savings and Credit Associations (ROSCAs), draw-down personal savings or sell property.

In Kenya, the use of urban public space is regulated by municipal by-laws or regulations that are outdated or are frequently changed. Until recently, there was no designated area for street trade within the CBD of Nairobi. Street vendors had to compete for trading space among themselves, with formal traders and with the municipality to use streets, roads and parking spaces. In 2003, in an effort to accommodate them within the CBD, the street vendors were relocated to back lanes that were no longer used as loading zones for formal businesses. Most of the lanes were not paved and had no streetlights. Some were used for dumping garbage, while others were used as homes for streetchildren or hide-outs for criminals. The move to relocate street vendors on these lanes was the first initiative towards an inclusive city that viewed street traders as part of its economy. But the conditions and reputation of the back lanes discouraged the flow of customers and the lack of lighting reduced the working hours of the vendors. Also, the available slots could not accommodate all of the 15,000 vendors in the CBD (Kiura 2005).

Since 2003, there have been two further attempts to relocate street vendors. In 2004, a new Minister for Local Government ordered them to move out of the back lanes to a five acre piece of land on the periphery of the CBD. To do this, the piece of land was cleared and street vendors were allocated spaces, but without the necessary infrastructure and services such as water, sanitation and security. The vendors refused to move to the new site and some of them (unsuccessfully) took the government to court. Endless street battles and protests ensued between the Minister, the municipal authorities and the traders.

Then, in 2005, the same Minister decided to reserve some streets in the CBD for street trading on Sundays; to allocate a parking lot within the CBD for use by vendors on Saturdays; and to allocate an undeveloped site on the periphery of the CBD for use on Tuesdays. However, the latter two markets serve the tourist trade, not the local residents who rely on street vendors for basic household supplies. Although the street vendors have not been fully relocated back in the CBD, the local government has conceded that they need to be accommodated (Winnie Mitullah, personal communication, 2005).

Domestic Workers

In most countries, domestic work is predominantly a female occupation. It is carried out in conditions similar to that of wage work, but for private households rather than an enterprise (Pok and Lorenzetti 2004). Although typically low-paid and informal, in some contexts domestic workers may be regulated and protected, that is, formal (Heyzer et al. 1994; Blackett 1998). For example, in 2002, after a 15-year struggle, domestic workers in South Africa were finally brought under the Unemployment Insurance Act covering employees (see Chapter 6). In many countries, domestic workers are from migrant communities or ethnic minorities. Some of these immigrants are recruited from overseas specifically to do domestic work, including some who immigrate with their employers to the host country.

Filipina Maids in Hong Kong. Since the 1970s economic crisis, low wages for even highly educated workers and high unemployment have caused many Filipinas to seek domestic work in Hong Kong and elsewhere in Asia and the Middle East. As of December 1995 there were over 130,000 Filipina 'domestic helpers' in Hong Kong, most between the ages of 20 and 30, with college degrees or high school diplomas, who had been employed in the Philippines before migrating and were supporting, on average, five family members via remittances.

The most common complaint among these workers is the long and arduous working hours with no overtime pay. A Standard Employment Contract for Foreign Domestic Workers was put in effect as early as the 1970s to govern the conditions of work, including the amount of time off and minimum wage (Heyzer and Wee 1994). However, enforcement is a problem; many workers are underpaid and forced to sign false receipts of payment. Surveys have also shown that many workers are required to do additional, and therefore illegal, work outside of their employer's home. Common forms of disciplining workers range from time-tabling all work activities and constant observation to the extension of employer control to workers' private domains – including curfews on days off, control of bank accounts and identity documents, rules on clothing and appearance and even rules on times and frequency of bathing (Constable 1997).

Filipina domestic workers have tried to resist certain types of employer and government control through political and legal channels, such as helping to organize the Filipino Migrant Workers' Union to bargain for rights, as well as engaging in public demonstrations or through quieter forms of protest. However, their ability to protect themselves against exploitative or abusive employers is limited. Although labour rights are guaranteed in the legal system, a high failure rate and the financial and personal costs involved in challenging an employer, as well as the onus on workers to prove their own innocence, effectively deters many workers from pursuing cases. Further, the balance of power in the employment relationship lies firmly with employers, given that most domestic workers are financially and emotionally indebted to family and friends for the payment of high registration and immigration fees and cannot risk the termination of employment and consequent repatriation. In the pursuit of profit recruitment agencies further compound the vulnerability of workers by encouraging employers to terminate contracts after two years (ibid).

Following the Asian economic crisis of the late 1990s, the Indonesian Government promoted the employment of Indonesian women as domestic workers in Asia. By 2005, there were over 90,000 Indonesian domestic workers in Hong Kong, and the number of Filipina domestic workers had decreased from a high of close to 150,000 to 124,000 in 2005 (Nicole Constable, personal communication, 2005).

Waste Pickers

In the developed world, most waste removal and recycling activities are carried out by municipalities. In the developing world, by contrast, these activities are mainly carried out by private individuals or enterprises. The only available estimate suggests that, in the late 1980s, about 1 per cent of the urban population in the developing world survived by scavenging for waste (Bartone 1988). While those who scavenge for waste often come from disadvantaged communities or are recent migrants to urban areas, and although the work is dirty, demeaning and demanding, waste pickers play an essential role in helping to clean cities and to supply raw materials to industry. And although those who collect and supply waste to contractors typically earn very little, others up the recycling chain often earn large amounts of money (Medina 2005).

Waste Pickers in Lucknow City, India. The intersection of caste, ethnicity and gender can be seen clearly in the case of waste pickers in Lucknow City in India. These are mainly migrants from the states of Uttar Pradesh, Bihar or Assam. Regional identity, slum environment and gender are key factors determining the relative vulnerability of waste pickers (Kantor and Nair 2005). All of the waste pickers are extremely vulnerable to injuries, infection and disease (especially skin diseases) given the type of waste they collect, their exposure to the elements and their risky picking and sorting practices – no shoes, no gloves, no hand washing before cooking and children playing among the waste during sorting (ibid.).

Migrants who have lived in Lucknow for a long time and have established ties fare better than newer migrants. The waste pickers from Assam are the worst-off socially and economically: the local language (Hindi) is not their mother tongue, they are ethnically different from the other two waste picking groups and they have fewer local ties. As a result, they are more dependent on subcontractors to provide them with living space and picking areas. Those who live in older slums and/or in occupationally-heterogeneous slums have better access to infrastructure and services. However, they may not be able to take advantage of this as they are more likely to face insults and rudeness from neighbours who do not pick waste, and they remain isolated and marginalized.

While both women and men pick garbage, more women than men sort it, adding to their exposure to waste and related health risks. Mostly men are involved in selling the waste. Since they have to move around different neighbourhoods, women face teasing, touching and other forms of sexual harassment while out picking. To avoid harassment, they try to pick in groups, remove girls from picking when they reach adolescence, and limit their mobility. They also limit their mobility to enable return trips home during the day to cook meals and look after children (Paula Kantor, personal communication, 2005).

A Causal Model of the Informal Economy

In examining the costs and benefits of working informally, it is important to look not only at generic costs and benefits, but also at which categories of informal workers tend to incur the costs or enjoy the benefits and under what circumstances. It is often the case that formal corporations choose to hire workers under informal employment relations in the interest of maintaining a flexible and low-cost workforce. In other words, *formal* firms or employers – not only the 'informals' themselves – may choose informal economic arrangements. Also, the policies and regulations of the state as well as social norms and institutions all serve to determine the costs and benefits of working informally.

With this perspective in mind, we can posit an integrative *causal model* of the informal economy that includes informal employment *by choice*, informal employment *by necessity*, and informal employment *by tradition*. Within this model, those who work informally by *choice* include:

- those who deliberately choose to avoid taxes and registration, such as many micro-entrepreneurs who hire others;
- those who prefer the flexibility and convenience of informal work, such as the professional and technical self-employed.

Those who operate in the informal economy by *necessity* include:

- those who cannot find a formal job, as when not enough jobs are created to keep up with the supply of labour, when retrenchments take place, when companies shift their location of production, when mechanization displaces workers or when companies decide to 'outsource' production or services;
- those who do not get sufficient income from their existing job, for example, when poorly-paid public sector employees have to earn a supplemental income in the informal economy to make ends meet;
- those who are forced to change their employment or commercial relationships: for instance, former employees who are re-contracted as seasonal workers; and independent producers who are forced to work under sub-contracts when they lose their market niche.

And those who operate in the informal employment *by tradition* include:

- those who follow in the hereditary occupation of their family or social group, which is passed down from one generation to the next (such as caste-specific occupations in India);
- those who receive a 'calling' to take up a traditional occupation (such as traditional healers in southern Africa);
- those who face labour supply constraints due to restrictions on their physical mobility (e.g., due to patriarchal norms) and/or competing demands on their time (e.g., due to the gender division of labour).

Some of those in the final category could be seen as operating informally due to necessity as well as tradition. This is because the constraints they face might not be due to gender-ascribed roles and responsibilities but, rather, to wider structural dimensions of the economy, such as asset ownership and gender segmentation of labour markets. Of course, some of these structural constraints may also reflect the gender norms of the society.

Poverty, gender and informal employment

Where the working poor, especially women, are located in the global workforce has consequences for persistent poverty and gender inequality. Development planners need to look at poverty from the perspective of the working poor – especially women – in the informal economy and consider the ways in which gender intersects with other sources of disadvantage in the realm of work. Finally, mainstream economists and others who advise policy makers need to revisit their assumptions regarding how labour markets are structured and behave to incorporate the reality of informal employment.

Money matters

Increased global attention to poverty has rekindled the debate on what constitutes poverty. There is renewed focus on its broader dimensions, which are not captured in the standard measures of what is now called 'income poverty', including: health, education, longevity and other human capabilities; political participation and social inclusion; and human rights, entitlements and empowerment (Sen 1985, 1993; UNDP 1997, 2001; Rodgers et al. 1995). While all of these dimensions are critical to the well-being of the poor, they should not obscure the centrality of earned income in the lives of the poor.

From the perspective of poor people, money matters: both how much cash flows *into* the household as well as how much cash flows *out of* the household. As the data presented in Chapter 3 indicate, average earnings are higher in the formal than in the informal economy, with the result that if one or more members of the household is formally employed the total income of the household tends to be above the poverty line. And, as the evidence presented in this chapter has shown, formal workers are more likely than informal workers to have secure work and access to social protection with the result that if one or more members of the household is formally employed, cash flows out of the household to cover common contingencies or periodic shocks tend to be relatively low.

From the perspective of poor women what also matters is the flow or distribution of income *within* the household. Who receives the money within the household? Do women control their own earnings? Women's control over their income and their role in the allocation of household budget expenditures are critical to their empowerment. Women's bargaining power within the household depends in large part on their earnings and bargaining power outside the household; yet their ability to earn outside the home depends on gender roles and relationships within the home (see Chapter 2). Women who do paid work from their homes are not likely, despite their earnings, to increase their bargaining power either outside or within the household. Women who do paid work outside their homes and, in the process, learn to bargain with wholesale traders and government officials, are more likely to be able to bargain within the household, whatever their level of earnings. Women workers who are organized are more likely to exercise bargaining power both within and outside their homes, no matter where they work or how much they earn (Chen and Snodgrass 2001).

To devise effective strategies for reducing poverty, development planners need to better understand and measure the costs and benefits of working informally, taking into account the flows of money into and out of the pockets of informal workers or their household budgets. That means confronting the problems with household income and expenditure measures, particularly households that depend on irregular wage employment and/or self-employment. It also means taking into account both out-of-pocket expenses and lost income associated with illnesses, accidents and work stoppages as well as the monetary and other costs to workers of flexible labour-market policies and business practices. Needed also are measures that capture women's contribution to the household income (e.g., female earnings as a percentage of total household earnings) as well as women's access to and control over income within the household.

Beyond income poverty

The consequences of working informally go far beyond the income – or money metric – dimensions of poverty. Compared to those who work in the formal economy, those who work in the informal economy are likely:

- to have less access to basic infrastructure and social services;
- to face greater exposure to common contingencies;
- to have less access to the means to address these contingencies (e.g., health, property or life insurance);
- to therefore have lower levels of health, education and longevity;
- to face greater exclusion from state, market and political institutions that determine the 'rules of the game' in these various spheres;
- to have fewer rights and benefits of employment;
- to have less access to financial, physical and other productive assets;
- to have less secure property rights over land, housing or other productive assets.

Many of these deprivations are mutually reinforcing. Individuals or families who lack secure tenure over their home are more likely to lack basic infrastructure such as water, sanitation or electrical connections. Lack of basic infrastructure may compromise their health, which in turn, compromises their ability to work. Yet those who survive on their own labour cannot afford to be sick. The lack of water connections in their home means that women have to spend many hours each day standing in line to draw water from a public tap or fetching water from a village well or the nearest water source. For home-based workers, the lack of basic infrastructure compromises their productivity.

Gender matters

The evidence presented here and in the previous chapter highlights the reality that working women worldwide are concentrated not only in informal employment but also in the more precarious forms of informal employment:

- women are more likely than men to be own account operators, industrial outworkers and unpaid contributing family members;
- men are more likely than women to be informal entrepreneurs who hire others, employees of informal firms and heads of family businesses;
- women are more likely than men to be concentrated in export-oriented light manufacturing, at least in the early stages of trade liberalization when a premium is placed on low-skilled and low-paid workers;[8]
- women are more likely than men to be in street trade, except in societies that place constraints on women's physical mobility, and they are also more likely to sell from the street (rather than from push carts, bicycles or as hawkers) and to sell perishable goods (rather than non-perishables).

As a result, women workers in the informal economy face a significant gender gap in earnings, arguably greater than that faced by women workers in the formal economy. This is largely due to the fact that women are concentrated in lower-paid work arrangements even within given occupations. But even when women and men do similar kinds of informal work, they often earn differ-

---

8 In the second generation of trade liberalization, when these activities become more profitable and mechanized, men often take over (see Box 1.1 on the impact of NAFTA on employment in Mexico).

ent incomes. In part, this reflects differences in the time that women and men can spend in paid work. However, studies that control for hours and days of work, as well as for other factors such as education and experience, find that on average women earn less than men within the same type of work, often due to the perception of women as being somehow less skilled or as being able to rely on a male breadwinner (Kantor and Nair 2005).

While some forms of informal work are said to have benefits for women, these often reflect gender ascribed roles and responsibilities that are, in turn, used to justify gender segmentation: notably, the need to balance paid work and unpaid care work. Finally, women are over-represented in forms of informal work that are associated with significant costs, most notably as industrial outworkers who have to absorb all of the non-wage costs of production while enjoying very little of the value added.

Intersection of gender and other sources of disadvantage

In every country in the world, under every economic system, women face constraints in the realm of paid work simply because they are women: their access to property is typically less than that of men and often mediated through their relationship to men; they face greater social demands on their time than men do (notably to carry out unpaid care work); and they face greater social constraints on their physical mobility than men. But to fully understand the relationships between women's employment and their poverty status, we need to integrate an analysis of gender with an analysis of other relationships and other sources of disadvantage (ILO 2003c). After all, most working poor women are poor and disadvantaged not just because of gender roles and relationships. Class, religion, race/ethnicity and geography all intersect with gender to position many (though not all) women in precarious forms of work. In most regions of the world, certain communities – differentiated largely by religion, race, ethnicity or geography as well as by class – are over-represented among the poor: notably, rural communities and religious, racial, or ethnic minorities. In these communities, women are further disadvantaged by reason of their gender, but the fact that they are poor and disadvantaged stems in the first instance from their wider social identity and/or from where they live.

Market Failures and Market Interventions

Mainstream economists argue that markets fail to achieve socially desirable outcomes when there are external costs or benefits, when contracts cannot be enforced without costs, when information is not shared or when monopolistic power exists. Such market failures are endemic in informal labour markets. A strong case can be made for direct government intervention in informal labour markets to achieve social objectives. But mainstream economists also argue that the costs of enduring market failures are less than the costs of intervening to correct market failures, especially in labour markets.

In assessing whether to accept market failure or intervene in informal labour markets, labour should not be seen as simply an input that produces output but rather as a process through which people experience benefits, costs or risks; through which people's well-being and capacities can be enhanced or depleted; and through which people can be empowered or disempowered (Elson 1999). Decent work generates social benefits such as social inclusion and cooperation, as well as personal benefits that extend beyond production and the income generated. However, informal work is often not decent work.

Economic policies that are explicitly employment-oriented and address the costs of informal employment can achieve better social outcomes – in terms of reducing both poverty and gender inequality – than policies that narrowly target growth. The evidence presented in this book shows that most of the world's poor – especially in developing countries – are working but they are not able to work their way out of poverty. A key pathway to reducing poverty and gender inequality is to create more and better employment opportunities and to increase the benefits and reduce the costs of working informally. Chapter 6 presents an employment-oriented framework for future policies and action to create more and better employment opportunities for informal workers, particularly women. However, as Chapter 5 will show, strong organizations representing informal workers are needed to ensure that appropriate policies are developed and implemented and to engage a range of players in this effort.

CHAPTER 5
Women's Organizing in the Informal Economy

Women protest low pay and working conditions in Cambodia's garment sector, Phnom Penh.
Photo: Phillippe Lopez/AFP/Getty

"My friend used to tell me that we had rights. I told her that we do not, that we are like 'third grade potatoes' and that's life. Nobody teaches us that we are workers and have rights to work, to defend our stalls, to earn a living. But we do have rights."

Street vendor, Peru (Ospina, StreetNet 2003)

As noted in earlier chapters, work in the informal economy tends to have higher costs and risks than work in the formal economy. This adds up to a situation of precariousness for most informal workers, no matter what kind of work they perform. They do not fit neatly under the type of employee-employer relationship that is generally governed by rules and regulations at the local or national level. They are excluded from social as well as legal protections and from collective bargaining agreements. Women suffer additional difficulties based on gender. They are more likely than men in the informal economy to work in isolation in scattered physical locations such as their own or other person's homes. The women and their work are often hidden within long production chains. They are weighed down by the double burden of income-generating work and unpaid care work. The lack of protections and the constraints of gender contribute to the difficulties informal women workers face in trying to lift themselves out of poverty through work.

One of the most important ways for workers in the informal economy to counter the forces that contribute to their impoverishment is through organizing. Organizing and the act of creating responsive organizations are critical elements in their economic, social and personal empowerment. These enable them to take action to advance and defend their interests, formulate policies that will benefit them and hold policy makers accountable over the long term.

Although organizing is more common – and easier – in the formal economy, informal workers have begun to come together to demand better conditions. Their organizations have given collective voice to some of the world's most impoverished informal workers, such as waste pickers and street vendors, and achieved important victories. The many local and international policies and programmes in support of informal workers cited in this and in the following chapter would not have been possible without the informed and sustained policy efforts of member-based organizations of informal workers.

Despite the role of women informal workers in achieving these gains, many of their organizations are still in their early stages, in part because of the extra difficulties women face in organizing. They may be less able than men to attend meetings and take leadership roles in workers' organizations because of cultural limitations on their public role, as well as the demands of their unpaid care work. Nevertheless, women consistently seek to create and join groups that will provide them with critical economic and social benefits.

Along with these specific goals, less tangible concerns drive women workers to organize. Many of them are vulnerable to danger and exploitation; they work extremely hard for less pay than men on average. Although they deal with these conditions as best they can, they also strive for respect, dignity and justice. Ultimately, many women workers see that they can find none of these if they act individually.

Thus, organizing is both an end in itself – as women achieve a sense of empowerment and are able to support each other – and a means to leveraging wider impact on the local, national and international stage. It promotes and affects policies and supports women's efforts to become active members of their communities and equal partners in their homes. As a woman organizer in India put it:

> "When individual women from amongst the poorest, least educated and most disenfranchised members of society come together, they experience dramatic changes in … the balance of power, in their living conditions, in relationships within the household and the community. Perhaps the most important effect of empowerment is that the woman says, 'Now I do not feel afraid.'"

Organizing can begin to address the costs and risks of informal work as well as the vulnerability, insecurity and dependence commonly experienced by women whose lives are controlled by powerful cultural, economic and political forces. This is particularly true for poor women. Organizing can address the many limitations that poverty imposes on them, including a lack of knowledge about the outside world and how it works. For women whose world has been confined to home, family and work, the very act of joining an organization adds breadth to their lives. When women actively participate in an organization, or take on leadership roles, their self-confidence, knowledge and understanding of the world generally increases and they gain new skills.

But organizing alone is not enough to bring about needed changes. Workers need representative voice in those institutions and processes that set policies and the 'rules of the (economic) game'. In a global economy, improving conditions for informal workers in general – and informal women workers in particular – requires representative voice at the international level as well as the local and national levels. International, regional and national negotiations regarding free trade agreements, the Millennium Development Goals (MDGs) and Poverty Reduction Strategy Papers (PRSPs) all need to include the voices and concerns of informal workers, who are the majority of workers in most developing countries and the vast majority of the working poor. Ensuring a voice for informal workers at the highest level requires supporting the growth of their organizations, and building capacity for leadership in this endeavour. It is not an easy road to travel, but it is a vital one.

Benefits of Organizing

This chapter looks primarily at member-based organizations since these are where women working in the informal economy are most likely to be directly involved. A member-based organization (MBO) is one where the members are the users of the services of the organization as well as its managers and owners. Thus, while women are building and participating in organizations, they are simultaneously building their own capacity. A member-based organization is most likely to deliver benefits and minimize the constraints faced by the working poor, especially women, because it is directly controlled and run by informal economy workers themselves. This is especially true of MBOs in which women are fully represented in leadership, providing working poor women with a direct avenue to negotiate with, and influence, those with the power to affect their working conditions and lives. Being part of such an organization can provide a large number of benefits for women workers in the informal economy:

When day labourers, industrial outworkers, homeworkers or contract workers organize to bargain with those who 'employ' them, they can **increase their daily earnings and make their working conditions more secure**. In 1999, after many years of protests and organizing, homeworkers in the United Kingdom were included under national minimum wage legislation. In South Africa, after a 15-year struggle involving a domestic workers' union among others, domestic workers were brought under the Unemployment Insurance Act in 2003, which provides unemployment, death, health, and maternity benefits.

Organizing helps women who have few, if any, assets to pool resources, thereby increasing their economic power. Savings and credit groups may help the working poor access microfinance services. Producers with little capital may buy raw materials at wholesale prices by combining their purchases. Landless labourers may be able to buy land collectively, and farmers who are unable to enter markets individually may have greater access and bargaining power as a collective.

Organizing helps informal workers to access services or to build better and bigger systems of social protection in areas such as health care and pensions. These activities have grown in importance as informal employment has increased while legal and social protections and state social spending have decreased. Organizations of women workers have collectively run schools and childcare and health centres. For example, using funds provided by the Accra City Council, the Accra Market Women's Association in Ghana developed a childcare programme to keep children safe while their mothers conducted business. The Department of Social Welfare, Ministry of Health and Ministry of Water and Sewage collaborated in refurbishing an old building near the market for the centre, which cares for infants as well as older children (Wazir 2001).

In times of crisis, organizations can mobilize support and assistance for victims, as the Self-Employed Women's Association (SEWA) was able to do after the massive earthquake in Gujarat State, India, or the Siyath Foundation (a member of HomeNet South Asia) did in Sri Lanka after the 2004 tsunami. The Foundation, which works with coir weavers, distributed clothes, food, sanitary napkins and tools; linked individuals with legal experts; provided psycho-social support; and, working with UNIFEM, developed a long-term rehabilitation programme that involves organizing members into a cooperative and mechanizing coir production.

The collective strength of organizing helps women gain representation in local, national and international policy-making forums, allowing them to use their power and influence to make changes in policy and law. In Cambodia, during the 2002 national PRSP consultations, trade union representatives were asked to participate. This included the president of the National Independent Federation of the Textile Unions of Cambodia (NIF-TUC), representing a large group of both formal and informal women workers in the textile and leather apparel sectors. The union representatives successfully argued for keeping a minimum wage floor in place as a poverty reduction strategy (Raghwan 2004).

There is one other benefit worth mentioning. A number of gender scholars and women's rights advocates have maintained that working outside the household is one of the major ways in which women have been able to improve their personal bargaining power within the household (Petchesky and Judd 1996). While this very much depends on the nature and conditions of the work, it is certainly true that women *can* increase their bargaining power in the household by achieving greater bargaining power outside the household – which in turn may help them to improve the terms of their employment (Chen and Snodgrass 2001; Kabeer 1998).

Identifying as Workers

Work is central to the lives of both women and men. It takes up a substantial part of their daily activities, providing a source of identity and dignity as well as a livelihood. In general, men's identities as workers are more easily recognized and appreciated than women's. People will say of a man, "he is a miner, an accountant, a farmer", but describe women primarily in their roles as mothers or care-givers. Women often remain invisible and unrecognized as workers, both because they are women and because work in the informal economy is often hidden. As described in Chapter 2, the work and contributions of women to the economy, as well as in the family and community, are persistently undervalued, particularly when women are home-based workers, paid domestic or care workers, or unpaid contributing workers in family businesses or on family farms. Focusing on their role as workers rather than homemakers or childcare providers serves to underscore the fact that women are economic agents who contribute to their households and the economy and therefore should be considered a target of economic as well as social policies.

Just as women workers are often invisible, so too are their organizations. This is particularly true of organizations created by informal women workers. Most international and national forums, conferences and seminars tend not to invite them directly, and not much has been written about them. This is partly due to the fact that some organizations choose to operate 'under the radar' in order to protect members. But it is largely owing to the fact that the working poor, even if they are organized, remain invisible in mainstream development circles, leading to the assumption that organizations of informal women workers do not exist.

The reality is very different. For example, when UNIFEM and HomeNet started a programme for home-based workers in Asia, one of their first activities was to map organizations that served these workers. They found that there were at least 508 such organizations in Bangladesh (BHWA 2003/2004) and 307 in Pakistan, with a large percentage of women members (Haider and Tahir 2004). Similarly when StreetNet International attempted to identify organizations of street vendors in Brazil, they learned of 770 associations of women and men street vendors in the city of Sao Paulo alone.

Most organizations of informal workers tend to be small, which can affect their sustainability. The advantages of these small, localized organizations is that they are often directly involved in the issues affecting their members and encourage active participation and opportunities for leadership. The disadvantages may lie in their limited power and ability to make substantive gains for members, limited contributions from members

---

Box 5.1

The Self-Employed Women's Association (SEWA)

Supporting women's empowerment through member-based organizations

The Self-Employed Women's Association (SEWA) is a trade union with 700,000 members – all poor working women in the informal economy – in six Indian states. SEWA describes itself as a banyan tree, with the Union as the trunk, its many sister organizations and affiliated member-based organizations as the branches and the members themselves as the leaves. SEWA was the first trade union of informal workers – men or women – anywhere in the world. It started in 1972 in the state of Gujarat, seeking to unite urban and rural women informal workers around the issue of 'full employment', which it defines as work, income, food and social security. Its second objective is to make its members self-reliant, both individually and collectively, as measured along eleven 'points': employment, income, assets, nutrition, health, housing, childcare, organizing, leadership, self-reliance and education.

SEWA advocates at the national and international levels for policies that benefit informal workers. Among its successes are the National Policy for Street Vendors in India (2004) and lobbying conference delegates to adopt the ILO Convention on Homework (1996) (see Box 5.6). It has also co-founded a number of national and international networks that support informal workers, including the National Alliance of Street Vendors of India, Women in Informal Employment: Globalizing and Organizing (WIEGO), StreetNet and HomeNet.

Over the years, SEWA has built a sisterhood of member-based organizations in addition to the union. These include a cooperative bank; village-based savings and credit groups, producer groups and cooperatives; and a federation of local groups and cooperatives. All of these economic organizations are owned by the women who are members of SEWA. They put up the share capital and manage and control the organizations through democratically elected boards of worker representatives.

SEWA has also set up specialized institutions that provide services of various kinds to members, including health care, childcare and insurance; research, training and communication; marketing; and housing and infrastructure. Today SEWA Bank has 200,000 depositors and a working capital of 900 million rupees (US$20.6 million); SEWA Insurance provides coverage to 130,000 members; SEWA Marketing reaches 400,000 producers; and SEWA Academy trains 300,000 women per year.

Box 5.2

Siyath Foundation: Providing Multiple Services

Any organization of workers is only as good as the services it provides. For formal workers, collective bargaining and solidarity action may be sufficient. But for informal women workers excluded from employment-related social security and other benefits, their organizations may have to provide much more.

Siyath Foundation, the organization of women home-based coir workers in Sri Lanka, is one of many organizations that have found innovative ways of providing critical services to their members. Women in Sri Lanka's coastal regions work under extremely difficult conditions to harvest coir fibre, their main source of livelihood. Previously most of them sold their products individually to buyers and were unable to bargain for fair prices. Siyath Foundation has set up a centre where members can bring samples to display, negotiate deals with buyers, get market information and participate in collective marketing efforts. This facilitates the interface between buyers and sellers so the profit goes to the worker instead of to an intermediary, and individual women do not have to negotiate prices on their own without knowing what a fair price should be. Siyath Foundation also provides technical training, literacy classes and services to abused and battered women.

---

and poor financial resources, minimal skills base, isolation and inability to access support.

Several informal women workers' organizations have managed to reach beyond local structures to create larger organizations that benefit from economies of scale, greater access to resources and greater influence. One of the most successful of these is SEWA, the union of informal women workers in India (see Box 5.1). SEWA's size gives it the credibility and strength to bargain for concrete benefits, to access resources and to influence policy processes at local, national and international levels.

Strategies and Forms of Organizing

Whether informal women workers organize, and what types of collective organization best fit their needs, depends on a range of factors, including the broader social, political and economic environment in which they work and live. Geographical location and restrictions on women's physical mobility can influence the ability to organize. In small scale, family or home-based enterprises, workers are not as visible as part-time, temporary or contract workers in larger enterprises and hence more difficult to contact and mobilize. Migrant workers and workers in export processing zones (EPZs) often face extreme difficulty organizing because of strict control of their movements. In addition, many informal workers may hesitate to join organizations due to family-based alliances, loyalty to kinship networks or fear of job loss. Organizing must reflect the nature and conditions of work in the informal economy, including the different types of work informal workers perform, their uncertain hours and their dispersed workplaces.

Women must also confront issues of power and discrimination based on gender. Thus, in addition to specific work-related protections, women workers need guarantees of equal pay for equal or comparable work; adequate, safe and affordable childcare; income protection when giving birth; physical security while travelling; and freedom from sexual harassment and sexual exploitation in the workplace.

Because informal workers often cannot easily identify an 'employer' with whom to negotiate better conditions, or risk losing their jobs if they do make demands, they have utilized various forms of organizations and diverse strategies to attain their goals. Where there is no identifiable employer, for example, street vendors have negotiated with municipalities to protect their right to earn a living on the street.

In California, in the United States, consumers, workers, unions and the state collaborated in creating public authorities to supervise in-home health-care services. An innovative aspect of these authorities was the presence on their boards of the consumers of health care, who were concerned about high turnover rates and poor services. The health-care providers meanwhile were generally low-wage informal workers who received few if any benefits. Until they and the unions helped create the public authorities, they had no ability to bargain collectively. With the creation of the public authorities, unions such as the Service Employees International Union (SEIU) have been able to negotiate wage increases and improved benefits for health aides, while protecting consumers' rights to hire, train and terminate a health-care provider (SEIU 2005).

In cases where collective bargaining is difficult, informal workers may use collective action instead. Because they can be fired at will, informal workers do not generally take strike action. Instead, informal women workers have more frequently turned to public displays of power through marches, demonstrations, rallies and passive resistance, often coupled with media and other publicity. In Thailand, advocacy campaigns launched by HomeNet and its allies led to the Ministerial Regulation Protection Act, passed in Parliament in 2004, allowing home-based workers and other informal economy workers to participate in Thailand's social security system (Rakawin Lee, personal communication, 2005).

Organizations of informal workers are set up differently depending on their different objectives, and their structures and by-laws reflect the different legal requirements that govern them. Whether workers organize in cooperatives, issue-based organizations or trade unions depends on how they see their own needs and objectives.

Worker cooperatives

Worker cooperatives are generally the easiest to set up, especially for small numbers of people. Cooperatives provide a structure through which workers pool financial resources, equipment, skills and experience (to minimize transaction costs), enabling them to increase their earning power and/or to obtain goods and services by sharing the gains from these combined resources. Cooperatives typically focus on income generation through business development (Levin 2002) and pursue both economic and social objectives, a factor that has contributed to their success in empowering women and increasing their awareness of the benefits of organizing. They also provide a structure through which women can develop bargaining, managerial and other skills and gain the know-how to eliminate exploitative contractors and intermediaries. In some cases, cooperatives work together with traditional unions to provide additional benefits, organize new members, or increase their bargaining power, as in the case of SEWA (see Box 5.1).

In Burkina Faso, the Organisation Nationale des Syndicats Libres (ONSL), a trade union, has reached out to informal women workers involved in embroidery, knitting and soap production in the capital city, Ouagadougou. It set up a development centre that offers literacy, hygiene and nutrition courses to enable women to maintain their children's health records, which are of enormous benefit if a child falls ill (the mortality rate of children under 5 years of age is 50 per cent in Burkina Faso). The centre also runs training courses in basic accounting and administration. Through these activities the women have organized themselves, formed a cooperative and joined ONSL (ICFTU 1999).

Similarly, in Kenya, Rwanda, Tanzania and Uganda, national trade unions and cooperative organizations have formed partnerships to develop a common strategy to organize unprotected informal workers. Gender awareness is built into these initiatives, which have led to an increase in the number of informal workers organized, higher incomes and the establishment of a revolving loan fund (ILO 2005d).

Issue-based organizations

An alternative for informal women workers in many places is to form or join organizations around specific issues concerning their lives and livelihoods. By tackling such issues, women are generally also able to address many of their work-related concerns, even if these are not dealt with directly. For example, poor women in urban slums face problems because of poor infrastructure, including a lack of transportation in general (and safe transportation in particular) or a lack of clean water. In some cases, women have organized safe transport systems. In others, they have set up water users groups as well as health awareness associations to help women protect themselves and their families against diseases from unclean water. These organizations may work closely with worker organizations and NGOs. Although many are localized in their communities, several have begun to operate nationally and internationally, such as SPARC (Society for the Promotion of Area Resource Centres) in Mumbai, India, which is a founding member of Shack Dwellers International (D'Cruz and Mitlin 2005).

Trade unions

At some point in their effort to gain recognition and voice, workers' organizations often need to draw on the strengths of traditional trade unions. For example, they may affiliate with trade unions in order to struggle for the right to engage in collective bargaining. Worldwide, women are less likely than men to be in established unions, both because a larger share of male workers are in formal employment and because women face more problems in organizing. They may, for example, be required to tend to the family after work or be unable to travel alone to meetings. Nevertheless, women's presence in established unions is growing globally as their share of work increases. This growth is currently uneven, varying from country to country (ICFTU 2005a) and from industry to industry. Informal women workers benefit from the strengths of established unions by being part of a functioning and recognized organization with resources, skills, contacts and access to employers, government and international organizations.

Box 5.3 — Waste Picker Cooperatives in Latin America

Waste pickers, often the poorest of the poor, have joined together to form successful cooperatives in several Latin American countries. The most dynamic waste picker cooperative movement is in Colombia, where an NGO – Fundacion Social – has helped over 100 cooperatives around the country launch a National Recycling Programme. The movement's organizational structure includes national, regional and local cooperatives, one of the most successful of which is the Cooperativa Recuperar. This cooperative was created in 1983 and today has 1,000 members, 60 per cent of them women. Members earn 1.5 times the minimum wage and receive health benefits through the Colombian national health-care system. The cooperative offers loans, scholarships and life and accident insurance to members. When Argentina's economic crisis resulted in factory closings and massive layoffs, many formerly salaried employees were forced to become scavengers in order to survive. A number of them are now organized into cooperatives such as the 14 set up by cardboard recyclers in Buenos Aires. One of these – Cooperativa El Ceibo – was founded by women, who make up the majority of its 102 members. The cooperative has signed an agreement with the city government to provide recycling services to an area covering 93 city blocks. In Brazil waste pickers have formed cooperatives around the country, including 14 in Rio de Janiero, with a total of 2,500 members. Coopamare is one of the most successful of these, collecting 100 tons of recyclables a month. Members earn twice the country's official minimum wage (Medina 2005).

Box 5.4: Women's Unions Around the Globe

Latin America – Brazil: Associação do Movimento Interestadual de Quebradeira de Coco Babaçu (Interstate Movement of Babassu Coconut Splitters), founded in 1989, is a union of women who harvest, shell and market coconuts in the Amazonas region. The union has formed alliances with environmental protection groups to fight over-exploitation of the crop by private and public companies. Members can join cooperatives set up by the union which is linked to trade union federations.

Africa – Chad: Syndicat des Femmes Vendeuses de Poisson (Union of Women Fish Vendors) was founded in 2002 and currently has 500 female fish vendors as members. Its aim is to protect the vendors' economic interests by increasing the price of fish and improving storage facilities. It also seeks to build women's solidarity through education and social activities.

Europe – the Netherlands: Vakwerk De Rode Draad (Red Thread Union) is a sex workers' union established in 2002, not long after sex work was legalized in the Netherlands. It is affiliated with the Netherlands Confederation of Trade Unions (FNV). In 2004 Red Thread established an organization for trafficked women and began negotiations with the Association of Brothel Owners for a national agreement. Negotiations stalled when the brothel owners insisted that sex workers were self-employed (Gallin and Horn 2005).

In some cases, informal women workers have banded together to create their own unions rather than join existing ones that may not be as responsive to their needs. For women, the advantages of organizing in 'new' unions is that they can set up innovative structures and programmes that are less patriarchal and more open to change than traditional unions. For example, women's unions are generally more creative in finding solutions to issues such as childcare and meeting times.

These unions are considered new – even though some of them, such as Working Women's Forum in India, are over 25 years old – because they are different in structure and function from established trade unions and have grown outside the formal trade union structure. Some new unions organize by sector, while others are general unions of informal workers. Some primarily organize waged workers in the informal economy, while others are made up of own account workers. As with cooperatives, some of these new unions are supported by established trade unions, which are increasingly reaching out to informal women workers as the formal workforce shrinks owing to relocation and restructuring by employers.

Influencing Policy Decisions: National, Regional and International Networks and Alliances

Along with improving immediate conditions on the ground, a major goal of organizing is to give informal workers, especially women, the ability to influence the forces that dictate the terms of work and to affect the policies that can regulate these forces. At a national level, informal workers need to have a voice in policy-making forums and with government and business. At an international level, they need to be heard in institutions that deal with trade, labour and economic policies. Once agreements are reached, a further challenge for women and their organizations is to ensure that what was agreed upon is implemented and enforced. Networks and alliances among women's organizations and NGOs, civil society, multilateral agencies and international policy-setting groups help women make their voices heard at the level of policy-making and rule-setting institutions and provide links to supportive NGOs and grant-making agencies.

Networks and alliances can help influence policy by conducting research and leveraging resources that would be beyond the scope of an individual organization, allowing informal workers to develop common strategies and campaigns and providing information on other women and their struggles.

Social change organizations in the developed world are often concerned about conditions for informal workers. Networks built around these issues may be able to support workers in distant countries. The Clean Clothes Campaign (CCC), for example, was created in Europe to improve the working conditions of and empower workers in the global garment industry, most of whom are women. Operating out of nine European countries, the CCC is made up of autonomous national coalitions of trade unions and NGOs linked to an international network of NGOs, unions, individuals and institutions in many countries where garments are produced. The Campaign works with consumers to put pressure on corporations that subcontract gar-

Box 5.5: StreetNet International

StreetNet International is an alliance of street vendor organizations, launched in 2002. Member-based organizations that directly organize street vendors are entitled to affiliate to StreetNet, which promotes the exchange of information and ideas on critical issues facing street vendors; develops practical organizing and advocacy strategies; promotes local, national and international solidarity between organizations of street vendors, market vendors and hawkers (who are often in competition); and stimulates the development of national alliances of such organizations.

To date, 19 street vendor organizations – with a combined total membership of approximately 200,000 – have affiliated with StreetNet. The alliance has attempted to ensure that men do not dominate its leadership through its constitution, which stipulates that at least 50 per cent of both its international council and its office holders must be women (StreetNet 2004).

ment work to the developing world, demanding that they improve employment conditions and prevent environmental degradation (Clean Clothes Campaign 2005).

At the global level, the umbrella organization of national trade union federations, the International Confederation of Free Trade Unions (ICFTU), and global unions such as the International Federation of Food, Tobacco, Agriculture and Allied Workers (IUF), the International Textile Garment and Leather Workers Federation (ITGLWF) and the International Federation of Building and Wood Workers (IFBWW), are now committed to supporting and organizing workers in the informal economy. They have put in place resolutions, projects and campaigns to support this commitment. For example, ICFTU launched a campaign on International Women's Day 2004, *Unions for Women, Women for Unions*, that focuses on organizing women in the informal economy and EPZs. This campaign is beginning to see results, most notably in Africa where, for example, the number of women members in the Mauritania affiliate increased by 30 per cent over a period of six months (ICFTU 2005b). In addition, the World Confederation of Labour (WCL) has prepared a training guide to familiarize trade unionists with informal economy issues and has undertaken work on regulatory frameworks (WCL 2004).

In another international alliance, the IUF, the ILO and the International Federation of Plantation, Agricultural and Allied Workers (IFPAAW) joined together to develop innovative projects in Ghana, Uganda, Zambia and Zimbabwe to bring more women into unions. Concerned about the total absence of women in leadership positions and their low participation in union activities, the three organizations helped create programmes that used songs, drama and role-playing to teach both male and female rural workers about trade unions and gender issues. By the end of the project, female membership had increased in all four countries, as had the number of women office holders.

In Central and Eastern Europe, trade unions were taken by surprise by the explosion of the informal economy in the transition from planned to free market economies. With support from the ICFTU, three pilot campaigns are underway in Bulgaria, Lithuania and Moldova, built around awareness-raising, organization, representation and social dialogue. The campaigns are developing cooperative links with NGO networks such as Solidar and the International Restructuring Education Network Europe (IRENE) (ILO 2005b).

HomeNet Asia is one of the best examples of how member-based organizations can collaborate with international agencies and networks to change policies and build voice. In the 1980s, when home-based women workers in different countries began

Box 5.6 — ILO Home Work Convention #177

Homeworkers, including industrial outworkers who work at home under a sub-contract, are often not recognized as having workers' rights and are seldom covered by labour or social protections. An alliance of organizations of homeworkers, trade unions, NGOs and international partners, including UNIFEM, lobbied conference delegates to adopt the only ILO Convention specifically targeted to the informal economy: ILO Convention #177 on Home Work. Adopted in 1996, the Convention calls for a national policy on home work aimed at improving the conditions of homeworkers, most of whom are women. A related Recommendation, passed the same year, details a full programme to improve the conditions of homework. To date, only four countries – Albania, Finland, Ireland and the Netherlands – have ratified the Convention, although several other countries are considering national legislation in line with the Convention and its Recommendation, and the EU has encouraged its member states to consider ratification (see Chen et al. 2004).

organizing, several of their organizations came together to explore common issues and strategies. In 1992, these groups formed HomeNet International to formalize their relationship.

One of their first concerns was to join the effort to push for international recognition of home-based workers. In addition to labour organizations and the members of HomeNet, the campaign drew in a variety of like-minded organizations and individuals. UNIFEM convened regional workshops for government policy makers from different countries, while researchers compiled statistics on the number of homeworkers in various countries and sectors (Chen et al. 1999). In 1996, the International Labour Conference adopted the ILO Convention on Home Work (#177).

The Convention opened an important space for home-based workers to expand their organizing efforts. In 2000, a UNIFEM/WIEGO conference for government officials, representatives of member-based organizations of informal workers, and researchers from five countries in South Asia resulted in the passage of the Kathmandu Declaration, which committed governments to promote national policies in support of home-based workers.

UNIFEM then worked closely with organizations in Asia to develop regional networks of national associations of home-based worker organizations, including HomeNet South Asia and HomeNet South East Asia. At present these networks include over 500 organizations of home-based workers that are working to influence national policies on issues such as social security and fair trade practices. Due to the promotion and support of UNIFEM, as well as the international trade union movement (in particular FNV in the Netherlands), HomeNet in Asia is growing rapidly and making visible the issues of the estimated 60 million home-based workers of the region (excluding China).

Women apply for small business loans through an NGO, Kyrgyzstan. Photo: Caroline Penn/Panos

The Next Stage

As this report has shown, a complex mix of challenges stands in the way of poor women's ability to improve their conditions of work: their frequently isolated working arrangements; their double day of paid and unpaid work; the multiple disadvantages women face by reason of their gender, race, religion, caste and class; as well as the wider political, economic, social and legal factors discussed throughout this report that restrict the rights of informal workers in general, and informal women workers in particular. Although organizing can make a difference, women's comparative lack of education and resources, as well as their inability to move about freely in some regions, make it particularly difficult for them to join organizing efforts. Discrimination and a general disregard for women may contribute to the reluctance of policy makers to bargain with women, especially poor women.

Despite the enormous difficulties, however, informal women workers have created effective strategies and real partnerships that involve communities and local leadership. These efforts need to be built up and expanded through financial backing, capacity building and support for women's leadership. As Dan Gallin, chair of the Global Labour Institute, has stated: "It is only by putting themselves in the position of exercising power through organizations that workers can gain voice. Without organization, voice becomes an ineffectual 'squawk'" (Gallin 2002).

Women in the informal economy must be supported in their efforts to gain voice and build capacity so they have the skills to negotiate and influence policy. Organizations such as trade unions, NGOs and multilateral agencies can provide financial and technical support to help women build and sustain member-based organizations at the local, national, regional and international levels. They can provide ways through which these organizations can increase their numbers, scale up their initiatives, and network to increase visibility and power. They can assist them to improve organizational effectiveness through deepening democracy, implementing innovative strategies, empowering women leaders and members and attaining financial sustainability. Trade unions can make even greater efforts to join with organizations of informal workers to maximize the voice of workers at the international level and to insert employment issues into the general debate on poverty reduction. There are three main areas where increased support and activism can have a profound effect: (1) strengthening grassroots, member-based organizations, (2) promoting the right to organize and (3) creating an enabling environment by increasing informal women workers' representation in policy and law processes.

Strengthening member-based organizations

Member-based organizations depend on the commitment and active participation of their members. **Education and awareness** play an important role in building participation. NGOs, agencies, trade unions and others could provide support at this very basic level of organizing. In partnership with member-based organizations, they could offer to support or provide education classes for women workers to build solidarity, self-esteem and confidence. For example, the International Federation of Worker's Education Associations (IFWEA), a global worker education institute, is working on a number of projects targeting workers in the informal economy, particularly women. These include projects with the ILO Asia sub-regional office in Bangkok to develop a training manual on organizing in the informal economy.

Generally, women in the informal economy have not had much chance to learn different types of skills. This contributes to the difficulty their organizations have sustaining themselves and influencing employers and policy makers. **Building capacity and skills** at the grass-roots level through partnerships with other organizations and various supportive agencies can help remedy this. It is also increasingly important for organizations, especially larger ones and networks, to learn how to use communication techniques and modern information technology to link with each other.

The ILO emphasizes the importance of membership-based organizations that are democratic and independent (ILO 2002c). However, organizations of informal workers, consisting as they do of poor people, are often unable to sustain their organizations through member dues. Moreover, they are rarely able to obtain the needed additional financial support through loans, revolving capital, matching grants or investment in physical resources. For this reason, **alternative financial resources** are critical in order to support creative approaches to bringing informal workers into the protection of employment regulations. Direct, appropriate and sustained financial support must be made available if organizations are to grow, develop and stabilize.

Promoting the right to organize

Most informal women workers do not have *full* rights as workers. This includes the basic rights to freedom of association, and thus to organize, and to enjoy legal protections. Employers and governments often deliberately seek to suppress or avoid granting or implementing rights, sometimes by violent means. Even in the formal economy, workers may have to struggle for these rights; for workers in the informal economy, both self-employed and wage workers, who have no clear or ongoing relationship with an employer, the challenges are even greater.

The freedom to organize when organizations are not recognized can be a hollow right. Many organizations struggle for recognition and registration – often over many years – seeking to acquire legitimacy and status in the eyes of potential members, opponents, governments and funders. Organizations must grow and be active to successfully engage in such struggles and to put rights into practice.

Given the many constraints described above, informal women workers and their organizations have adopted different ways of recruiting and retaining members and of working to build their rights. The organizations may reach out to workers in innovative ways: to homeworkers in their homes, at a group workplace or at a community centre; to migrant workers in dormitories; to domestic workers in training centres; to street and market vendors at their workplaces or nearby open spaces, and so on.

The ILO has recognized the rights of informal workers to freedom of association and to organize both as employees and as the self-employed to improve their condition (see Box 5.7). Employers, government bodies and policy makers must do the same. Informal worker organizations, as we have seen, come in a variety of forms, and all are important and must have formal recognition. Organizations of informal women workers should have representation in all forums, from the local to the international, that influence the economic and social position of their members, most critically in labour, trade and civil society forums. Representation should be permanent rather than ad hoc, and statutory rather than informal. Negotiation and collective bargaining must be *genuine*, with clear agreements and effective implementation and monitoring, whether bargaining on income, policy or other issues.

Box 5.7

Freedom of Association and the Informal Economy

The ILO fundamental conventions on freedom of association (Nos. 87 and 98) explicitly state that all workers, without distinction, enjoy this fundamental right. Thus workers in the informal economy have the right to organize and, where there is an employer, engage in collective bargaining. They should be able to freely establish and join trade unions of their own choosing. Workers' organizations should be able to carry out their trade union activities (elections, administration, formulating programmes) without intervention from public authorities. The right of freedom of association is equally applicable to the self employed. Thus the self employed who work in the informal economy should also be free to create organizations of their own choosing, such as small business associations, and enjoy the same rights as described above. Complaints regarding infringement of the right to associate can be brought to the ILO via its Committee on Freedom of Association (CFA). These complaints should emanate from a trade union or an employers' organization, although theoretically they can also come from a government. The trade union or employers' organization does not have to be registered or recognized at the national level in order to bring a complaint, nor does the country in question have to have ratified the ILO Conventions on freedom of association.

More information on the CFA, its procedures and cases can be found at: http://webfusion.ilo.org/public/db/standards/normes/libsynd/index.cfm?Lang=EN&hdroff=1 (Katerina Tsotroudi, personal communication, 2005).

Tobacco picker, member of a work gang, Gujarat state, India. Photo: Martha Chen

Increasing representation in policy and law processes

The lives of poor informal women workers are affected by policy and law at every level, from the local to the international. In order for organizations of women workers to flourish, an enabling environment is required that gives these organizations space to grow. Currently, laws that guarantee freedom of association and recognize organizations vary considerably from country to country. For example, existing labour law in some countries allows for many different forms of trade unions, while in others only enterprise-based unions are allowed.

In some countries cooperative law allows genuine and independent self-help organizations to develop, while in others they become quasi-governmental organizations. Policies in different areas can encourage the growth of these organizations or can be so unfavourable that organizations are unable to take root. Thus finance and banking policies can promote or retard the growth of women's financial institutions, trade policies can encourage or discourage the growth of women's cooperative marketing and social security policies will affect organizations that provide services such as childcare.

Women are developing strategies through their organizations to ensure their participation in policy-making and rule-setting bodies at the different levels. This is a slow process, with gains and setbacks along the way, but women continue to build alliances, coalitions and networks backed up by research and technical assistance to jointly advocate and/or negotiate. The adoption by the International Labour Conference of the conclusions on decent work and the informal economy marked an important consensus among employer, worker and government delegates. It also reflected an alliance involving trade unions, organizations of informal workers and researchers (ILO 2002a).

At the national level in many countries, informal women and men workers are demanding changes to labour laws in order to guarantee their rights as workers. In some cases they have succeeded, especially where they have been organized or supported by recognized trade unions. In Ghana, the Ghana Trade Union Congress (GTUC) fought for, and won, a broader definition of 'worker' and 'workplace' in an attempt to include more informal workers. It also won the extension of rights, minimum wages and benefits to casual and temporary workers (Kofi Asemoah, personal communication, 2004). In South Africa, a new labour law provides legal protections for domestic and farm workers, and was negotiated in a tripartite forum that included major trade union federations.

As the Millennium Declaration recognized, gender equality and women's empowerment are critical to efforts to eliminate poverty, hunger and disease and to stimulate sustainable development. It is essential therefore that working poor women in the informal economy are recognized at all policy-making levels. Supporting their efforts to attain voice and recognition is a large task that will require concerted efforts over a long period. International agencies, governments, trade unions, women's organizations and other NGOs all have roles to play in helping to increase the visibility and voice of informal workers and their organizations. The opening of institutional and political space brought about by multi-stakeholder development frameworks such as the MDGs or the PRSPs can provide new opportunities for the working poor to influence policy and decision-making from the local to the international level (see Chapter 6).

In order to take advantage of these opportunities, partnerships and coalitions are already forming at the grassroots level, developing strategies for informal working women's advocacy and participation in the MDG and PRSP processes. For example, in Kenya, UNIFEM, working with NGOs and informal women workers, and supported by UNDP, built a coalition to include poor women's voices in the MDG process. The coalition met with rural and urban women around the country to determine what they needed to improve their lives. The information from these discussions was presented to the media, government and policy makers. Although at the early stages of implementation, this coalition is now participating in MDG needs assessments and working to promote gender responsive budgeting.

In Kyrgyzstan, women's groups used lessons learned from work on women and land reform to engender the MDG process. Supported by UNIFEM, women's groups and legal experts had worked at the local level to build capacity and awareness around women's right to land and property. Several thousand rural women attended seminars, as did government staff, on land and property ownership issues. Legal centres were set up to advise women about their rights, and amendments to the existing land code were drafted and submitted to Parliament. The organizing and capacity-building involved in this effort resulted in a cadre of informal agricultural women workers who could give voice to women's economic and social concerns when economic policy was being debated. Women leaders were able to mainstream women's issues into MDG, PRSP and CEDAW reporting and monitoring, which was then fed into the National Action Plan, successfully aligning all four processes. They also succeeded in proposing new indicators on gender equality in the workforce for Goal 3 of the MDGs (see Chapter 3).

International agencies have an important role to play in these alliances. They are in a unique position to strengthen the efforts of organizations representing informal women workers to engage in policy dialogues. There are numerous actions international agencies, national governments, global unions, policy research networks, NGOs and academic institutions can take to promote an enabling environment. They can recognize and acknowledge the importance of member-based organizations representing informal workers in their own policies and documents. They can help research and develop innovative policy and law options on issues such as the rights of informal women working on their own account or institutionalizing new bargaining forums. In partnership with local organizations, they can work with governments to make changes and provide technical and funding support. Finally, they can facilitate linkages among women's and workers' organizations, and between informal workers' organizations and trade unions. This support at every level will help to ensure that organizations representing informal workers build the power to exert influence over the forces that affect the lives and work of their members.

Box 5.8 — Where Informal Women Workers Need to be Represented

Local level
Community councils: social, political, administrative
Collective bargaining bodies, tripartite boards
Municipal planning, zoning and advisory boards
Rural planning bodies and resource allocation bodies

National level
Planning commissions and advisory committees
Tripartite bodies
Chambers of commerce
Trade union federations
Collective bargaining bodies
Sector-specific associations or boards
National MDG and PRSP negotiations

Regional level
Inter-governmental commissions
Bilateral trade negotiations
Development banks and agencies
Trade union bodies

International level
UN specialized agencies/funds (UNIFEM, UNCTAD, ILO)
ICFTU, global unions, worker networks
Finance institutions, IMF and World Bank
Trade negotiations
Fair and ethical trade initiatives
Codes of conduct and international framework agreement negotiations
Civil society movements

CHAPTER 6
A Framework for Policy and Action

Vendors selling phones and cigarettes on a street in Bogota, Colombia.
Photo: Gerardo Gomez/AFP/Getty

> **"The police** used to harass us a lot. They would take away our vegetables. They would take away our bundles. Since we joined SEWA, they have stopped harassing us. No police or anyone else harasses us now."
>
> Street vendor, India (cited in Chen and Snodgrass 2001)

The premise of this report is that promoting decent work for the working poor, both women and men, is a critical pathway to reducing poverty and advancing gender equality. With most of the working poor in the informal economy, the critical question is: What can be done to promote decent work for informal workers, especially women?

This chapter presents a framework for policy and action to reduce the costs and increase the benefits of informal employment in order to combat poverty and gender inequality. It recommends strategies and provides examples of what different stakeholders – governments, international organizations, private firms and business associations, workers' organizations and non-governmental organizations (NGOs) – have done to promote decent work for the working poor, especially women. But first it takes up some of the ongoing debates around the informal economy that inform all policy discussions.

Policy Debates on the Informal Economy

Historically, policy makers, economists and other observers have differed about the role of the informal economy. As noted in Chapter 1, some look at it positively, as a 'cushion' during economic crises or a dynamic source of entrepreneurial growth – provided it is free to operate without government regulations. Others see it more problematically, arguing that informal entrepreneurs deliberately operate outside the reach of government regulations in order to avoid taxation and registration. Still others focus on the working poor within the informal economy, regarding them either as a vulnerable group who need social assistance or as unprotected workers who need legal protections.

Underlying these varying perspectives are ideological differences about whether and how to regulate the informal economy, and the larger issue of whether or not government should get involved in regulating the economy at all. A second ideological divide, related to the first, has to do more specifically with whether and how to formalize the informal economy, and the related issue of whether and how the informal economy, the formal economy and the formal regulatory environment are linked.

Whether to regulate

There is a fundamental debate in international development circles about the role of government in regulating the economy or the operation of markets. Neo-classical economists are trained to think of government interventions in labour markets – in setting wages or regulating hiring and firing – as creating distortions that lead to either unemployment or informal employment. But governments can and do intervene in labour markets. To make labour markets operate more efficiently, they can and do help facilitate market information and match labour demand with supply by facilitating information-exchange and providing training on the skills required. To make labour markets more equitable, they can and do help correct the unequal balance of power between employers and workers, reduce discrimination against disadvantaged groups such as women or ethnic minorities and/or provide protection against work-related risks and uncertainties.

A parallel debate concerns whether and how governments should regulate the informal economy in particular. One approach, championed by Hernando de Soto of Peru, argues for reducing the burden of bureaucracy that leads entrepreneurs to operate informally and for extending the 'rule of law', in particular property rights, so that informal entrepreneurs can convert their informal assets into real assets (de Soto 2000, 1989). Another approach, promoted by Alejandro Portes and others who take a structuralist view, sees a government role in regulating the unequal relationship between 'big business' and informal producers and traders in order to address the imbalance of power within markets (Portes et al. 1989). A third approach, promoted by the ILO, UNDP and UNIFEM among others, sees a government role in promoting economic opportunities, developing appropriate legal and regulatory frameworks, extending social protection and promoting social dialogue to increase representation of informal workers.[1]

---

1 The International Labour Conference which sets ILO policies has stressed a comprehensive approach involving the "promotion of rights, decent employment, social protection and social dialogue" (ILO 2002c: 59). 'Social dialogue' refers to all types of negotiation or consultation among representatives of governments, employers and workers on issues of common interest; its practice varies by country.

In reality the informal economy has been variously over-regulated, under-regulated and completely ignored. As part of economic restructuring and market liberalization, there has been a fair amount of *deregulation*, particularly of financial markets, labour markets and international trade. Deregulation of labour markets is associated with the rise of informalized or 'flexible' labour markets. Some labour advocates have argued for *re-regulation* of labour markets to protect informal wage workers from the economic risks and uncertainty associated with flexibility and informalization.

Moreover, the regulatory environment often overlooks whole categories of the informal workforce. A *missing* regulatory environment can be as costly to informal operators as an *excessive* regulatory environment (Chen et al. 2004). For example, some governments do not guarantee informal workers freedom of association or the right to organize. In such cases, informal workers may fall into a legal void when they try to form associations or join trade unions simply because the law does not provide an appropriate legal framework (ILO 2004b). Also, few cities have adopted a coherent regulatory approach towards street trade (Bhowmik 2005; Mitullah 2004), typically trying either to eliminate it or to turn a 'blind eye' to it. Both have a punitive effect: eviction, harassment and the demand for bribes by police, municipal officials and other vested interests. The best practice would be to situate informal trade in local economic development or small enterprise support departments. The worst practice – as in many cities – is situating street traders in law enforcement departments, such as traffic control and police.

In considering the appropriate role for government in regulating labour markets, it is important not to overlook the private sector. Private firms decide whether or not to comply with existing government regulations when they hire or fire workers, set wages and manage working conditions. Further, in today's global economy, transnational corporations (TNCs) often have more power than local governments, given their control over resources, their access to markets and new technologies and their ability to locate and relocate production as circumstances suit them.

In sum, what is needed is *appropriate regulation*, not complete deregulation or the lack of regulation. An appropriate response would strike a balance between efficiency and equity concerns and take into account the specific interests of formal and informal firms, formal and informal workers, men and women, and the behaviour of the corporate sector.

For instance, it is important to take into consideration the capacity of different sizes of firms to comply with business regulations. However, a balanced approach should not undermine respect for fundamental principles and rights at work for people in the informal economy, since these are basic human rights.

Whether to formalize

At the core of the debates on the informal economy is the oft-repeated question of whether the informal economy should be 'formalized'. It is unclear, however, what is meant by 'formalization'. To many it means that informal enterprises should obtain a license, register their enterprises and pay taxes. But to the self-employed these represent the *costs of entry* into the formal economy. If they pay these costs, they expect to receive the *benefits of operating formally*, including enforceable commercial contracts, legal ownership of their place of business and means of production, tax breaks and incentive packages to increase competitiveness, membership in trade associations and statutory social protection. In reality, many microenterprises are neither completely formal nor informal when it comes to regulations (Reinecke and White 2003). The issue is whether those who comply with regulations receive the benefits of compliance.

To informal wage workers, however, formalization means obtaining a formal wage job or converting the job they have into a formal wage job, with a secure contract, worker benefits and social protection, along with the right to organize. In the case of wage workers, it is their employers who decide whether or not to comply with regulations.

The formalization debate should be turned on its head by recognizing that formalization has different meanings for different segments of the informal economy and by acknowledging that it is unlikely that most informal producers and workers can be formalized – although efforts should be made to do so. Formalization of informal enterprises requires bureaucracies that are able to simplify registration requirements and to offer informal businesses the incentives and benefits that formal businesses receive. Formalization of informal wage labour requires creation of more formal jobs and extension of formal legal and social protection to informal workers. However, recent trends suggest that employment growth is not keeping pace with the demand for jobs – there simply are not enough jobs to go around. And employers are more inclined to convert formal jobs into informal jobs than the other way around.

Finally, those who work on the informal economy are often asked two additional questions. First, do you promote informal employment, despite its consequences? Our answer is that informal employment is a widespread feature of today's global economy that needs to be upgraded: the goal is to reduce the costs and increase the benefits of working informally. Second, are there any 'magic bullets' for improving conditions of informal employment? Our answer is that while some interventions (such as microfinance) are seen as magic bullets to improve conditions in some cases, no single intervention can address all of the constraints and needs faced by the working poor in the informal economy. What is needed is a context-specific mix of interventions, developed in consultation with working poor women and men and informed by an understanding of their significance in the labour force and their contribution to the economy.

In sum, we are calling for:

- renewed focus on expanding formal employment – by putting employment creation and decent work at the centre of macroeconomic policy;
- increased efforts to formalize informal enterprises and informal jobs by creating incentives and simplifying procedures for entrepreneurs to register and by persuading employers to provide more benefits and protections to their workers; and
- a series of interventions to help those who work in the informal economy get higher returns to their labour – by increasing their assets and competitiveness and by assuring better terms and conditions of work (Diez de Medina 2005).

Framework for Policy and Action

In setting priorities for policy and action, it is important to underscore why policy and action are needed. As shown in Chapter 3, those who work in the informal economy, especially women, have lower average earnings and a higher poverty risk than those who work in the formal economy. And, as shown in Chapter 4, the benefits of informality are usually not sufficient and the costs are often too high for most informal workers to achieve an adequate standard of living. Moreover, they lack worker rights, social protection and representative voice. As such, informal employment should be considered from a rights perspective. The 1998 ILO Declaration on Fundamental Principles and Rights at Work highlights the key areas of freedom of association and collective bargaining, and the elimination of discrimination, forced labour and child labour. As State parties to the Convention on the Elimination of All Forms of Discrimination against Women (CEDAW) and the International Covenant on Economic, Social and Cultural Rights (ICESCR), governments have a duty to enable all workers, including women and men in informal employment, to claim their rights as workers, including the right to organize, to receive employee benefits and to negotiate formal contracts. Beyond this, international agencies, civil society and the private sector all have an obligation to help informal workers, especially women, achieve an adequate standard of living, claim their rights and gain representative voice.

In the following framework, the goals for policy and action are presented as a set of six strategic priorities, involving a range of possible interventions from policy reform and institutional development to service delivery. Implicit in this framework is the need for current economic development strategies to be reoriented in order to improve employment opportunities and reduce poverty. As discussed in Chapter 1, the current Poverty Reduction Strategy Papers (PRSPs) fail to include a coherent approach to employment with concrete policy interventions, raising questions about the feasibility and sustainability of their poverty reduction goals. Addressing this problem requires restructuring the PRSPs so that macroeconomic policies, sectoral interventions, governance and social policy are coordinated to deliver more and better employment opportunities, particularly for women.

Similarly, it is crucial to recognize that the current policies endorsed by global institutions, such as the International Monetary Fund (IMF) or the World Trade Organization (WTO), may limit the effectiveness of strategies to generate better employment. For example, a narrow focus on inflation-targeting frequently has collateral impacts on interest and exchange rates, and can create an economic environment hostile to an expansion of decent employment opportunities. Successful implementation of the policy framework proposed here would require adjustment in the focus and targets of the strategies promoted by these institutions.

Strategic priorities

The three overarching goals – to expand formal employment, to formalize informal enterprises and jobs and to increase the returns to their labour of informal workers—are linked to a set of more specific goals aimed at promoting economic opportunities, economic rights, social protection, and representative voice for the working poor, especially women, in the informal economy. Achieving these requires a favourable economic policy environment as well as targeted interventions, reflected in the following strategic priorities:

#1 –To Create a Favourable Policy Environment

The economic policy environment needs to be supportive of the working poor, rather than blind to them or biased against them. This requires addressing biases in general policies as well as designing and implementing targeted policies.

#2 - To Increase Assets and Access

For the working poor to be able to take advantage of the opportunities offered by a more favourable policy environment, they need greater market access as well as the relevant assets and skills with which to better compete in the markets.

#3 – To Improve Terms of Trade

To compete effectively in markets, in addition to having the requisite resources and skills the working poor need to be able to negotiate favourable prices and wages for the goods and services they sell, relative to their cost of inputs and their cost of living.

#4 – To Secure Appropriate Legal Frameworks

The working poor in the informal economy need new or expanded legal frameworks to protect their rights and entitlements as workers, including the right to work, rights at work and property rights.

#5 – To Address Risk and Uncertainty

The working poor need protection against the risks and uncertainties associated with their work as well as the common contingencies of property loss, illness, disability and death.

#6 – To Strengthen Representative Voice and Increase Visibility

To demand their rights and influence the policy decisions that shape their lives, the working poor need stronger organizations and a voice in policy-making as well as greater visibility in national data and statistics.

Most of these strategic priorities have been on the international development agenda for some time. But several points about them do not get sufficient attention. First, poverty and inequality cannot be reduced by simply expecting that economic policies will generate sufficient employment and that social policies will compensate those left out. Economic growth often fails to generate sufficient employment, and social policies to address this failure are inadequate where they exist and often neglected altogether. Second, poverty reduction requires a major reorientation in economic priorities to focus on employment, not just growth and inflation (Lee and Vivarelli 2004). And third, to be effective, strategies to reduce poverty and promote equality should be *worker-centred*.

In recent years, many in the international development community have called for a people-centred approach to poverty reduction. The framework proposed here focuses on the needs and constraints of the working poor, especially women, *as workers*, not only as citizens or members of poor households. A worker focus will provide coherence and relevance to poverty reduction strategies because most poor people are economically active, because earnings represent the main source of income in poor households and because working conditions affect all dimensions of poverty (i.e., income, human development, human rights and social inclusion).

Interventions

These broad strategies require targeted interventions. First, policy reforms are needed to correct for biases in existing policies against the working poor, especially women, in the informal economy and to develop policies to support specific groups of informal workers. Second, relevant institutions need to become more inclusive of the informal workforce; and organizations representing informal workers need to be strengthened to have effective voice. Third, a range of services are needed, including microfinance, business development, infrastructure, social services, occupational health and safety and social protection (insurance, safety nets, disability and pensions).

To successfully pursue these broad strategies and implement the interventions requires concerted action by a range of players—including governments, international trade and financial institutions, intergovernmental agencies, the donor community, the private sector, consumers and the public, unions and other worker organizations and NGOs.

Given the variety of interventions and players, coherence is crucial. At the international level, international trade and financial systems need to operate in accordance with widely agreed-upon UN commitments, especially as regards poverty reduction, gender equality and labour standards (Floro and Hoppe 2005; World Commission on the Social Dimension of Globalization 2004). At the national level, governments should take a lead role in ensuring that the efforts of different actors are consistent. Too often interventions in support of the informal economy – and of women workers in particular – are made in a piece-meal fashion by different actors, which can produce sub-optimal, if not contradictory, effects. It is also important that the government's own policies are coherent: this requires accountability for and monitoring of progress towards shared goals and priorities, as well as inter-departmental coordination.

Strategies and interventions for each of these strategic priorities are outlined below.

#1 – To Create a Favourable Policy Environment

Most if not all economic and social policies – both macro and micro – affect the lives and work of the working poor in various direct ways.

As workers: government policies and regulations influence hiring and firing, minimum wages, benefits, working conditions, training and long-term prospects of informal workers; create incentives and benefits for enterprises; and determine whether the working poor have the right to organize, strike and be represented in collective bargaining negotiations or rule-setting institutions.

As consumers: government policies affect the accessibility, variety and costs of goods and services, including those consumed by the working poor.

As users of infrastructure, finance and property and natural resources: government policies regarding infrastructure investments, financial markets, property rights and the use of urban space, utilities and natural resources all affect the economic opportunities available to the working poor and their ability to take advantage of them.

As potential recipients of tax-funded services or transfers: whether or not the working poor, especially women, receive public services or public transfers depends in large part on whether these services and transfers are targeted to specific groups of the working poor, the locations where the working poor live and the particular activities from which they earn their livelihoods (World Bank 2005).

A Kurdish family during harvest, Iraq. Photo: Behrouz Mehri/AFP/Getty

Creating a favourable policy environment involves both addressing biases in existing policies that disadvantage the working poor and developing new policies targeted to them.

Addressing biases

A recent seven-country study sponsored by the ILO identified biases against micro- and small enterprises (MSEs) and made a set of recommendations as to how to address them, including setting up lines of credit for MSEs, streamlining licensing arrangements and simplifying taxation policies (Reinecke and White 2003). Ideally, such an analysis should look at the intersection of different biases: those that favour the rich over the poor, some ethnic groups over others, the formal over the informal economy and men over women.

Women's rights advocates have pointed out that women's location in the economy means that general economic policies cannot be assumed to be gender neutral simply because they are gender blind. To make policies more gender-sensitive, they have developed a set of analytical tools: gender assessments, gender impact assessments and gender-responsive budgeting. *Gender assessments* (see Box 6.2) involve the analysis of national data and research findings to assess the situation of women and men/girls and boys in order to develop gender-sensitive national policies. *Gender impact assessments* are designed to assess the impact of specific policies, such as trade or investment, on women and men/girls and boys. *Gender-responsive budgeting* integrates a gender perspective into the budget process and tracks how government revenues and expenditures affect women and men/girls and boys. A gender budget is not a separate budget for women but an attempt to disaggregate expenditure and revenue according to their different impacts on women and men (UNIFEM 2000).

As with gender, economic policies that are 'blind' to how labour markets are actually structured and function cannot be assumed to be 'neutral' towards labour. Economic planners should take into account the size, composition and contribution of both the formal and informal labour markets in different countries, and recognize that their policies are likely to have differential impacts on informal and formal enterprises, on informal and formal workers, and on women and men within these categories. To assess and address how economic policies affect the working poor, especially women, it is important to analyse how class, gender and other biases intersect in labour markets, including biases that favour capital over labour, formal over informal enterprises, formal over informal workers, and men over women within each of these categories.

A newer tool, *informal economy budget analysis,* views budget allocations (or the lack thereof) as an expression of policy approaches. Informal economy budgets are designed to do three things. First, they examine the extent to which the state budget shows an awareness of the existence and situation of informal workers and their enterprises. Second, they identify measures of direct and indirect state support, and thus have the potential to raise the visibility of informal workers and their enterprises and encourage advocacy for

> **Box 6.1**
>
> ## Multi-Sectoral Approach to Informal Economy Budget Analysis
>
> **Statistics:** Good data is a first step towards improving policies for informal workers and enterprises. Time and money invested in data collection that focuses on the size, composition and contribution of informal workers and enterprises will increase visibility.
>
> **Economic policy and employment creation:** Informal workers will benefit from policies and allocations that support smaller rather than larger business. Special attention to and support for very small enterprises will reach poorer people and especially women.
>
> **Regulation of labour and employment conditions:** Labour departments regulate conditions of work and employment. Special efforts should be made to extend the regulatory reach to include informal workers and their enterprises and to ensure labour laws are progressive with respect to the informal labour force.
>
> **Land entitlements:** Budgetary allocations to land reforms that are redistributive, and in which women have entitlements in their own right, will be of direct benefit to women informal workers.
>
> **Agricultural support:** Support for informal and poorer workers will be reflected in budget allocations to extension officers with an orientation to very small producers, in employment of women extension officers and in training in methods of reaching women producers.
>
> **Communications:** A telecommunications policy that supports cheaper telecommunications will give informal workers easier access to information about markets and prices, and can specifically address the exclusion of women from the informal circuits of information-sharing and price-setting that are dominated by men.
>
> **Education:** Informal workers benefit from policies that allocate resources to literacy, to adult and further education and to primary and secondary education geared to the real world of work. Resources for affordable early childhood education can enable the mothers of young children to work, and can create significant (albeit low-waged) employment opportunities for women.
>
> **Health:** Informal women workers are assisted by health services that emphasize reproductive health and are alert to occupational health and safety issues, and by services that are safe, affordable and near the place of work.
>
> **Housing:** Private homes are used by millions of people, especially women, as places to earn a living. Allocations of land for housing development that are near markets and industrial nodes, and housing subsidies for poorer people will directly benefit informal women workers.
>
> **Infrastructure:** Water, sanitation and electricity are essential for most informal as well as formal work activities, and policies should ensure quality, accessibility and affordability.
>
> **Transport:** Governments should support affordable and accessible public and private transport so workers and their products can reach markets and work sites.
>
> **The safety and protection services:** National and local policing policies that see informal and formal business as linked, and that are funded in a way that enables their safety, will help improve the general investment or business environment.
>
> Source: Budlender, Skinner and Valodia 2004; Budlender 2000.

greater support. Third, they can be used to assess the gap between policies, budget allocations, and policy implementation.

Two pioneering informal budget initiatives in South Africa (Budlender et al. 2004; Budlender 2000) showed the need to analyse budget allocations across all government agencies, not just those dealing with 'economic development' or 'support for small businesses' (see Box 6.1).

Some policies or regulations that may have benefits and/or costs to informal workers are not found in budgets themselves. For example, zoning policies can restrict or promote the accommodation of economic activities in residential areas; urban planning can integrate or restrict sites for informal operators in urban renewal plans, or exclude them altogether; and municipal and national governments can design tendering and procurement policies (which will be reflected in budgets) to include or exclude very small businesses.

In brief, informal economy budget analysis links the rhetoric of policy to the allocation of resources, enabling us to see assessments of the costs and benefits of policy decisions for informal workers. In addition, this analysis offers a method for integrating poverty, gender and labour market analysis in assessing the impact of economic and social policies on working poor women and men.

Targeted policies

To help redress biases in existing policies and to complement existing policies, targeted policies in support of informal workers are also needed. In India, for example, the Government, in consultation with organizations of informal workers, has recently adopted targeted policies in support of street vendors and informal workers more generally. In Kenya, the Government formulated a national policy in support of micro- and small enterprises. And in South Africa, one outcome of negotiations between labour and Government has been the extension of labour rights to 'vulnerable workers', defined as those not covered by existing collective bargaining agreements, including agricultural and domestic workers (see Close-up).

#2 - To Increase Assets and Access

Over the past three decades, there has been a proliferation of projects and programmes designed to support microenterprises, including microfinance services and business development services. Far less attention has been paid to informal wage workers and their need for skills, assets and competitiveness in labour markets.

Support to the self-employed

Many of the working poor who are self-employed, both women and men, are unable to take advantage of new opportunities opened up by trade liberalization or economic growth because they lack access to credit, business skills or technologies, productive assets, or market information. And self-employed women face additional problems not faced by self-employed men, including less access to property due to unequal inheritance laws; less access to formal sources of credit due to lack of collateral; and fewer opportunities for apprenticeship and skills training. They may also be treated as dependents in tax and benefit systems and confront a lack of business development and marketing services for female-dominated industries or sectors (Mayoux 2001).

Microfinance – Beginning in the early 1970s, there has been what has been called a 'microfinance revolution'. Microfinance has shown that poor people are bankable – they can save regularly and borrow and repay loans at interest rates at or above commercial rates of interest. At the heart of the microfinance movement the world over are working poor women, who make up around 80 per cent of all clients of microfinance institutions. They have proved to be credit worthy and good savers and, in general, they have better repayment rates than men. Microfinance has led to fundamental changes in the lives of many (though certainly not all) women, who now have increased access to resources, improved material well-being and enhanced identity and power (Kelkar et al. 2004; Chen and Snodgrass 2001; Kabeer 1998).

In addition, women-led microfinance institutions such as SEWA Bank and Women's World Banking (WWB) have helped push the frontiers of microfinance, pioneering many of the innovative services and methodologies in the field. Founded in 1974, SEWA Bank is a women's cooperative bank in which clients – all working poor women – comprise the majority of the board. It was the first microfinance institution to start as a full-fledged bank rather than a microfinance project, and to include a focus on savings, not just loans; it was also one of the first to add insurance to its financial services.

Founded in 1980, WWB is the first global women's financial institution. Its affiliates and associates provide financial services to over 15 million low-income women entrepreneurs in some 40 countries. In addition, WWB has linked its clients, affiliates and associates to formal banking institutions and influenced financial sector policies worldwide.

Despite the importance of microfinance in recognizing and supporting women's economic roles, however, it should not be seen as a magic bullet for women's economic security. To date it reaches less than 13 per cent of the estimated 550 million working poor worldwide. As different types of financial institutions become involved in microfinance – and formal banks go into 'untapped' markets – it is important to keep a focus on women's participation as well as products and services that address the needs of working poor women. Equally important, the formal financial sector needs to develop financial policies and systems that work for the poor majority

Business development services – Business development services (BDS) are aimed at increasing the business skills and market access of microenterprises. Those offered by government generally do not reach the smallest enterprises, especially those run by women, and while BDS provided by NGOs have been more successful at targeting the most disadvantaged producers and traders, they have limited outreach. More critically for our purposes, few if any of these focus on working poor women.[2] This is an area in which governments can play a role in facilitating service provision through private firms or through public-private partnerships of various kinds.

A key issue is whether to provide generic BDS (such as preparing a business plan) or more specific services (such as marketing specific products). Both are needed, but sector-specific services are more likely to be effective for self-employed women, who tend to be concentrated in certain sectors and face a variety of sector-specific disadvantages (Chen et al. 1998).

The term 'sub-sector' is used to refer to each of the tasks, enterprises and actors linked to the production and distribution of a particular final product (e.g., silk) or commodity (e.g., vegetables) along a value chain. The sub-sector approach to microenterprise development refers to efforts to address common constraints or opportunities facing the targeted clients – in this case, women micro-entrepreneurs – within a given sub-sector. Depending on the sub-sector, common constraints might include barriers to accessing existing infrastructure and services, poor quality – or lack – of existing infrastructure and services and unfavourable prices. As such, the sub-sector or value-chain approach typically involves more than the provision of business development services: it often involves negotiating prices, enforcing contracts and balancing power relations within markets (ibid.). Good practice examples on sub-sector development range from coconut oil producers in Samoa to traditional medicine dealers in South Africa (see Close-up).

---

2 A review of 28 evaluations of enterprise development projects that involved small or microenterprises found that, across the board, the gender impacts of projects were not addressed. At most, a few provided a breakdown of beneficiaries by sex. In addition, human and social dimensions did not feature in any of these evaluation approaches. The focus was almost entirely on enterprises, markets, institutional capacity; not on entrepreneurs, knowledge and skill acquisition. While some considered the projects' economic and institutional context, none considered their human and social context (Zandniapour et al. 2004).

Support to informal wage workers

It is important to note that virtually all business development services and most microfinance services are targeted at the self-employed. Recently, some microfinance institutions have begun to offer loans and savings products to deal with the consumption as well as the investment needs of their poorer clients. These products should continue to be extended to all the working poor, including those who are wage employed. The counterpart to business development services for the wage employed is workforce or human resource development services. However, to date, most of these initiatives – such as training and retraining programmes – have focused on formal employees in the private or public sector or those who have lost their formal jobs. In part for this reason, the International Labour Conference (ILC) 2004 recommended that governments should develop policies and programmes aimed at "creating decent jobs and opportunities for education and training, as well as validating prior learning and skills gained to assist workers and employers to move into the formal economy" (Human Resources Development Recommendation, No. 194, adopted by the ILC 2004).

#3 – To Improve the Terms of Trade

For the informal self-employed, more favourable terms of trade mean more favourable prices for their products relative to the cost of their inputs. For informal wage workers, they mean more favourable wages relative to their cost of living. Changing these terms of trade clearly requires more than service delivery. It involves changing specific government policies, government-set prices or institutional arrangements, as well as the balance of power within markets or value chains.

Consider the unfavourable terms of trade for small farmers producing for the domestic market in Ghana, where urban food prices are relatively high while the price farmers get is relatively low (Heintz 2004), and the difference gets captured by various intermediaries. Targeted interventions such as finance for storage facilities, rural-to-urban transport infrastructure or market facilitation services could cut out the intermediaries (or at least lower the rents they get) and improve returns to small farmers.

At the global level, the fair trade movement seeks to promote more equitable trading relationships, particularly for small producers, by improving market access, strengthening producer organizations, negotiating better prices and supporting consumers to use their purchasing power to help counter the imbalances in international trade. The Fairtrade Labelling Organisation (FLO) provides a fair trade standard, indicating that producers have achieved the principles set out by FLO for their particular product. These principles include setting a minimum price and a creating a social premium to pass back for community investment.

#4 – To Secure Appropriate Legal Frameworks

Whether formal or informal, workers and entrepreneurs are entitled to respect for fundamental principles and rights at work, as expressed in the 1998 ILO Declaration of that name (www.ilo.org/declaration). Yet informal workers are often denied these basic human rights (ILO 2004c). Strategies to ensure their legal rights include the development, ratification and enforcement of international labour conventions and recommendations; changes in national labour legislation, including extending the scope of the employment relationship (ILO 2005a); the implementation and monitoring of corporate codes of conduct; and collective bargaining agreements and grievance mechanisms.

International labour standards – It is often assumed that international labour standards do not apply to workers in the informal economy. While some of these standards are aimed at formal enterprises, those that embody fundamental human rights are, in principle, to be enjoyed by all workers whether they work in formal or informal settings (Trebilcock 2004). To date, only one ILO convention applies to a specific category of informal worker: the Home Work Convention #177, passed in 1996, which has been ratified by only four countries (see Chapter 5).

Even when they are not widely ratified or enforced, ILO conventions can be used as advocacy tools in promoting national policies or programmes in support of informal workers in general or specific groups of informal workers. In Southern and South-Eastern Asia, national and regional organizations of home-based workers – linked through the HomeNet network – have used Convention #177 to lobby for supportive policies and programmes for home-based workers in their respective countries and regions.

A joint project of UNIFEM, SEWA and Home-Net South Asia seeks to ensure safe and secure livelihoods for home-based workers in the region. Its primary objective is to assist with organizing and networking of home-based workers and their organizations; ratification of the ILO Home Work Convention; supporting the development of policy frameworks and advocacy on key issues; demonstrating pilot approaches for social protection; and promoting fair trade practices. To achieve these goals, HomeNet South Asia has been mapping organizations of home-based workers, helping to build national networks, consulting with relevant national ministries to advocate on behalf of home-based workers, disseminating information and increasing the visibility of the national HomeNet associations through workshops and media (HomeNet South Asia 2004).

Domestic labour laws and policies – Limitations in existing labour laws contribute to the fact that more and more workers worldwide are not legally protected. These limitations include how labour law defines and classifies the employment relationship; how the definitions or classifications encoded in labour law are interpreted and applied; and whether the law, as interpreted, is enforced or complied with. In some cases the employment relationship is objectively ambiguous (e.g., in the case of many so-called 'independent contractors', such as truck drivers who drive their own trucks on behalf of another person or a firm). In other cases the employment relationship clearly exists but it is not clear who the employer is, what rights the worker has and who is responsible for securing these rights (e.g., in the case of temporary workers hired through agencies). To address these problems as they relate to migrant workers, some governments such as those in Hong Kong in the 1970s and Jordan in 2003 have created standard contracts for migrant workers that guarantee benefits and minimum wages.

However, no matter how labour law is defined, interpreted, applied or enforced, some employers will continue to deliberately disguise or change the employment relationship in order to avoid their obligations as employers. They may disguise the employment relationship, for example, by claiming that their outworkers are actually commercial partners who buy raw materials from them and sell finished goods to them. In other cases, employers seek to change existing employment relationships through legal means to less secure and protected relationships. For instance, a management consultancy in South Africa assists companies to restructure their workforces so that they no longer have to adhere to collective agreements on minimum wages or contribute to benefit or training schemes (Skinner and Valodia 2001). When employers deliberately disguise the employment relationship, workers can and have successfully challenged this practice, as in India, where several cases have gone all the way to the Supreme Court.

Codes of conduct – Globalization has led to a significant increase in the global sourcing of goods, generating increased employment for many women workers in export production. However, the conditions of employment of these workers are often poor and lacking in basic rights. Global sourcing is often undertaken by large brand name companies and retailers, who do not own production but can exert great control over their suppliers. NGOs and trade unions have put increasing pressure on large corporate buyers to act more responsibly and improve employment conditions within their supply chains. An important mechanism for this are codes of conduct.

Since the early 1990s, there has been a marked emergence of these codes—voluntary agreements drawn up at a company, industry or multi-sector level to establish basic social or ethical standards. Their proliferation reflects the decline of state regulation of transnational corporations, the rise of corporate self-regulation and pressure from adverse publicity regarding poor working conditions or environmental standards. Various players are 'driving' the development of the codes: women's organizations, trade unions, NGOs, companies and business associations – as well as multi-stakeholder networks or initiatives such as the Ethical Trade Initiative (ETI) (see Close-up). However, organizations of informal workers have generally not been actively represented in the negotiations around corporate codes of conduct (Jenkins et al. 2002).

Recently, there has been a growing focus on public/private partnerships between business and the non-profit world as a way to develop corporate codes of conduct that businesses can support but that also allow monitoring of implementation. Including businesses among the stakeholders increases the likelihood of implementation. Public/private partnerships also provide a forum for focusing on the benefits of codes of conduct to profit-making entities. These range from increased sales among consumers who are concerned about worker conditions in production chains beyond their borders to more committed workers, less turnover and less absenteeism. Many companies have their own codes, which cover issues such as health, safety and child labour. However, codes can include other rights such as union organization, wages, working hours and discrimination.

In 2004, Calvert, a socially responsible investment firm; Verité, an independent, nonprofit social auditing and research organization; and UNIFEM collaborated on a pioneering code of conduct relating to gender equality. The Women's Principles, which focus on empowering women worldwide, are a set of goals for companies to aspire to and measure their progress against. They address such issues as employment and income; health, safety and violence; management and governance; and education and training. Over the course of several years, the three entities plan to design a verification regime for companies endorsing the principles; develop curriculum, surveys and training methodologies for social compliance; and conduct research to build a case for the financial return from investing in women's empowerment. (UNIFEM 2004a).

The better codes are based on the four principles of the ILO Declaration on Fundamental Principles and Rights at Work – freedom of association and freedom from forced labour, child labour, and discrimination – which are enshrined in the following core ILO Conventions:

- No. 87 on freedom of association and No. 98 on collective bargaining;
- No. 29 and No. 105 on forced labour;
- No. 100 and No. 111 on eliminating discrimination;
- No. 138 and No. 182 on child labour.

Occupational safety and health as well as hours of work are common features of these codes. Some codes include the more controversial provision that workers should receive a living wage. This recognizes that legally set minimum wages, which are included in many company codes, are often not adequate to meet the basic needs of workers (Burns and Blowfield 2000).

At the international level, several hundred large companies have pledged to respect the four principles encompassed in the ILO Declaration on Fundamental Principles and Rights at Work under the Global Compact, an initiative launched by the United Nations Secretary-General and the business community in 1999.

Labour standards and trade agreements.

Despite resistance from both developing countries and multinational corporations, labour standards (including workplace safety) have been incorporated into some international trade treaties. The North American Free Trade Agreement (NAFTA) and its side agreement the North American Agreement on Labour Cooperation (NAALC), which went into effect in 1994, were the first formal attempt to do this. The NAALC does not oblige the parties (Canada, Mexico and the United States) to modify their national labour legislation but requires them to guarantee effective application of their own legislation. It also provides an institutional framework to secure compliance, including a special system for dispute resolution (Lopez-Valcarcel 2002).

However, a decade after these agreements went into effect, few if any of the labour rights of Mexican *maquiladora* workers have been protected by the NAALC due to "inherent weaknesses of the agreement, a lack of political will to implement either the letter or the spirit of the agreement, and the economic disincentives for Mexico to enforce labour rights that would 'discourage foreign investment'" (Brown 2004, cited in Lund and Marriott 2005). None of the 28 labour standards complaints submitted to the National Administrative Offices has got beyond the second stage of a seven-step investigative process and "not a single workplace hazard has been corrected as a result of NAFTA and the NAALC" (ibid.). While there are clear scope, enforcement and public participation problems within the NAALC and other labour agreements within trade treaties, the Maquiladora Health and Safety Support Network and expert observers remain optimistic that these can be overcome if a number of essential components are incorporated into future trade agreements (ibid.).

Securing rights for migrant workers

Women migrant workers, many of whom work informally, are especially vulnerable to abuse and exploitation because they often have no rights within the country to which they migrate. UNIFEM is one of several organizations that are focusing on empowering women migrant workers, informing them of their rights under international agreements and helping them to secure work contracts in host countries. A UNIFEM briefing kit, *Empowering Women Migrant Workers in Asia,* includes information on several initiatives as follows:

Policy and legal reforms have been undertaken at local, provincial, national and international levels to protect workers. These include projects such as the successful effort, supported by UNIFEM, to mainstream gender concerns in migration into Nepal's National Development Plan (this was the first time that migration was discussed in the Plan) and UNIFEM's work in support of bringing non-resident workers under the protection of employment laws in Italy and Jordan.

Organizing initiatives to provide voice to migrant workers include the formation of the Filipino Migrant Workers Union (FMWU) and the Indonesian Migrant Women's Union (IMWU) in Hong Kong. In addition, UNIFEM has helped create partnerships between traditional trade unions and migrant worker unions as in the case of the Indonesian Migrant Workers Union, which receives technical support and shared office space from the Hong Kong Confederation of Trade Unions.

Public awareness campaigns, such as a local campaign in greater Jakarta, Indonesia, a national one initiated by the Nepalese Government and an Asian regional campaign supported by UNIFEM, helped raise awareness about the problems facing migrant workers, highlighted good practices and provided a framework for strategic intervention.

Provision of direct services to migrant workers which generally involves such things as travel assistance, interest-free loans and life insurance and promoting regional collaboration between countries of origin and countries that receive migrants. The ILO is proposing a non-binding Multilateral Framework on Labour Migration (ILO 2004b).

Securing rights for the self-employed

It should be noted that while some international labour laws and standards apply to self-employed workers, these workers have specific concerns that differ from those of wage workers and that are often not covered by international standards or national labour law. These include the right to do their particular line of work and the right to use urban space or common properties. The right to work is enshrined in the constitutions of some countries and thus can be used to defend the right of occupational groups to do the kind of work they do. For example, the Supreme Court of India, in two landmark judgements, has upheld the right of street vendors to vend and, therefore, to a secure place from which to vend. These rights also include the right of access to credit, land and natural resources and the right to a fair share in the benefits of their intellectual property.

Securing property rights for informal workers

People who own and control assets such as land and housing tend to enjoy some degree of economic security and, if they have legal rights over their assets, are able to use them to access credit and other economic resources. However, the working poor face several handicaps in this regard. First, many poor families own few assets other than their labour. Those who do own assets, often do not have legally recognized rights to them (de Soto 2000). Finally, women face even greater constraints since in many countries they are far less likely than men to own or control assets.

A mix of strategies is needed to secure property rights for poor women. First, efforts are needed to increase the assets of the poor, such as (a) policies to allocate land and other resources more equitably across social groups and (b) microfinance services to increase financial assets (through savings) and physical assets (through loans). Second, efforts must be made to help the poor secure legal property rights to the assets that they do own, including land, housing, equipment, livestock or natural resources. Finally, efforts should be made to help women make claims to a share of the land, housing or other property owned by their families. In Viet Nam, for example recent revisions to the marriage and family laws require that both husband and wife sign any documents registering family assets, including land and property. (Ravallion and van de Walle 2004; Posterman and Hanstad 2003).

#5 – To Address Risk and Uncertainty

With the global expansion of informal employment, the number of workers who do not have employment-based protections such as health or unemployment insurance, retirement or disability benefits has grown markedly. A health crisis, for example, can plunge a family into poverty and keep it there. Meanwhile, trade liberalization brings new risks and vulnerabilities, such as less-secure contracts and work orders, at the same time that governments in many countries have reduced social spending. There is, in brief, a real crisis in social protection for the global workforce.

A common policy prescription to address income insecurity in the informal economy is public works programmes (World Bank 1995). One of the best-known and respected is the Employment Guarantee Scheme in Maharashtra state, India. This is unique in that it not only guarantees gainful employment for all adults above 18 years but also requires that this employment contribute to building productive community assets. It has been successful in generating significant employment, especially for women, and in creating productive community assets including temporary dams to conserve water, paved roads and more (Krishnaraj et al. 2003). A draft national Employment Guarantee Act, which would mandate the provision of a minimum of 100 days of work to poor households, is currently being debated in India (Dreze 2005).

But public works, important as they are, are not enough to protect informal workers, who need additional social protection measures such as relief payments or cash transfers; health, property, disability and life insurance; and pensions or long-term savings schemes. Governments, the private sector, NGOs, trade unions and other membership-based organizations can all play active roles in providing social protection to informal workers. Although informal workers are able to contribute, they should not have to bear sole responsibility.

Around the world, a wide range of alternative management and financing arrangements for providing social protection to informal workers have been put successfully in place. These include:

- **mutual health insurance schemes**: for example, in Mali, Senegal and other countries.
- **voluntary self-insurance schemes financed through premiums**: e.g., integrated social security of SEWA in India (see chapter 5).
- **voluntary insurance schemes financed through worker and state contributions**: for example, voluntary health and pension scheme for informal workers in Costa Rica (see Close-up).
- **means-tested government-funded pensions**: for example, old-age pensions for agricultural workers with incomes below the poverty line, such as the Rural Social Insurance Scheme in Brazil that extends pensions and disability insurance to the rural poor.
- **universal health insurance or pension schemes**: e.g., the national scheme in Japan that provides health insurance and pensions for more than 90 per cent of the population; the

South African pension scheme for the elderly poor; and the 30-baht health scheme in Thailand (see Close-up).

- **schemes funded by contributions from both employers and workers**: e.g., the extension of South Africa's Unemployment Insurance Act to cover domestic workers.
- **extension of existing statutory schemes**: e.g., the extension of the statutory social security system in Portugal to cover home-based embroiderers on the island of Madeira for old age, disability, maternity and sick days.
- **schemes financed by taxes on industries**: e.g., welfare schemes in India for informal workers in specific sectors (see Close-up).

Recently, the ILO has launched a Global Campaign to extend social security to all and proposed a Global Social Trust (see www.ilo.org/protection).

Finally, in designing services for informal workers, it is important to note that it may not make sense to apply policies from the formal sector without reframing them to fit the reality of informal employment or making them more inclusive to include informal workers. In the case of occupational health and safety (OHS), for example, ensuring OHS protections for both formal and informal workers would require a multi-layered response that includes collecting comprehensive data on work-related health and safety; extending the definition of 'place of work' to include informal work settings; broadening the conceptualization of worker vulnerability to include issues affecting informal workers such as long hours and intense pace; and recognizing and reframing the interdependent links between public, environmental and occupational health so that all three sectors can work together to benefit each other (Lund and Marriott 2005).

In Thailand, HomeNet, the Ministry of Labour and the ILO have joined forces to train home-based workers to recognize and deal with hazards they face while carrying out their tasks. They are using the WISH (Work Improvement for Safe Homes) methodology, which uses graphics to demonstrate safety and health concerns so that illiterate workers can participate. The women involved have organized to lobby the government for primary health-care units at the local level and to obtain further technical support. The ILO has recently introduced the WISH methodology in other countries, such as Viet Nam (Anne Trebilcock, personal communication, 2005).

#6 - To Strengthen Representative Voice and Increase Visibility

To advocate effectively for policies and programmes that address poverty and increase gender equality, the working poor, especially poor women must organize to strengthen representative voice beyond the local level to all levels of planning and policy-making. Recent international initiatives to combat poverty such as MDGs and PRSPs, have opened up political space for informal workers involvement in the development process. Taking advantage of this space, however, is difficult for informal workers with limited resources and capacity for advocacy beyond a local agenda. It requires creative and sustained linkages between women's and social justice organizations and trade unions, along with governments and UN partners, such as UNIFEM, UNDP and ILO.

For informal workers to become visible to policy makers, however, also requires the collection and application of better data and statistics. As this report has highlighted, relatively few countries have comprehensive statistical data on the informal economy and fewer still have data on the links between informal employment, gender, and poverty. Therefore, more countries need to include statistics on informal employment in their national labour force surveys, and countries that do so already need to improve the quality of statistics they collect. Expanding the collection and improving the quality of data on the various types of informal employment will facilitate future research on the linkages between informal employment, gender and poverty, as well as more informed policy decisions at the local, national and international levels.

Gender assessments and MDGs

The participatory processes mandated in the preparation of national MDG reports and PRSPs provide the opportunity to advocate for and provide improved data on women's role in the informal economy. In partnership with other international, regional and national organizations, UNIFEM has played a lead role in preparing gender assessments in Cambodia and in several countries in Latin America that can be used to advocate for a gender and employment focus in national planning related to the MDGs and more broadly.

These reports can sensitize and train officials on how to mainstream gender and employment in national planning around the MDGs, the PRSPs as well as national development objectives. They also provide a guide to women's groups showing how they can frame their own advocacy efforts within the MDG framework — in this way bringing women's voices into MDG-related processes at the national level. Future assessments can draw on both the proposed new employment indicators for MDG Goal 3 – employment by type and earnings – and informal economy budget analysis to assess the impact of economic and social trends on different segments of the labour market and their effect on poverty and gender.

Close-up: Good Practice Cases

Following are the six strategic priorities that require targeted interventions in order to promote economic opportunities, economic rights, social protection and representative voice for the working poor, especially women, in the informal economy.

Strategy # 1 – To Create a Favourable Policy Environment

The economic policy environment needs to support the working poor in the informal economy, rather than be blind to them or biased against them. This requires addressing biases in existing policies and designing and implementing targeted policies.

National policy on street vendors, India. The overarching objective of this policy is to provide a supportive economic environment for street vendors while limiting congestion and maintaining standards of hygiene in public spaces. Jointly drafted by the Government of India and the National Association of Street Vendors (NASVI), the policy was officially adopted in early 2004 with specific provisions in the following areas:

- *Legal:* Vendors will be given legal status by amending, enacting, repealing and implementing appropriate laws and providing legitimate hawking zones in urban development/zoning plans.
- *Space:* Arrangements will be made for the appropriate use of identified space, including creating special hawking zones.
- *Regulation:* Instead of numerical limits for licensing vendors, the Government will move to fee-based regulations.
- *Role in urban trade:* Street vendors will be treated as a special component of the urban development/zoning plans by being recognized as an integral and legitimate part of the urban trading system.
- *Organization:* Organizations of street vendors such as unions, cooperatives and associations will be promoted.
- *Participation:* Participatory mechanisms for orderly conduct of urban vending will be created, with joint representation from vendors' organizations, voluntary organizations, local authorities, the police and residents' welfare associations.
- *Social security and financial services:* Social security benefits (pensions, insurance, etc.) and access to credit will be encouraged through vendor self-help groups, cooperatives and microfinance institutions.
- *Rehabilitation of child vendors:* Various measures will be adopted to promote a better future for child vendors by making appropriate interventions for their rehabilitation and schooling. (Government of India, Ministry of Urban Development and Poverty Alleviation 2004)

National and local policies for micro- and small enterprises, Kenya. The Government of Kenya has for many years incorporated the informal economy into its national economic planning, focusing on areas such as credit, training and marketing services to micro and small enterprises (MSE) and government procurement from the MSE sector. A recent strategic plan for economic recovery notes the importance of this sector in creating employment and seeks to provide infrastructure and services to it while receiving taxes in exchange. A number of policies relating to the informal economy have also been adopted by local governments, most notably a Single Business Permit that simplifies the procedures for registering businesses. In several cities and towns around the country, suitable locations for street vendors are under review, and informal transport operations are being encouraged to coordinate their operations (Winnie Mitullah, personal communication, 2005).

New Labour Act, Ghana. In a review of national labour laws, the Ghana Trade Union Congress (GTUC) found that the laws were outdated, fragmented and did not fit with work realities or the Ghanaian Constitution. The resulting New Labour Act (2003) was negotiated through a tripartite process involving the Government, trade unions and employers. The Act applies to all workers (excluding armed forces, police, etc.). A key objective of the GTUC was to extend to informal workers important protections that formal workers had secured for themselves. The Act allows temporary and casual workers to benefit from provisions of collective agreements on equal pay for work of equal value, access to the same medical provisions available to permanent workers and a full minimum wage for all days in attendance and public holidays. In addition, a temporary worker employed by the same employer for a continuous period of six months or more must be treated as a permanent worker (Owusu 2003; Kofi Asemoah, personal communication, 2004).

Strategy # 2 - To Increase Assets and Access

To be able to take advantage of the opportunities offered by a more favourable policy environment, the working poor need greater market access and the relevant assets and skills for competing in markets.

Export links for coconut oil producers, Samoa. While the Samoan economy overall has outperformed its Pacific neighbours, the rural economy of this small island country has lagged far behind, resulting in migration to urban areas. In response, Women in Business Development Incorporated (WIBDI), a Samoan NGO, has introduced technological improvements to better enable rural women to tap into export markets. While WIBDI has supported a range of projects, including organic farming, beekeeping and handicraft production, perhaps its most innovative project has been its work on virgin coconut oil production. It introduced an innovative, small-scale processing method and trained rural women to produce virgin coconut oil suitable for export. The oil resulting from the new processing method is not only of higher quality but it can be produced within a much shorter time period than previous techniques. The processing method is also less labour intensive. WIBDI has established the Pure Coconut Oil Company to market and export the virgin oil on behalf of the villagers and assists with quality control (Cretney and Tafuna'i 2004).

Upgrading the supply chain for dairy producers, Nicaragua. In Nicaragua, the United Nations Industrial Development Organization (UNIDO) worked with local partners through its Women's Entrepreneurship Development (WED) programme to analyse and upgrade a dairy production chain. The analysis identified bottlenecks in the stages of production, which the collaborative programme then addressed through a mix of interventions: lobbying the Government to introduce technical standards for handling fresh milk and processing milk products; establishing a cooperative to improve the supply of milk to cheese producers; establishing a laboratory for quality assurance; creating a technical service centre for the producers; and establishing links with large enterprises outside the production chain for distribution, sales and technology. The programme also helped form the Nicaraguan Chamber of the Milk Sector and a Milk-Cluster Commission in cooperation with the National Programme for Competitiveness and the Milk Federation of Central America (Tran-Nguyen and Zampetti 2004).

Traditional medicine support programme, South Africa. A significant component of the informal economy in South Africa is the traditional medicine (or *muthi*) sector, which is utilized by 80 per cent of black South Africans, often in parallel with modern medicine. It is estimated that 61 million rand (approximately US$8.7 million) of medicinal plant material is traded in KwaZulu Natal annually, with Durban/eThekwini the primary trading and dispensing node. Over 30,000 people, most of whom are women, work in this sector, mainly as rural gatherers. The volume and value of *muthi* transactions convinced the Durban/eThekwini City Council to develop a broad range of interventions to support this sector. In consultation with traders, traditional health practitioners, cultivators, farmers, various research institutions and private sector companies, the Council has initiated and facilitated support strategies across the traditional medicine value chain.

A market building that can accommodate 550 stallholders has been developed to support the retail level, with shelter, storage, water and toilet facilities. The building, which now includes consultation booths and a processing plant, has significantly improved the working environment for traders.

The Council supports environmental sustainability by training gatherers in sustainable harvesting techniques. This has led to the establishment of a sustainable bark harvesters association, the first organization of its kind in South Africa. It also supports a medicinal plant nursery that produces seedlings for farmers and trains traditional healers in growing methods. Since the nursery alone was unable to meet the demand for medicinal plants, five labour-intensive pilot nurseries and small farms have been established across the municipality since 2004.

Training facilities have also been expanded. Given the long growing time needed for many medicinal plants and the need to generate sustainable livelihoods, the pilot farms also produce seedlings for subsistence food crops as well as landscaping plants that the municipality has agreed to buy.

The municipality has also invested substantial funds in research and development of traditional medicine in partnership with the Traditional Healers Organization, the Medical Research Council, the Nelson Mandela School of Medicine at the University of KwaZulu Natal and the Regional Biotech Innovation Centre. The intention is to develop home-grown, patented, mainstream preventive and curative medicines. A feasibility study is exploring the potential of a public-private economic empowerment partnership to invest in a processing facility, to protect indigenous knowledge and to process, package and market traditional pharmaceutical products for both the national and international markets (Institute for Natural Resources 2003; Mander 1998; Fred Pieterson, personal communication, 2005).

Strategy # 3 – To Improve the Terms of Trade
To compete effectively in the markets, the working poor need to be able to negotiate favourable prices and wages for the goods and services they sell, relative to their cost of inputs and their cost of living

Gum collection and marketing, India. In the state of Andhra Pradesh, the Chenchu people, a hunter-gatherer tribe, collect gum and other forest products. In June 2002, UNIFEM and the NGO Society for the Elimination of Poverty launched a project in partnership with a local NGO, the Kovel Foundation, to support the Chenchu in collecting gum, bark, seeds and other non-timber forest products. The main innovations in this project include training both women and men in sustainable collection and processing methods and the organization of women's groups to run community-based procurement centres. These centres buy products collected by the Chenchu and sell them to the state government forest corporation or on the open market. Previously, the local community was unaware of the quality or price of what they sold and were often cheated by private traders or government officials. The pilot project, which started with one product in one district, has expanded to cover nearly 60 products and 17 districts in Andhra Pradesh. It has shown that rural women, empowered by market knowledge and collective solidarity, can perform well in the market place (Meenashki Ahluwalia, personal communication, 2005).

Buy-back centres for waste collectors, South Africa. In South Africa, waste collectors are predominantly very poor black women and, increasingly, male immigrants from other African countries. In the mid 1990s the Self Employed Women's Union (SEWU) began organizing women cardboard collectors in the inner city of Durban/eThekwini. The union found that the women were largely innumerate and often exploited by unscrupulous middlemen. It lobbied for assistance from the local government, which responded by helping to build a buy-back centre in the inner city. The municipality provided a small plot of land for the centre, while a large private sector recycler provided scales, storage containers and trolleys for the collectors. SEWU worked alongside city officials to design the intervention and trained the cardboard collectors in weights and measurements. The collectors now sell their cardboard directly to the recycling company, which has substantially increased their (albeit still low) incomes. The success of this buy-back centre has led the Municipal Council to establish a number of similar centres throughout the city (Mgingqizana 2002).

Improved terms of trade for a cocoa bean cooperative, Ghana. A UK fairtrade organization (Twin Trading) joined with an NGO in the Netherlands (SNV) to assist Kuapa Kokoo, a cocoa bean cooperative in Ghana, to join the cocoa producers' register of the Fairtrade Labelling Organization (FLO). This enables the 45,000 producers in the cooperative – a third of whom are women – to market to importers and chocolate companies who wish to buy under fair trade conditions, and it also gives smallholders a guaranteed fair price plus a premium of $150 per ton. The premium is used by cooperative members to invest in community development projects, many of which are priorities for women, such as wells, corn mills and schools. In addition, the cooperative has established the Day Chocolate Company as a joint venture in the UK that markets its own brand of chocolate to retailers. The cooperative provided 33 per cent of the company's equity and receives 66 per cent of the profits (Tiffin et al. 2004; Redfern and Snedket 2002). The cooperative is now the fifth largest licensed cocoa buying company in Ghana, which means it can negotiate with the Government to set fair prices for the crop. Twin Trading has also assisted the cooperative to obtain funds to set up a credit union, which has turned out to be a source of security during the lean season between cocoa harvests (Tiffin et al. 2004).

Strategy # 4 – To Secure Appropriate Legal Frameworks

The working poor in the informal economy need legal recognition as workers and the legal entitlements that come with that recognition, including the right to work (e.g., to vend in public spaces), rights at work (i.e., workers' rights) and rights to property.

Women's land rights in Central Asia. Central Asia is considered the poorest area in the Commonwealth of Independent States (CIS) region, with lack of land a major reason for poverty. The majority of the population in both Kyrgyzstan and Tajikistan, where UNIFEM is working on initiatives to increase women's land rights, live in rural areas and earn their livelihood through agricultural work. In both countries, Government initiatives aimed at reducing poverty through land reform have been introduced, but women have not benefited as much as men both because of a widespread belief that women should not own or inherit land and limited awareness among women about their economic rights. To ensure women's land rights, UNIFEM is working with the Governments, civil society and women's groups to raise awareness and amend laws. In Tajikistan, amendments to the land reform act that improve women's access were signed into law in 2004. In Kyrgyzstan, UNIFEM has supported the work of legal experts in drafting and submitting to the Government amendments to the existing land code, and has created training programmes to build awareness and negotiating skills among women at the local level (UNIFEM 2004b).

National Union of Domestic Employees (NUDE), Trinidad and Tobago. Initially established in 1982 to organize domestic workers, NUDE began including other low wage workers who had no protections or guaranteed benefits in 1992. As of 2002, the union had 450 members – 65 of whom were men – and an all-female executive. The union has been campaigning against discrimination against domestic workers in labour legislation and to have women's housework counted in the national budget. It has hosted meetings on domestic workers' issues that have brought together unions, NGOs, Government agencies, UN agencies, universities and individual researchers and has convened meetings of domestic workers' organizations at the Caribbean regional level to define common demands (Global Labour Institute 2003).

Ethical Trading Initiative, United Kingdom. The Ethical Trading Initiative (ETI) in the UK is an independent multi-stakeholder initiative that supports labour codes. It involves companies, trade unions and NGOs and has developed independent labour codes for informal workers based on core ILO Conventions. The ETI has brought together over 35 companies with NGOs and trade union federations in support of the ETI Base Code, which must be included as a minimum in the codes of member companies. The ETI has a number of working groups that share learning and information on how to advance the code and work with local stakeholders – including home-worker – in developing countries. A similar initiative in the US, Social Accountability International (SAI), provides an auditable standard, SA 8000, against which companies can be certified as compliant. (Stephanie Barrientos, personal communication, 2005)

Application of ETI Base Code, South Africa. Most UK supermarkets are members of the ETI. This means, for example, that wine and fruit growers in South Africa producing for the UK market understand that they need to comply with UK labour legislation and the code. Improved labour standards have led to better conditions for some women workers, especially those with permanent contracts. However, under competitive pressure to keep costs low, some growers are switching from permanent labourers to temporary ones, making it easier to avoid providing employment benefits, and conditions for these workers are often quite bad. The lack of union organization among rural workers in general and women in particular makes it difficult for workers to address these conditions (Barrientos et al. 2004).

Strategy # 5 – To Address Risk and Uncertainty

The working poor need protection against the risks and uncertainties associated with their work as well as the common contingencies of property loss, illness, disability and death.

Government-initiated voluntary scheme for health and pension provision for informal workers, Costa Rica. An increasing proportion of Costa Rica's labour force is not covered by occupationally related social insurance. However, voluntary insurance is available for independent workers, own account workers and non-remunerated workers (family workers, housewives and students). It is aimed at workers who have either never contributed to a health or pension plan or who did not do so for long enough to accumulate adequate benefits. Workers may join the plan if they have a per capita family income lower than a basic basket of food products, as determined by the Statistics Institute. Although joining has been voluntary, it is becoming statutory in 2005. The plan is funded by contributions from the State and the individuals who join. This is an interesting example of a country with a good history of social provision attempting to adjust in flexible ways to increasing numbers of informal workers in the labour market (Lund 2004, drawing on Martinéz and Meso-Lago 2003).

Government sponsored social protection, Thailand. The formal contributory social security scheme in Thailand covers sickness, disability, death and survivor grants, maternity benefits for 90 days, old age pensions and child allowances. In the late 1990s and early 2000s, it covered only about 15 per cent of the workforce, mostly formal workers. Plans to extend the social insurance scheme to informal workers were actively under review in mid-2005. Apart from this scheme and additional programmes covering pensions and health care for civil servants, the Government of Thailand has developed voluntary subsidized health cards for those not covered by the formal scheme and labour protection laws. To provide universal health coverage within 10-15 years, it has instituted a '30 Baht Health Scheme,' in which poor people pay a minimal co-pay (30 baht is approximately US$0.75) for health care and the Government funds the rest of the costs through taxation (Lund and Nicholson 2003). This plan has become the basic social protection scheme in Thailand, covering some 47 million people out of a total population of 62 million (Rakawin Lee, personal communication, 2005).

Industry-specific welfare funds for informal workers, India. In India, the Government has set up a number of welfare funds for workers in specific industries. These funds are created by special Acts of Parliament. For example, the Building and Other Construction Workers' (Regulation of Employment and Conditions of Service) Act was passed in 1996. Unlike previous legislation, this bill extended coverage to small construction sites that employed as few as 10 people in a 12-month period. The law requires builders to issue identity and attendance cards to workers, create a welfare fund, provide insurance coverage, pay medical expenses and pay minimum wages. Building sites with more than 50 workers are required to set up crèches for workers' children.

The Cigarette (*Bidi*) and Cigar Workers (Conditions of Employment) Act, also from 1996, expanded the definition of 'employee' to those who work under the 'sale-purchase system' (i.e., the worker buys raw materials and sells finished goods to a trader or contractor) and created a national minimum wage to be adopted by all states in India. The Bidi Workers Welfare Tax Act generates welfare funds for bidi workers, 90 per cent of whom are women. (Jhabvala and Kanbur 2002; Subrahmanya 2000).

Strategy #6 – To Strengthen Representative Voice and Increase Visibility

To advocate effectively for supportive policies and programmes, the working poor, expecially women, need to be organized and gain representative voice in all levels of planning and policy-making. To have informed policy and action, the working poor in the informal economy must be 'visible' in national statistics. Therefore, greater priority needs to be given to the collection of data on informal employment.

Working with internal migrant women workers, China. The Chinese Working Women Network (CWWN) is a non-profit NGO, whose mission is to better the lives of Chinese migrant women workers by helping them fight for labour rights in China's export processing zones. Because of difficulties organizing migrant workers in the workplace, CWWN organizes through local communities and dormitories for migrant women. It builds labour networks and encourages collective action among the women CWWN also runs organizing and training centres to help women take on leadership roles, a mobile health centre, a community occupational health centre, a support group for injured workers, and a women workers' cooperative for economic activities (Ngai 2005).

Developing statistics on the informal economy, Moldova. Moldova, in common with other transition countries, has seen a rise in informal employment both inside and outside the informal sector (i.e., small unregistered enterprises) as they shift to a market economy. As a result, statistical data, particularly gender-disaggregated statistics on the informal economy, have become increasingly necessary to aid policy makers in creating appropriate policies. In response to this, a collaborative project was developed between the Department for Statistics and Sociology of the Republic of Moldova, the National Institute of Statistics and Economic Studies of France and the ILO. The project has cleared up misunderstandings about the concept of informality and its activities, collected and disseminated gender-disaggregated statistics in quarterly reports, and served as an example to a number of countries that seek to replicate the Moldovan process (ILO Bureau of Statistics 2004).

The Way Forward

Such an approach requires a major reorientation of economic thinking, economic planning, and economic policies. The global community needs to recognize that that there are no short-cuts to reducing poverty and gender inequality; and that economic growth alone – even if supplemented by social policies to compensate the losers – cannot eliminate poverty and inequality. The global community needs to set more and better employment – especially for working poor women and men – as a core priority and target of all economic policies. It should also recognize that economic policies that are narrowly focused on inflation-targeting, such as those promoted by the IMF and the World Bank, can create an economic environment that is hostile to an expansion of more and better employment opportunities. Successful implementation of the policy framework proposed here would require adjustment in the focus and targets of the economic policies promoted by these institutions and, therefore, adopted by many national governments.

As part of this reorientation, the greater focus on employment proposed here should be incorporated into national poverty reduction and development strategies, including the national MDG reports and PRSPs. The fact that employment creation is neither one of the Millennium Development Goals, nor an indicator under the goal of eradicating extreme poverty and hunger is reflected in the relative neglect of employment in most of the national MDG reports as well as the PRSPs. Even in those PRSPs that include a focus on employment, the role of informal employment and women's employment in poverty reduction receive scant attention.

Improving the employment content of the national MDG reports, PRSPs and other national policies requires four broad interventions. First, employment must be regarded as a target in itself, not as a by-product of growth and investment. Second, national economic plans and macroeconomic management must support the ultimate objective of generating employment for poverty reduction. This requires a coherent employment policy framework within the policy documents. Currently, such policy coordination is absent. Third, strategies must be devised to insure that poor and disadvantaged groups, particularly women, have access to the improved employment opportunities generated by the revised policy approach. That is, policies must be put in place to create employment opportunities and labour markets that work for the poor and disadvantaged, particularly women: as detailed in strategies # 2 to 5 in this chapter. Finally, the policies that are put in place must provide resources to improve labour market data in order to make monitoring and implementation of employment policies possible.[5]

To ensure that these four broad interventions are effectively pursued requires policy coherence

---

Box 6.2

National Gender Assessments: The MDGs, National Planning and Gender

Latin America

UNIFEM and ECLAC commissioned six gender assessments - in Bolivia, Colombia, Ecuador, Nicaragua, Peru and Venezuela - to analyse the MDGs from a gender perspective. Each report analysed national statistical data using a common framework, in which gender equality was regarded both as an end in itself, and as a requirement for meeting all of the other goals. The reports considered employment as a determining factor in achieving Goal 1, the eradication of extreme poverty and hunger:

> The areas of employment and social protection, among others, are fundamental to determine standards of living in our region, in which under-employment, precarious work, prevalence of the informal sector, almost absolute absence of social safety nets to protect against unemployment and insufficient income are widespread phenomena (ECLAC 2002).

The reports present indicators in addition to those now specified for international monitoring of progress toward achieving the MDGs. These include data on the links between gender inequality and different dimensions of poverty, including: access to the labour market and forms of employment, remuneration in employment, the contribution that women make to reducing poverty.

The UNIFEM-ECLAC Peru report, "Las Metas del Milenio y la Igualdad de Género: El Caso de Peru" was launched jointly with UNDP in a public session of the Peruvian Congress which had the effect of informing civil society as well as strengthening UNIFEM-UNDP collaboration (ECLAC 2004b). It was used to prepare a national report on the implementation of the MDGs. Numerous copies were printed to use as national advocacy material and for use in several workshops being held with the national women's organization, Flora Tristan, throughout the country.

Cambodia

A Fair Share for Women: Cambodia Gender Assessment is the result of several years of collaboration between UNIFEM and UN partners in cooperation with the Ministry of Women's and Veteran's Affairs of Cambodia (UNIFEM et al. 2004). The assessment is based on information on gender issues collected as part of national economic and social planning, specifically in connection with the National Poverty Reduction Strategy (NPRS) report, national planning to achieve the MDGs as well as on economic empowerment, livelihood and employment. Extensive data are reviewed and recommendations are included on gender and national policies, including those related to putting in place mechanisms to collect and analyse gender-responsive information as part of the monitoring process for both the NPRS and the MDGs.

Employment issues feature prominently in both the analysis and recommendations, which include attention to the role of women in agriculture and the sex industry. The gender assessment led to the formulation of policy briefs to guide policy makers and other officials in addressing gender dimensions in their respective sectors.

---

5 For a detailed discussion of how the employment content of the Ghana Poverty Reduction Strategy (GPRS) could be strengthened, see Heintz (2004).

at all levels and the concerted action of a range of players. At the international level, international trade and finance institutions need to operate in accordance with widely agreed-upon UN commitments, including the MDGs. Also, the international institutions overseeing national MDG and PRSP processes, including the UNDP and the World Bank, need to coordinate their efforts. At the national level, this means that existing efforts to harmonize MDG and PRSP processes – including making the policy goals and monitoring indicators of national PRSPs and MDG reports more consistent - need to be maintained and intensified. It is also important that the national policies of specific countries are coherent: this requires accountability for progress towards shared goals as well as inter-departmental coordination. Also, private firms need to operate in compliance with widely-agreed upon UN commitments as well as national policies, including the recommendations of national MDG reports and PRSPs. Finally, organizations of informal workers, women, and other disadvantaged groups need to participate in international and national policy processes to ensure that the policies that are put in place are responsive to their needs as workers.

In sum, promoting decent work for the working poor, both women and men, is a key pathway to reducing both poverty and gender inequality. This requires re-inserting employment on the poverty reduction and development agenda. Specifically, it requires:

- creating more and better employment opportunities
- creating incentives for informal enterprises to register and for employers to extend benefits to workers
- increasing the returns to labour of those who work in the informal economy

However, reorienting policies, planning, and practices towards creating more and better employment will not be possible unless two preconditions are met. First, the visibility of workers – especially working poor women and men – in labour force statistics and other data used in formulating policies needs to be increased. Second, the representative voice of workers – especially informal workers, both women and men – in the processes and institutions that determine economic policies and formulate the 'rules of the (economic) game' needs to be increased. This requires pursuing an inclusive development policy process that promotes the participation of the poor, both men and women, as *workers*: that is, a *worker-centred policy process*.

Core Priorities

What is needed is a critical mass of institutions and individuals at all levels to work together on a core minimum set of interventions and to move forward in a collaborative and incremental way towards the broader strategies and goals outlined above.

We recommend that UNIFEM and the UN system more generally pursue the following core priorities to promote decent work for working poor women:

Core Priority # 1 - To promote decent employment for both men and women as a key pathway to combating poverty and gender inequality. A concerted effort is needed to ensure that decent employment opportunities are viewed as a target rather than an outcome of economic policies, including national MDG strategies and Poverty Reduction Strategies.

Core Priority # 2 - To increase visibility of informal women workers in national labour force statistics and in national gender and poverty assessments, using the employment by type and earnings indicators proposed for Millennium Development Goal 3.

Core Priority #3 - To promote a more favourable policy environment for the working poor, especially women, in the informal economy through improved analysis, broad awareness building and participatory policy dialogues.

Core Priority # 4 - To support organizations representing women informal workers and help them gain effective voice in relevant policy-making processes and institutions.

In conclusion, this report shows that workers in the informal economy, especially women, have lower average earnings and a higher poverty risk than workers in the formal economy. The meagre benefits and high costs of informal employment mean that most informal workers are not able to work their way out of poverty. In the short term, they are often forced to 'over-work' to cover these costs and still somehow make ends meet. In the long term, the cumulative toll of being over-worked, under-compensated and under-protected on informal workers, their families, and their societies undermines human capital and depletes physical capital.

So long as the majority of women workers are informally employed, gender equality will also remain an elusive goal. Progress on both of these goals therefore demands that all those committed to achieving the MDGs, including the UN system, governments and the international trade and finance institutions, make decent employment a priority – and that corporations be made more socially responsible. Informal workers, both women and men, organized in unions, cooperatives or grassroots organizations, are ready to partner with them in this vital endeavour.

References Cited

Akintola, Olagoke. 2004. *A Gendered Analysis of the Burden of Care on Family and Volunteer Care-givers in Uganda and South Africa*. Durban: Health Economics and HIV/AIDS Research Division, University of KwaZulu Natal.

Antrobus, Peggy. 2005. "Gender Critique of the Implementation of the Millennium Development Goals (MDGs) in the Caribbean." Christ Church, Barbados: UNIFEM Caribbean Office. Unpublished.

Armstrong, Pat. 1996. "The Feminization of the Labour Force: Harmonizing Down in a Global Economy." In Isabella Bakker, ed., *Rethinking Restructuring: Gender and Change in Canada*. Toronto: University of Toronto Press.

Bakker, Isabella. 1996. "Introduction: The Gendered Foundations of Restructuring in Canada." In Isabella Bakker, ed., *Rethinking Restructuring: Gender and Change in Canada*. Toronto: University of Toronto Press.

Bangladesh Homeworkers Women's Association (BHWA). 2003/2004. *Newsletter*, 2(1), April-June.

Barrientos, Armando. 2004. "Women, Informal Employment, and Social Protection in Latin America." In Claudia Piras, ed., *Women at Work: Challenges for Latin America*. Washington DC: Inter-American Development Bank.

_____ and Stephanie Barrientos. 2002. "Extending Social Protection to Informal Workers in the Horticulture Global Value Chain." *Social Protection Discussion Paper* No. 0216. Washington, DC: World Bank.

Barrientos, Stephanie, Andrienetta Kritzinger and Hester Rossouw. 2004. "National Labour Regulations in an Informal Context: Women Workers in Export Horticulture in South Africa." In Marilyn Carr, ed., *Chains of Fortune: Linking Local Women Producers and Workers with Global Markets*. London: Commonwealth Secretariat.

Bartone, Carl. 1988. "The Value in Wastes." *Decade Watch*. Washington, DC: The World Bank.

Benería, Lourdes. 2003. *Gender, Development and Globalization*. New York and London: Routledge.

_____. 1992. "Accounting for Women's Work: The Progress of Two Decades." *World Development*, 20(11).

_____ and Maria Floro. 2004. "Deconstructing Poverty: Labor Market Informalization, Income Volatility and Economic Insecurity in Bolivia and Ecuador." http://www.unifemandina.org/documentos/june04.doc

_____ and Martha Roldán. 1987. *The Crossroads of Class and Gender: Industrial Homework, Subcontracting, and Household Dynamics in Mexico City*. Chicago: University of Chicago Press.

Bhatt, Ela R. 2004. "Interview with Rick Pantaleo." On *Talk to America*. Voice of America. 9 September.

Bhattacharya, Debapriya and Mustafizur Rahman. 2002. "Female Employment Under Export-Propelled Industrialization: Prospect for Internalizing Global Opportunities in Bangladesh's Apparel Sector." Geneva: UNRISD.

Bhowmik, Sharit. 2005. "Street Vendors in Asia: A Review" in *Economic and Political Weekly*. May 28-June 4.

Blackett, Adelle. 1998. *Making Domestic Work Visible: The Case for Specific Regulation*. Geneva: ILO.http://www.ilo.org/public/english/dialogue/ifpdial/pub l/infocus/domestic/

Breman, Jan. 1996. *Footloose Labour: Working in India's Informal Economy*. Cambridge: Cambridge University Press.

Brown, Garrett D. 2004. "Why NAFTA Failed and What's Needed to Protect Workers' Health and Safety in International Trade Treaties." Maquiladora Health and Safety Support Network. http://mhssn.igc.org/trade_2004.pdf

Buchan, James and Julie Sochalski. 2004. "The Migration of Nurses: Trends and Policies." *Bulletin of the World Health Organization*, 82(8), August.

Budlender, Debbie. 2004. "Expectations Versus Realities in Gender Responsive Budget Initiatives." Paper commissioned by UNRISD. http://www.gender-budgets.org/uploads/user-S/10999485211

_____. 2003. "Home-based Care in Botswana, Mozambique and Zimbabwe." Draft regional report, UNIFEM.

_____. 2002. *Why Should We Care About Unpaid Care Work?* Guidebook prepared for the UNIFEM Southern Africa Region Office, Harare, Zimbabwe.

_____. 2000. "The Political Economy of Women's Budgets in the South." *World Development*, 28(7).

_____, ed. 1996. *The Women's Budget*. Cape Town: Institute for Democracy in South Africa.

_____, Caroline Skinner and Imraan Valodia. 2004. "South African Informal Economy Budget Analysis." School of Development Studies Working Paper, University of KwaZulu Natal, Durban, South Africa.

Burn, Nalini. 2004. "The 'Feminization of Poverty': What Currency for Sub-Saharan Africa?" Report commissioned by UNIFEM, July.

Burns, Maggie and Mick Blowfield. 2000. *Approaches to Ethical Trade: Impact and Lessons Learned*. London: Ethical Trade and Natural Resources Programme, Natural Resources Institute.

Campbell, Iain and John Burgess. 2001. "Casual Employment in Australia and Temporary Employment in Europe: Developing a Cross-National Comparison." *Work, Employment and Society*, 15(1).

Carr, Marilyn, Martha Chen and Jane Tate. 2000. "Globalization and Home-based Workers." *Feminist Economics*, 6(3).

Carré, Françoise, Marianne Ferber, Lonnie Golden and Stephen Herzneberg, eds. 2001. *Nonstandard Work: The Nature and Challenges of Changing Employment Arrangements*. Champaign, IL: Industrial Relations Research Association.

_____ and Joaquín Herranz, Jr. 2002. "Informal Jobs in Industrialized 'North' Countries." Background paper for *Women and Men in the Informal Economy: A Statistical Picture*. Geneva: International Labour Office.

CELA-PUCE. 2002. "Evaluación de Los Impactos Economicos y Sociales de las Politicas de Ajuste Estructural en el Ecuador 1982-1999." http://saprin.org/ecuador/research

Chant, Sylvia. 2003. "New Contributions to the Analysis of Poverty: Methodological and Conceptual Challenges to Understanding Poverty from a Gender Perspective." Comisión Económica para América Latina (CEPAL) 47.

Charmes, Jacques and Mustapha Lekehal n.d. "Industrialization and New Forms of Employment in Tunisia." Cambridge, MA: WIEGO

Chen, Martha Alter. 2005. *Towards Economic Freedom: The Impact of SEWA*. Ahmedabad, India: Self-Employed Women's Association. http://www.sewaresearch.org/Impact.pdf

_____. 2000. *Perpetual Mourning: Widowhood in Rural India*. New Delhi: Oxford University Press.

_____. 1995. "A Matter of Survival: Women's Right to Employment in India and Bangladesh." In Martha Nussbaum and Jonathan Glover, eds., *Women, Culture and Development*. Oxford: Clarendon Press.

_____ and Donald Snodgrass. 2001. *Managing Resources, Activities, and Risk in Urban India: The Impact of SEWA Bank.* Washington, D.C.: United States Agency for International Development (USAID) AIMS Project.

_____, Jennefer Sebstad and Lesley O'Connell. 1999. "Counting the Invisible Workforce: The Case of Homebased Workers." *World Development*, 27(3).

_____, Joann Vanek and Marilyn Carr. 2004. *Mainstreaming Informal Employment and Gender in Poverty Reduction.* London: Commonwealth Secretariat.

_____, Yassine Fall, Rosa E. Montes de Oca and Jennefer Sebstad. 1998. "An Empowerment Approach to Women's Enterprise Development: A Review of UNIFEM's Enterprise Development Programme." New York: UNIFEM.

Chen, Shaohua and Martin Ravallion. 2004. "How Have the World's Poorest Fared Since the Early 1980s?" Policy Research Working Paper, No. WPS3341. Washington, D.C.: The World Bank. http://econ.worldbank.org/files

Clean Clothes Campaign. 2005. "How is the Clean Clothes Campaign Structured?" Clean Clothes Campaign website. http://www.cleanclothes.org

Constable, Nicole. 1997. *Maid to Order in Hong Kong: Stories of Filipina Workers.* Ithaca, NY: Cornell University Press.

Cook, Sarah. 2003. "After the Iron Rice Bowl: Extending the Safety Net in China." In Sarah Cook, Naila Kabeer and Gary Suwannarat, eds., *Social Protection in Asia.* New Delhi: Har-Anand Publications.

Cranford, Cynthia and Leah Vosko. 2005. "Conceptualizing Precarious Employment: Mapping Wage Work Across Social Location and Occupational Context." In Leah Vosko, ed., *Precarious Employment: Understanding Labour Market Insecurity in Canada.* Montreal: McGill-Queen's University Press.

Cretney, John and Adimaimalaga Tafuna'i. 2004. "Tradition, Trade and Technology: Virgin Coconut Oil in Samoa." In Marilyn Carr, ed., *Chains of Fortune: Linking Local Women Producers and Workers with Global Markets.* London: Commonwealth Secretariat.

Dasgupta, Sukti. 2002. "Organizing for Socio-Economic Security in India." InFocus Programme on Socio-Economic Security. Geneva: International Labour Office.

Daza, José Luis. 2005. "Informal Economy, Undeclared Work and Labour Administration." *Dialogue Paper* No. 9. Geneva: International Labour Office.

D'Cruz, Celine and Diana Mitlin. 2005. "Shack/Slum Dwellers International: One Experience of the Contribution of Membership Organizations to Pro-poor Urban Development." Paper presented at WIEGO/Cornell/SEWA/EDP conference, Ahmedabad, India, January.

Deaton, Angus and Jean Dreze. 2002. "Poverty and Inequality in India: A Re-Examination." *Economic and Political Weekly*, 7 September.

de Soto, Hernando. 2000. *The Mystery of Capital: Why Capitalism Triumphs in the West and Fails Everywhere Else.* New York: Basic Books.

_____. 1989. *The Other Path: The Economic Answer to Terrorism.* New York: HarperCollins.

Diez de Medina, Rafael. 2005. "A Model of Change for the Informal Economy." PowerPoint presentation. Geneva: International Labour Office.

Dimova, Lilia and Polina Radeva. 2004. "Women in the Informal Economy of Bulgaria 2004." UNIFEM Central and Eastern Europe. Unpublished paper.

Doane, Donna, Rosalinda Ofreneo and Daonoi Srikajon. 2003. "Social Protection for Informal Workers in the Garment Industry: Philippines and Thailand." In Francie Lund and Jillian Nicholson, eds., *Chains of Production, Ladders of Protection.* Durban: School of Development Studies, University of Natal.

Dorrington, Rob E. and Leigh Johnson. 2002. "Impacts: Epidemiological and Demographic." In Jeff Gow and Chris Desmond, eds., *Impacts and Interventions: The HIV/AIDS Epidemic and the Children of South Africa.* Pietermaritzburg: University of Natal Press.

Dreze, Jean. 2005. "Employment Bill Lacks Teeth." *Times of India.* 21 May. http://timesofindia.indiatimes.com/articleshow/1117848.cms

du Toit, Andries and Joachim Ewert. 2002. "Myths of Globalisation: Private Regulation and Farm Worker Livelihoods on Western Cape Farms." *Transformation*, Vol. 50.

Economic Commission for Latin America and the Caribbean (ECLAC). 2004a. "Panorama Social de América Latina 2004." November.

_____. 2004b. "Las Metas del Milenio y la Igualdad de Género: El Caso de Peru." *Serie Mujer y Dessarrollo*, No. 55.

_____. 2002. Note prepared by ECLAC for the international seminar on Latin America and the Caribbean, Challenges Posed by the Millennium Development Goals, organized by the Inter-American Development Bank (IDB), World Bank, UNDP and ECLAC, Washington, DC, June.

El Mahdi, Alia and Mona Amer. 2003. "The Workforce Development Research: Formal Versus Informal Labor Market Developments in Egypt during 1990-2003." Report to the Economic Policy Institute-Global Policy Network. Cairo: University of Cairo.

Elson, Diane. 1999. "Labor Markets as Gendered Institutions: Equality, Efficiency, and Empowerment Issues." *World Development*, 27(3).

Esim, Simel and Monica Smith, eds. 2004. *Gender and Migration in Arab States: The Case of Domestic Workers.* Beirut: ILO.

Fleck, Susan. 2001. "A Gender Perspective on Maquila Employment and Wages in Mexico." In Elizabeth G. Katz and Maria C. Correia, eds., *The Economics of Gender in Mexico.* Washington D.C.: World Bank.

Floro, Maria and Hella Hoppe. 2005. "Engendering Policy Coherence for Development: Gender Issues for the Global Policy Agenda in the Year 2005." *Dialogue on Globalization,* Occasional Paper No. 17, April. Berlin: Friedrich Ebert Stiftung. http://www.igtn.org/pdfs

Flyn, Don and Eleonore Kofman. 2004. "Women, Trade and Migration." *Gender and Development*, 12(2).

Folbre, Nancy. 1990 "Women on Their Own: Global Patterns of Female Headship." In Rita S. Gallin and Ann Ferguson, eds., *Women and International Development Annual*, Vol. 2. Boulder, CO: Westview.

Fudge, Judy and Leah Vosko. 2001 "By Whose Standards? Re-regulating the Canadian Labour Market." *Economic and Industrial Democracy*, 22(3).

Fultz, Elaine, Markus Ruck and Silke Steinhilber. 2003. *Gender Dimensions of Social Security Reform.* Budapest: ILO Subregional Office.

Gallin, Dan. 2002. "Organizing in the Informal Economy." *Labour Education,* 2(127). "Unprotected Labour: What Role for Unions in the Informal Economy?" Geneva: ILO. http://www.ilo.org/public/english

_____ and Pat Horn. 2005. "Organizing Informal Women Workers." Paper prepared for UNRISD *Gender Policy Report.* http://www.global-labour.org/pat_horn.htm

Gereffi, Gary.1994. "The Organization of Buyer-Driven Global Commodity Chains: How U.S. Retailers Shape Overseas Production Networks." In Gary Gereffi and Miguel Korzeniewicz, eds., *Commodity Chains and Global Capitalism.* Westport, CT: Praeger.

Global Labour Institute. 2003. *Note on Domestic Workers' Unions.* Geneva: Global Labour Institute.

Government of India. 2001. *Census of India 2001: General Population Tables.* New Delhi: Government of India. http://www.censusindia.net/results

Government of India, Ministry of Urban Development and Poverty Alleviation. 2004. *National Policy on Street Vendors.* New Delhi: Government of India. http://urbanindia.nic.in/mud-final-site

Grown, Caren, Geeta Rao Gupta and Aslihan Kes. 2005. *Achieving Gender Equality and Empowering Women.* Report of UN Millennium Project Task Force on Education and Gender Equality. Sterling, VA: Earthscan.

Grown, Caren, Geeta Rao Gupta and Zahia Khan. 2003. *Promises to Keep: Achieving Gender Equality and the Empowerment of Women.* Washington, DC: International Center for Research on Women. http://www.mdgender.net

Haider, Mehnaz and Misbah Tahir. 2004. *Mapping Organizations Working For Women Homeworkers In Pakistan.* Lahore: Aurat Publication and Information Service Foundation.

Hallward-Driemeier, Mary and Andrew Stone. 2004. "The Investment Climate for Informal Firms." Background Paper for *World Development Report 2005*. Washington, DC: World Bank.

Heintz, James. 2004. "Elements of an Employment Framework for Poverty Reduction in Ghana." Report of a Joint ILO/UNDP Mission. http://www.undp.org/poverty/docs/employment

Heyzer, Noeleen. 2004. "Beyond Cancun: Whose Access Counts?" Panel Presentation, XV International AIDS Conference. Bangkok, Thailand. July. http://www.unifem.org/news_events

_____. 2002. "Indigenous Women's Rights in the Context of Globalization." Speech delivered to the First Indigenous Women's Summit of the Americas. Oaxaca, Mexico. November. http://www.unifem.org/news

_____. 2001a. "Progress for Women, Progress for All." Presentation. Santiago, Chile. April. http://www.unifem.org/news

_____. 2001b. "Globalization, Gender Equality and State Modernization." Presentation. Santiago, Chile. April. http://www.unifem.org/news

_____. 1986. *Working Women in Southeast Asia*. London: Open University Press.

_____ and Vivienne Wee. 1994. "Domestic Workers in Transient Overseas Employment: Who Benefits, Who Profits." In Noeleen Heyzer, Geertje Lycklama à Nijeholt and Nedra Weerakoon, eds., *The Trade in Domestic Workers: Causes, Mechanisms and Consequences of International Migration*. London: Zed Books.

_____, Geertje Lycklama à Nijeholt and Nedra Weerakoon, eds. 1994. *The Trade in Domestic Workers: Causes, Mechanisms and Consequences of International Migration*. London: Zed Books.

HomeNet South Asia. 2004. *HomeNet South Asia at the World Social Forum*. May. Ahmedabad: HomeNet South Asia.

Hussmanns, Ralf. 2004. "Notes Prepared for Inter-agency and Expert Meeting on MDG Indicators." United Nations Statistics Division and Economic Commission for Europe, Geneva. 29 September.

Institute for Natural Resources. 2003. "Strategy and Business Plan for Development of the eThekwini Medicinal Plants Industry." Report prepared for the Durban Unicity Council.

International Confederation of Free Trade Unions (ICFTU). 2005a. "Great Expectations…Mixed Results." February. http://www.icftu.org

_____. 2005b. "International Women's Day." ICFTU OnLine, 8 March. http://www.icftu.org

_____. 1999. "Claiming Our Rights –Women and Trade Unions."Background document. http://www.icftu.org

International Labour Office. 2005a. "The Employment Relationship." *Report V(1), International Labour Conference, 95th Session*, 2006. Geneva: International Labour Office. http://www.ilo.org/public/english/standards

_____. 2005b. *Exhibition Guide*. Knowledge Fair on Decent Work and the Informal Economy. International Labour Office.

_____. 2005c. *World Employment Report 2004-05: Employment, Productivity and Poverty Reduction*. Geneva: International Labour Office.

_____. 2005d. *Knowledge Fair Newspaper:* Decent Work and the Informal Economy. Geneva: International Labour Office.

_____. 2004a. *Economic Security for a Better World*. Geneva: International Labour Office.

_____. 2004b. "Towards a Fair Deal for Migrant Workers in the Global Economy." *Report VI, International Labour Conference, 92nd Session*. Geneva: International Labour Office.

_____. 2004c. "Organizing for Social Justice." *Global Report under the Follow-up to the ILO Declaration on Fundamental Principles and Rights at Work*. Geneva: International Labour Office.

_____. 2004d. "Youth: Pathways to Decent Work." *Report VI, International Labour Conference, 92nd Session*. Geneva: International Labour Office. http://www.ilo.org/public/english/standards/relm/ilc/ilc93/pdf/rep-vi.pdf

_____. 2003a. "Working Out of Poverty." *Report of the Director General, International Labour Conference, 91st Session*. Geneva: International Labour Office.

_____. 2003b. "Scope of the Employment Relationship." *Report IV, International Labour Conference, 91st Session.* Geneva: International Labour Office.

_____. 2003c. "Time for Equality at Work." *Global Report under the Follow-up to the ILO Declaration on Fundamental Principles and Rights at Work.* Geneva: International Labour Office.

_____. 2002a. "Decent Work and the Informal Economy." *Report VI, International Labour Conference, 90th Session*. Geneva: International Labour Office.

_____. 2002b. *Women and Men in the Informal Economy: A Statistical Picture*. Geneva: Employment Sector, International Labour Office.

_____. 2002c. "Conclusions Concerning Decent Work and the Informal Economy." International Labour Conference, 90th Session, Geneva, 2002, *Provisional Record* No. 25. Geneva: International Labour Office.

_____. 2002d. *Employment and Social Policy in Respect of Export Processing Zones (EPZs).* ILO Governing Body document GB.285/ESP/5. Geneva: International Labour Office. http://www.ilo.org/public/english/standards

_____. 2001. "Organizing the Unorganized: Informal Economy and Other Unprotected Workers." *Promoting Gender Equality - A Resource Kit for Trade Unions.* http://www.ilo.org/public/english/employment/gems

_____. 1999. "Decent Work." *Report of the Director General, International Labour Conference, 87th Session.* Geneva: International Labour Office. http://www.ilo.org/public/english/standards

_____. 1998. *ILO Declaration on Fundamental Principles and Rights at Work.* Geneva: International Labour Office. http://www.ilo.org/public/english

International Labour Office Bureau of Statistics in collaboration with the Department for Statistics and Sociology of the Republic of Moldova. 2004. "Employment in the Informal Economy in the Republic of Moldova." *Working Paper,* No. 41. Geneva: International Labour Office. http://www.ilo.org/public

Jenkins, Rhys, Ruth Pearson, and Gill Seyfang, eds. 2002. *Corporate Responsibility and Labour Rights: Codes of Conduct in the Global Economy*. Sterling, VA: Earthscan Publications Ltd.

Jhabvala, Renana and Ravi Kanbur. 2002. "Globalization and Economic Reform as Seen from the Ground: SEWA's Experiences in India." Paper presented to the Indian Economy Conference, Cornell University, 19-20 April.

Kabeer, Naila. 1996. "Agency, Well Being and Inequality: Reflections on the Gender Dimensions of Poverty." *IDS Bulletin*, 27(1).

_____. 1998. "Money Can't Buy Me Love? Re-evaluating Gender, Credit and Empowerment in Rural Bangladesh." IDS Discussion Paper, No. 363. Brighton, UK: Institute of Development Studies (IDS), University of Sussex.

_____ and Simeen Mahmud. 2004. "Globalization, Gender and Poverty: Bangladeshi Women Workers in Export and Local Markets." *Journal of International Development*, 14(1).

Kantor, Paula and Padmaja Nair. 2005. "Vulnerability to Crisis in Lucknow, India: The Role of Assets in Mitigating Risks." Project Overview, Study Methodology, Findings and Summary. Delhi: Oxfam Great Britain in India.

Kelka, Govind, Dev Nathan and Rownok Jahan. 2004. "Redefining Women's 'Samman': Microcredit and Gender Relations in Rural Bangladesh." *Economic and Political Weekly*, 39(32).

Kidder, Thalia and Kate Raworth. 2004. "Good Jobs and Hidden Costs: Women Workers Documenting the Price of Precarious Employment." *Gender and Development*, 12(2), July.

Kiura, C. Munene. 2005. "Integrating Street Vendors in Urban Development: A Case Study of Hawkers in Nairobi, Kenya." Dissertation in partial fulfilment of the requirement for the award of a Masters of Arts degree in Development Studies, University of Nairobi.

Kofman, Eleonore. 2004. "Gendered Global Migrations." *International Feminist Journal of Politics*, 6(4).

Krishnaraj, Maitreyi, Divya Pandey and Aruna Kanchi. 2003. "Gender Sensitive Analysis of Employment Guarantee Scheme." *Follow the Money Series South Asia*, No. 5. Mumbai: UNIFEM.

Lee, Eddy and Marco Vivarelli. 2004. *Understanding Globalization, Employment, and Poverty Reduction*. New York: Palgrave Macmillan.

Levin, Mark. 2002. "Cooperatives and Unions – Joint Action for Informal Workers." *Labour Education*, 2(127): "Unprotected Labour: What Role for Unions in the Informal Economy?" Geneva: ILO. http://www.ilo.org

Lewis, Jane. 2002. "Gender and Welfare State Change." *European Societies*, 4(4).

Lopez-Valcarcel, Alberto. 2002. "New Challenges and Opportunities for Occupational Safety and Health in a Globalized World." April. Geneva: International Labour Office. http://www-ilo-mirror.cornell.edu/public/english

Lund, Francie. 2004. "Informal Workers' Access to Social Security and Social Protection." Background paper for UNRISD Report on *Gender Equality: Striving for Justice in an Unequal World*.

_____ and Cally Ardington. 2005. "Employment Status, Security and the Management of Risk: A Study of Workers in Kwansane, KwaSulu Natal." Unpublished paper.

_____ and Anna Marriott. 2005. "Health and Safety and the Poorest." Research report prepared for Department for International Development, UK.

_____ and Smita Srinivas. 2000. *A Gendered Approach to Social Protection for Workers in the Informal Economy*. Geneva: ILO.

_____ and Jeemol Unni n.d. "Reconceptualizing Security." Cambridge, MA; WIEGO.

_____ and Jillian Nicholson, eds. 2003. *Chains of Production, Ladders of Protection*. Durban: School of Development Studies, University of Kwazulu Natal.

Maher, Kristen Hill and Silke Staab. 2005. "Nanny Politics." *International Feminist Journal of Politics*, 7(1).

Maloney, William F. 2004. "Informality Revisited." *World Development,* 32(7), July.

Mander, Myles. 1998. "Marketing of Indigenous Medicinal Plants in South Africa: A Case Study of KwaZulu Natal." Rome: Food and Agricultural Organization of the United Nations (FAO).

Martínez Franzoni, Juliana and Carmelo Mesa-Lago. 2003. *La Reforma de la Seguridad Social en Costa Rica en Pensiones y Salud: Avences, Problemas Pendientes y Recomendaciones.* April. San José, Costa Rica: Fundación Freidrich Ebert.

Mayoux, Lynda. 2001. "Jobs, Gender and Small Enterprises: Getting the Policy Environment Right." *SEED Working Paper No 15*. Geneva: International Labour Office.

Medina, Martin. 2005. "Waste Picker Cooperatives in Developing Countries." Paper presented at WIEGO/Cornell/SEWA/EDP conference on Membership Based Organizations of the Poor, Ahmedabad, India, January.

Mitullah, Winnie. 2004. *A Review of Street Trade in Africa.* WIEGO. Unpublished manuscript.

Mgingqizana, N. 2002. "Running a Drop-off Recycling Centre and Buy-Back Centre: What to Expect." Conference Proceedings of the International Waste Congress and Exhibition of the Institute of Waste Management South Africa (IWMSA).

Narayan, Deepa, ed. 2000. *Voices of the Poor: Can Anyone Hear Us?* New York: World Bank and Oxford University Press.

Ngai, Pun. 2005. "A New Pro-active of Labour Organizing: Community-based Organization of Migrant Women Workers in South China," paper presented at the Membership-Based Organization of the Poor Workshop, organized by WIEGO/SEWA/EDP, Ahmedabad, India.

Nussbaum, Martha. 2005. "Care, Dependency, and Social Justice: A Challenge to Conventional Ideas of the Social Contract." In Peter Lloyd-Sherlock, ed., *Living Longer: Ageing, Development and Social Protection.* New York: Palgrave MacMillan.

Ogden, Jessica, Simel Esim and Caren Grown. 2004. *Expanding the Care Continuum for HIV/AIDS: Bringing Carers into Focus*. Washington D.C: International Center for Research on Women.

Orloff, Ann. 2000. "The Significance of Changing Gender Relations and Family Forms for Systems of Social Protection." Background paper prepared for the *World Labour Report 1999-2000,* Social Security Department, International Labour Office, Geneva.

Osmani. S. R. 2005. "The Role of Employment in Promoting the Millennium Development Goals." Paper prepared under the joint ILO-UNDP Programme on Promoting Employment for Poverty Reduction.

Ospina, Estela. 2003. "Trade Unions Work for Women in the Informal Economy." *StreetNet News*, No. 2, October. http://www.streetnet.org.za

Owusu, Francis X. 2003. "Ghana: Where the Strong Help the Weaker." In Federatie Nederlandse Vakbeweging (FNV), ed., *From Marginal Work to Core Business: European Trade Unions Organising in the Informal Economy.* Amsterdam: FNV.

Oxfam International. 2004. *Trading Away Our Rights: Women Working in Global Supply Chains.* Oxford: Oxfam International.

Pascall, Gillian and Jane Lewis. 2004. "Emerging Gender Regimes and Policies for Gender Equality in a Wider Europe." *Journal of Social Policy*, 33(3).

Pearson, Ruth. 2004. "The Social is Political: Re-Politicization of Feminist Analysis of the Global Economy." *International Feminist Journal of Politics*, 6:4.

Petchesky, Rosalind P. and Karen Judd, eds. 1996. *Negotiating Reproductive Rights: Women's Perspectives Across Countries and Cultures*. International Reproductive Rights Research Action Group (IRRRAG). London and New York: Zed Books.

Pocock, Barbara, John Buchanan and Iain Campbell. 2004. "Securing Quality Employment: Policy Options for Casual and Part-time Workers in Australia." Chifley Research Centre, Adelaide. http://www.chifley.org.au/publications

Pok, Cynthia and Andrea Lorenzetti. 2004. "Los Perfiles Sociales de la Informalidad en Argentina." Paper presented at the workshop "Informalidad y Genero en Argentina" sponsored by WIEGO and Centro Interdisciplinario para el Estudio de Politicas Publicas (CIEPP), Buenos Aires, Argentina, May.

Polaski, Sandra. 2004. "Jobs, Wages, and Household Income." In John Audley, ed., *NAFTA's Promise and Reality: Lessons from Mexico for the Hemisphere*. Washington DC: Carnegie Endowment for International Peace.

Pollert, Anna and Eva Fodor, eds. 2005. *Working Conditions and Gender in an Enlarged Europe*. Dublin: European Foundation for the Improvement of Living and Working Conditions. http://www.eurofound.eu.int/publications/EF04138.htm

Portes, Alejandro, Manuel Castells and Lauren A. Benton, eds. 1989. *The Informal Economy: Studies in Advanced and Less Developed Countries*. Baltimore: John Hopkins University Press.

Prosterman, Roy L. and Tim Hanstad. 2003. "Land Reform in the 21st Century: New Challenges, New Responses." *RDI Reports on Foreign Aid and Development,* No. 117. Seattle: Rural Development Institute.

Raghwan, Raghwan. 2004. "Uncomfortable but Taking Part – Cambodia's Unions and the PRSP." *Labour Education*, 1-2(134-135): "Special Issue on Trade Unions and Poverty Reduction Strategies." http://www.ilo.org/public/english

Rani, Uma and Jeemol Unni. 2000. "Urban Informal Sector: Size and Income Generation Processes in Gujarat, Part II." SEWA-GIDR-ISST-NCAER Contribution of the Informal Sector to the Economy, Report No. 3, National Council of Applied Economic Research, New Delhi.

Ravallion, Martin and Dominique P. van de Walle. 2004. "Breaking Up the Collective Farms." *Economics of Transition*, 12(2), June.

Redfern, Andy and Paul Snedker. 2002. "Creating Market Opportunities for Small Enterprises: Experiences of the Fair Trade Movement." *SEED Working Paper,* No. 30. Geneva: International Labour Office.

Reinecke, Gerhard and Simon White. 2004. *Policies for Small Enterprises: Creating the Right Environment for Good Jobs*. Geneva: International Labour Office.

Rodgers, Gerry, Charles Gore and Jose Figueiredo, eds. 1995. *Social Exclusion: Rhetoric, Reality, Responses*. Geneva: Institute for Labour Studies.

Sastry, N. S. 2004. "Estimating Informal Employment and Poverty in India." Discussion Paper Series, No. 7. Delhi: UNDP India.

Säve-Soderbergh, Bengt. 2005. "What About Employment, Decent Work and Labour Markets as Parts of the International Agenda for Fighting Poverty and Promoting Development Cooperation?" A Memorandum for Discussion and Consultations, Ministry of Foreign Affairs, Sweden. 17 March.

Sebstad, Jennefer and Monique Cohen. 2001. *Microfinance, Risk Management, and Poverty*. Washington, DC: The Consultative Group to Assist the Poorest (CGAP), the World Bank.

Sekhamane, Neo. 2004. "Impact of Urban Livelihoods on Women's Caregiving Behaviours, Household Food Security and Nutrition of Children in Lesotho: A Community Case Study." Unpublished Masters dissertation, School of Development Studies, University of KwaZulu Natal.

Sen, Amartya K. 1985. *Commodities and Capabilities*. Amsterdam: North-Holland.

_____. 1993. "Capability and Well-being." In Martha Nussbaum and Amartya K. Sen, eds., *The Quality of Life*. Oxford: Oxford University Press.

Service Employees International Union (SEIU). 2005. "Working Together for Quality Personal Care: How SEIU Has Worked in Coalition with Consumers and Advocates to Win Workforce Improvements for Consumer-Directed Personal Care through Workforce Councils." http://s67.advocateoffice.com/vertical/Sites

Sinha, Shalini. 2004. "Laws for Informal Economy in India." WIEGO. Unpublished manuscript. Cambridge, MA: WIEGO.

Skinner, Caroline and Imraan Valodia. 2001. "Labour Market Policy, Flexibility, and the Future of Labour Relations: The Case of Clothing." *Transformation*, Vol. 50.

Standing, Guy. 1999. "Global Feminization Through Flexible Labour: A Theme Revisited." *World Development*, 27(3).

_____. 1989. "Global Feminization Through Flexible Labour." *World Development,* 17(7).

Stellman, Jeanne Mager 1998. *Encyclopaedia of Occupational Health and Safety*, 4th ed., Geneva: ILO.

Stone, Katherine V. W. 2004. *From Widgets to Digits: Employment Regulation for the Changing Workplace*. New York: Cambridge University Press.

StreetNet International. 2005: "General Information." http://www/streetnet.org.za

_____. 2004. "Constitution of StreetNet International." 17 March. http://www.streetnet.org.za/english

_____. 2003. *StreetNet News*. No. 2, October. http://www.streetnet.org.za/english

Subrahmanya, R. K. A. 2000. "Strategies for Protective Social Security." In Renana Jhabvala and R. K. A. Subrahmanya, eds., *The Unorganised Sector: Work Security and Social Protection*. New Delhi: Sage Publications.

Tiffin, Pauline, Jacqui MacDonald, Haruna Maamah and Frema Osei-Opare. 2004. "From Tree Minders to Global Players: Cocoa Farmers in Ghana." In Marilyn Carr, ed., *Chains of Fortune: Linking Local Women Producers and Workers with Global Markets*. London: Commonwealth Secretariat.

Trade Union Congress (TUC). 2004. "Government Must Enforce Rights for Hidden Workers Say Oxfam, TUC and NGH." Press release. http://www.tuc.org.uk/law

Tran-Nguyen, Anh-Nga and Americo Beviglia Zampetti, eds. 2004. *Trade and Gender: Opportunities and Challenges for Developing Countries*. New York: United Nations.

Trebilcock, Anne. 2004. "International Labour Standards and the Informal Economy." In J. C. Javillier, B. Gernigon and G. Politakis, eds., *Les Normes Internationales du Travail: Un Patrimoine pour l'Avenir*. Geneva: ILO.

Ungerson, Clare. 2003. "Commodified Care Work in European Labour Markets." *European Societies*, 5(4).

UNAIDS, United Nations Population Fund (UNFPA) and United Nations Development Fund for Women (UNIFEM). 2004. *Women and HIV/AIDS: Confronting the Crisis*. New York: UNAIDS, UNFPA and UNIFEM.

United Nations. 2005. *The Millennium Development Goals Report*. New York: United Nations.

_____. 2000. *The World's Women 2000: Trends and Statistics*. New York: United Nations.

_____. 1995. *The World's Women 1995: Trends and Statistics*. New York: United Nations.

United Nations Development Fund for Women (UNIFEM). 2005a. "The Story Behind the Numbers: Women and Employment in Central and Eastern Europe and the CIS." Bratislava: UNIFEM Central and Eastern Europe.

_____. 2005b "Addressing Feminization of Poverty in Africa: A Concept Paper." Draft report commissioned by UNIFEM.

_____. 2004a. "The Calvert Women's Principles." Media Advisory and Briefing Kit. 23 June. http://www.unifem.org/news

_____. 2004b. "Women's Land Rights in Central Asia." In UNIFEM/CIS, *In the Right Hands: Land for Women*. Almaty, Kazakhstan: UNIFEM/CIS. http://www.unifemcis.org/?en=1

_____. 2003. *Empowering Women Migrant Workers in Asia: A Briefing Kit.* Bangkok: UNIFEM East and South-East Asia.

_____. 2002a. "Lesotho Mission Report." April. New York. Unpublished report.

_____. 2002b. *Progress of the World's Women 2002, Volume 2: Gender Equality and the Millennium Development Goals.* New York: UNIFEM.

_____. 2000. *Progress of the World's Women 2000.* New York: UNIFEM.

_____, the Commonwealth Secretariat and the International Development Research Centre (IRDC). Gender Responsive Budgets Initiatives website. http://www.gender-budgets.org

_____, et al. 2004. *A Fair Share for Women: Cambodia Gender Assessment.* Phnom Penh: UNIFEM, World Bank, Asian Development Bank, UNDP and Department for International Development (DFID), UK., in cooperation with the Ministry of Women's and Veterans' Affairs. http://web.worldbank.org

United Nations Development Programme (UNDP). 2005a. *In Focus*. On-line bulletin of the International Poverty Centre. http://www.undp-povertycentre.-org/ipcpublications.htm

_____. 2005b. *"Looking for Equality: A Gender Review of National MDG Reports."*

_____. 2001. *Human Development Report 2001.* New York: Oxford University Press.

_____. 1997. *Human Development Report 1997.* New York: Oxford University Press.

United Nations Millennium Project. 2004. "Task Force 3 Interim Report on Gender Equality". February. http://www.unmillenniumproject.org

United Nations Research Institute for Social Development (UNRISD). 2005. *Gender Equality: Striving for Justice in an Unequal World.* New York: UNRISD.

Unni, Jeemol. 2005. "Informal Sector, Unorganized Sector, and Informal Economy." PowerPoint presentation. New Delhi: National Commission on Enterprises in the Unorganized/Informal Sector.

_____. 2000. "Urban Informal Sector: Size and Income Generation Processes in Gujarat, Part I." SEWA-GIDR-ISST-NCAER, *Contribution of the Informal Sector to the Economy, Report No. 2.* New Delhi: National Council of Applied Economic Research.

_____ and Uma Rani. 2005. "Impact of Recent Policies on Home-based Work in India." Discussion paper Series 10. Human Development Resource Centre. New Delhi; UNDP.

_____ and Uma Rani. 2002. "Insecurities of Informal Workers in Gujarat, India." InFocus Programme on Socio-Economic Security Paper, No. 30. September. Geneva: International Labour Office. http://www.ilo.org/public/english

Vosko, Leah. 2005. "Precarious Employment: Towards an Improved Understanding of Labour Market Insecurity." In Leah Vosko, ed., *Precarious Employment: Understanding Labour Market Insecurity in Canada.* Montreal: McGill-Queens University Press.

_____. 2004. "Confronting the Norm: Gender and the International Regulation of Precarious Work." Ottawa; Law Commission of Canada, July.

_____. 2003. "Gender Differentiation and the Standard/Non-Standard Employment Distinction in Canada 1945 to Present." In Danielle Juteau, ed., *Patterns and Processes of Social Differentiation: The Construction of Gender, Age, 'Race/Ethnicity' and Locality.* Toronto: University of Toronto Press.

_____. 2002. "Rethinking Feminization: Gendered Precariousness in the Canadian Labour Market and the Crisis in Social Reproduction." Roberts Canada Research Chair Lecture, 11 April, York University, Toronto, Canada.

_____, Nancy Zukewich and Cynthia Crawford. 2003. "Precarious Jobs A New Typology of Employment." *Perspectives on Labour and Income,* October. Ottawa: Statistics Canada.

Wazir, Rekha. 2001. "Early Childhood Care and Development in India: Some Policy Issues." In Mary Daly, ed., *Carework - the Quest for Security.* Geneva: ILO.

Weiping, Wu. 2001. "Labor Mobility in China: A Review of Programs Redressing Discrimination against Labor Migrants 1997-2001." In *Labor Mobility in China: A Review of Ford Foundation Grant Making 1997-2001.* Beijing: Ford Foundation.

White, Marceline, Carlos Salas and Sarah Gammage. 2003. "NAFTA and the FTAA: A Gender Analysis of Employment and Poverty Impacts in Agriculture." November. Washington DC: Women's Edge Coalition.

World Bank. 2005a. *World Development Report 2005: A Better Investment Climate for Everyone.* New York: Oxford University Press.

_____. 2005b. *Global Development Finance*. March. Washington DC: World Bank.

_____. 2003. *Gender in Transition.* Washington, DC: World Bank.

_____. 1998. *The Social Consequences of the East Asian Financial Crisis.* Washington, D.C.: World Bank.

_____. 1995. *World Development Report: Workers in an Integrating World.* New York: Oxford University Press.

_____. 1990. *World Development Report, 1990.* Washington, DC: World Bank.

World Commission on the Social Dimension of Globalization. 2004. *A Fair Globalization: Creating Opportunities for All.* Geneva: ILO.

World Confederation of Labour. 2004. *10 Trade Union Actions to Strengthen the Status of Workers in the Informal Economy.*

Zambrano, Gloria Camacho and Katty Hernandez Basante. 2005. "Cambio Mi Vida - Migración Femenina, Percepciones e Impactos." February. Quito: UNIFEM and Centro de Planificación y Estudios Sociales (CEPLAES).

Zandniapour, Lily, Jennefer Sebstad and Donald Snodgrass. 2004. "Review of Impact Assessments of Selected Enterprise Development Projects." July. USAID/AMAP/DAI

Zuckerman, Elaine and Ashley Garrett. 2003. "Do Poverty Reduction Strategy Papers (PRSPs) Address Gender? A Gender Audit of 2002 PRSPs." Prepared for Gender Action. http://www.sarpn.org.za

About the Authors

Martha Chen is a Lecturer in Public Policy at the Kennedy School of Government and Co-ordinator of the global research policy network Women in Informal Employment: Globalizing and Organizing (WIEGO). An experienced development specialist, she received a Ph.D. in South Asian Regional Studies from the University of Pennsylvania and lived and worked for 15 years in Bangladesh and India. She lectures and writes widely on gender and poverty alleviation, with a focus on issues of employment and livelihoods and is the author, most recently, of *Mainstreaming Informal Employment and Gender in Poverty Reduction* (co-authored with Joann Vanek and Marilyn Carr), *Women and Men in the Informal Economy: A Statistical Picture* (co-authored with Joann Vanek) and *Perpetual Mourning: Widowhood in Rural India.*

Joann Vanek is the Director of the Statistics Programme of WIEGO. She worked with the United Nations Statistics Division for 20 years, where she led the development of the gender statistics programme and co-ordinated production of three issues of the global report, *The World's Women: Trends and Statistics*. Her most recent publications include *Mainstreaming Informal Employment and Gender in Poverty Reduction* (co-authored with Martha Chen and Marilyn Carr), and *Women and Men in the Informal Economy: A Statistical Picture* (co-authored with Martha Chen), which was prepared for the 2002 International Labour Conference.

Francie Lund is an Associate Professor at the University of KwaZulu Natal in Durban, South Africa, School of Development Studies. Currently Director of the Social Protection Programme of WIEGO, she specializes in social security, analysing the effects of different forms of social assistance on poor households. She chaired the Lund Committee on Child and Family Support which was convened after the transition to democracy in 1994.

James Heintz is an Assistant Research Professor at the University of Massachusetts at Amherst. He has written widely on economic policy issues, including job creation, global labour standards, macroeconomic strategies, and investment behaviour. He has been a consultant for the International Labour Organization and the United Nations Development Programme in Ghana and South Africa, focusing on employment-oriented development policy.

Renana Jhabvala has worked with the Self Employed Women's Association (SEWA) since 1977 and is currently SEWA's National Co-ordinator and Chairperson of SEWA Bank and SEWA Bharat. She serves as a policy adviser to, and a member of the steering committee of WIEGO. Her recent publications include *Informal Economy Centrestage: New Structures of Employment* (co-edited with Ratna M. Sudarshan and Jeemol Unni), and *The Unorganised Sector: Work Security and Social Protection* (co-edited with R.K.A. Subramanya).

Christine Bonner is the Director of the Organization and Representation Programme of WIEGO. She has spent 30 years working in and with the labour movement in South Africa. She was founding Director of the Development Institute for Training, Support and Education for Labour (DITSELA) focusing on trade union education and organizational development.

Index

Business development services, 12, 92, 93-94
Caste identity and work, 23, 33, 65, 67, 72, 81
Causal wage workers, see Employment status
Child care, 12, 25, 28, 29, 30, 64
Codes of conduct, 12, 67, 85, 94, 95
Community volunteer work, 23, 31
Cooperatives, see Member-based organizations of informal workers
Decent work
   ILO definition of, 19
   for informal workers, 8, 15, 73, 84, 87, 89,104
Domestic work/workers, 9, 24, 26, 30, 33, 34, 35, 39, 41, 44, 45, 47, 50, 51, 54, 55, 71-72, 76, 92, 97, 101
Earnings, see also Wages
   formal employment:
      private sector, 47
      public sector, 47, 54
   informal employment:
      employers, 9, 43-44, 47, 48, 50, 54
      industrial outworkers, 9, 10, 54
   informal wage workers:
      casual, 9, 47, 50, 53-54
      regular, 53-54
      own-account workers, 8-9, 47-48, 50
   gap 9, 18, 38, 48, 52, 66, 68
   indicator for MDG 3, 39-41, 98, 104
Employment
   by type, indicator for MDG Goal 3, 13, 21, 40-41
   formal, 45-46
   indicators for MDG 3, 39-41, 98, 104
   informal, 38-39
   rate, see Labour force participation rate
   relations of, 9, 10, 59, 61
   statistics on, 8-9, 40, 42, 44, 45, 46
   status, see Employment status
Employment-oriented development strategy, 12, 73, 86-104
Employment status
   definition, 38
   categories of:
      casual wage workers, 9, 39, 44, 46-47, 50, 53, 54
      employees, 9, 10, 18, 21, 32, 39, 41, 42, 44, 46, 48, 50-51, 55, 57, 61, 64, 67-71, 78-79, 83, 94
      industrial outworkers/homeworkers, 9-10, 39, 44, 45, 54, 60, 61, 62, 63, 66, 68, 69-70, 73, 76, 81, 101
      members of producer cooperatives, 39, 41
      self-employed:
         employers, 9, 10, 38, 41, 43-44, 47-48, 50-51, 54, 56, 61
         own-account workers, 9, 10, 38, 41, 44, 46-51, 56, 61, 80, 102
         unpaid contributing family workers, 9, 10, 38, 44-45, 51, 57, 61
Ethnic/racial identity and work, 21, 33, 34, 37, 65, 71, 73, 81, 87, 91
Export processing zones (EPZs), 18, 62, 78, 80,102
Female-headed households, 18, 37, 52-53, 54
Feminization of labour markets, 37-38, 55
Feminization of poverty
   definition and measures, 20, 37-38, 56
   association with female-headed households, 37
Flexibility/flexibilization of labour markets, see Labour markets
Formal economy, see Formal employment
Formal employment/job
   private sector, 46, 47
   public sector, 47, 48, 50, 51
   statistics on, 46, 47
Formalization of the informal economy, 88-89
Garment workers
   agency workers, 70
   EPZ factory workers, 18, 70
   group-based industrial outworkers, 70
   industrial outworkers, 69-70

Gender
   division of labour, 10, 67
   and other sources of disadvantage, 33-35
Gender assessments, 91, 98,103
Gender-Responsive Budget Analysis/gender budgets, 11, 91
Gender gap
   earnings, 9, 18, 35,40, 49-50, 68
   wages, 38, 66
   benefits, 35
   MDG indicators, 1, 16
Gender impact assessments, 91
Gender segmentation, see Labour markets
Hierarchy of earnings, 9, 53-54
Hierarchy of poverty risk, 9, 53-54
HIV/AIDS and work, 23, 27, 28, 31-32, 35
Homeworkers, see Industrial outworkers
Industrial outworkers, 9-10, 39, 44, 45, 54, 60, 61, 62, 63, 66, 68, 69-70, 73, 76, 81, 101
Informal economy, see Informal employment
Informal Economy Budget Analysis, 11, 91-92, 98
Informal employment/work
   benefits of, 59, 62-63, 87
   causal model of, 66-67
   costs of, 63-66
   definition of, 38
   nature of, 59-62
   regulation of, 87
   associated risks and uncertainties, 63-66
   statistical framework for, 38, 54-55
   statistics on, 38-39
Informal sector, see also Informal employment/economy
   1993 definition, 38
Informalization of labour force, see Labour force
Labour force
   feminization of, 37-38, 55-56
   flexibilization of, 63
   informalization of, 37-38, 42, 55, 59, 88
   participation rate, 16, 18, 25, 37-38, 41
   segmentation of 42-55
   statistics on, 54-56
Labour laws and policies
   domestic, 95
   and regional trade agreements, 96
Labour markets
   definition of, 55
   demand side factors, 55
   dualistic, 44
   flexibility of, 17, 42, 49, 59, 62-63, 67, 88
   gender segmentation of, 49
   interventions in, 73
   multi-segmented, 10, 55
   supply side factors, 55
Labour standards
   international, 8, 12, 70, 90, 94
   and trade agreements, 96
Legal frameworks for informal workers, 12, 89, 94, 101
Maquiladoras, see Export Processing Zones
Markets
   access to, 11, 88, 89, 93, 94, 99, 103
   bargaining power in,12, 19, 62, 63, 64, 76, 79
   competitiveness in, 11, 19, 62, 63, 65, 88, 95
Member-based organizations of informal workers
   cooperatives, 13, 39, 77, 78-79, 80
   issue-based, 78, 79
   trade unions, 78, 79-80
Microfinance, 12, 76, 88, 90, 92, 93, 94, 97
Migrant workers, 34, 69, 78, 83, 95, 96, 102
Millennium Declaration, 8, 15, 16, 19, 85
Millennium Development Goals
   Goal 1, 20, 41,103
   Goal 3, 10, 13, 20; indicators for, 16, 19, 21, 39-41, 56, 85, 98, 104
   Goal 8, 20; indicators for, 19, 27
Millennium Development Goals reports, 21, 103
Millennium Summit, 15
Occupational health and safety, 64, 65, 70, 90, 92, 98
Organizing of informal workers:
   benefits of, 76-77
   strategies for, 78-80

Organizations of informal workers, see Member-based organizations of informal workers
Own account workers, see Employment status
Part-time work/workers, 29, 30, 35, 39, 42, 43
Place of work
   categories of, 59-60
   associated costs, risks, and benefits, 9, 21, 59, 60
Poverty
   dimensions of, 10, 13, 15, 21, 56, 68, 90, 103
   income poverty, 21, 54, 56, 57, 67, 68
   measurement of, 51
Poverty reduction strategies, 13,19, 56, 90, 104
Poverty Reduction Strategy Papers (PRSPs), 12, 19-21, 76, 85, 89, 98, 103
Poverty risk
   definition of, 21
   of different employment statuses, 9, 10, 13, 15, 38, 53-54, 89
Precarious employment, 8, 9, 18, 20, 23, 29, 33, 34, 42, 43, 46, 47, 50, 54, 65, 68, 73
Religious identity and work, 21, 33, 35, 37, 73, 81
Representative voice, 11, 12,13, 76, 89, 90, 98, 99, 102, 104
Reproductive work, 24
Rights
   property, 10, 68, 87, 90, 97
   workers'
      right to work, 12, 90, 96, 101
      right to vend, 12, 96, 101
      right to organize, 82, 83, 88, 89, 90
Self-employment, see Employment status
Social protection for informal workers
   public works, 12, 97
   safety nets, 12, 90, 103
   insurance, 12, 90, 97, 102
   pensions, 12, 76, 90, 97
Street vendors
   policies for, 77, 92, 96, 99
   programmes for, 75, 77, 80, 99
Subsistence production, 23-24, 31
System of production
   global, 10, 17, 61-62
   industrial, 10, 62
   semi-industrial, 10
   traditional agriculture and artisan, 10, 62
Temporary work/workers, 9, 17, 18, 42-43, 84, 95
Terms of trade for informal workers, 12, 89, 94, 100,101
Trade unions, 12, 78, 79-80, 81, 82, 83, 84, 85, 88, 95, 96, 97, 98, 99, 101
Underemployment, 20, 49, 55
Unemployment, 20, 27, 34, 44, 55, 64, 66, 71, 87
Unpaid care work
   definition of, 24
   valuation of, 21, 23, 29
Unpaid contributing family members, see Employment Status
Value chains
   global value chains, 62, 69
Wage gap, 38
Waste pickers, 60, 65, 72, 75, 79
Women's work
   segmentation of, 9, 21, 23, 29
   spatial dimensions of, 21, 23, 29
   temporal dimensions of, 21, 23, 29
   totality of, 21, 23
   types of, 21, 23
   valuation of, 21, 23, 24, 29
Women's identity as workers
   organizing around, 77-80
Women's organizations, 77-80
Worker-centred policy processes, 76, 77, 82, 83-85, 104
Working arrangements, 21, 37, 42, 59-63, 67, 68, 81
Working conditions, 10, 13, 17, 30-31, 62, 63, 76, 80, 81, 88, 90, 95
Working poor, 11-13, 15, 19, 21, 23, 35, 50-53, 57, 59, 65, 67, 73, 76, 77, 85, 87, 89-91, 92, 93, 94, 97, 98, 99, 100, 101, 102, 104